D1583855

WITHDRAWN FROM STOCK
DUBLIN CITY PUBLIC LIBRARIES

# In My Gut,
# I Don't Believe

Leabharlann Baile Formaid
Ballyfermot Library
01-2228422

## Also by JOE ARMSTRONG

### BOOKS
*In My Gut, I Don't Believe*
*Write Way to Stop Smoking*
*Men's Health, The Common Sense Approach*
*Men's Health, The Common Sense Course*
*The NUJ and Your Rights at Work*
*From Special Care to Specialist Treatment: A History of Muckamore Abbey Hospital* (with Ian Montgomery)
*Workplace Stress in Ireland*

### PLAY
*Mother Earth*, a play for children

### COLUMNS
*After God* in *The Irish Freethinker & Humanist*
*Soul Food* in *Reality*
*Bookshelf* in *Reality*
*Health & Wholeness* in *Reality*
*Life Coach* in *Face Up*
*Body, Mind & Spirit* in *Face Up*
*The Collector* in *The Irish Times*
*Health Matters* in *The Irish Times*
*Man Alive* in *The Irish Times*
*Dad's Diary* in *SQ*
*Successful Meath People* in *The Meath Weekender*

### FEATURES
*The Irish Times, The Sunday Times,*
*The Sunday Business Post, The Sunday Tribune*

### RADIO DOCUMENTARY
*From Belief to Unbelief,* RTE

### PODCAST
*Losing My Religion*

# In My Gut, I Don't Believe

A Memoir

Joe Armstrong

GLEBE

# In My Gut, I Don't Believe

Published by GLEBE
Kells, Co. Meath. A82 E190

© Joe Armstrong 2020

The moral right of Joe Armstrong to be identified as the author of this work has been asserted in accordance with the Copyright, Designs and Patents Act 1988.
First published in 2020 by GLEBE.

All rights reserved. No part of this publication may be reproduced or transmitted in any form or by any means, electronic or mechanical, including photocopying, recording or otherwise, or stored in a retrieval system, or transmitted, in any form or by any means without the prior written permission of the above publisher, nor be otherwise circulated in any form of binding or cover other than that in which it is published and without similar condition being imposed on the subsequent purchaser. The publishers have made every reasonable effort to seek permissions from copyright holders whose work has been quoted in this book. We welcome hearing from any copyright holders who have not been acknowledged.

Cover artwork and design by
3D Artist John Armstrong:
JohnArmstrong3@gmail.com

ISBN: 978-0-9546610-1-4

A CIP catalogue record for this book is available from the British Library.

# Dedication

*For Ruth, love always*

# Disclaimer

Being human, my memories are imperfect. I'm sharing to the best of my knowledge. I recognise that other people's memories of people, things, events and conversations mentioned in this book will differ.

# Epigraph

*'If you would be a real seeker after truth, it is necessary that at least once in your life you doubt, as far as possible, all things.'*

– René Descartes

# Contents

Leabharlann Baile Formaid
Ballyfermot Library
01-2228422

# Preface

## #1

I spent nine years of my one and only life studying for the Roman Catholic priesthood. Aged 18 in 1980, I entered the novitiate of the Marist Fathers, also known as the Society of Mary, a religious congregation of priests, at Mount St Mary's, Milltown, Dublin, Ireland. By 1989, the year that the Berlin Wall came down, I took two years' leave of absence, needing only one: I left for good in 1990.

Now approaching 60, I'm a husband, father, writer, podcaster and Humanist celebrant. As a writer and communicator, I want to explore my humanity, believing that, when I am most personal and vulnerable, I am most universal. As a celebrant, I'm doing what I set out to do when I was 18, celebrating with people the milestones of their lives – birth, marriage and death – shorn of religious artifice.

I needed to write this book, to examine myself, understand myself and to see how I transitioned, if not from believer to unbeliever, at least from aspirant priest to leaving the seminary.

Leabharlanna Poiblí Chathair Baile Átha Cliath
Dublin City Public Libraries

# IN MY GUT, I DON'T BELIEVE

One of the problems in the mindset of many religious people is their propensity to impose their views on others. I know – I was such a believer. I voted against the introduction of divorce and in favour of the constitutional ban on abortion in Ireland in the 1980s.

As a pious teenager, I had a row with a school friend who thought that the laws of the State shouldn't reflect the laws of any Church. He wondered if we religious people would prefer those with differing views to emigrate.

Yes, I thought, to my shame. As the Church reflected the mind of God, I thought it would have been better if those who disagreed emigrated, leaving behind a society more attuned to God's plan. Having what you see as God's higher values on your side blinds people – it blinded me – to rational debate.

Abortion is now allowed in Ireland. But I wonder if anyone could have said anything back in the 1980s for me to reconsider my position. I believed a unique human soul was formed at the moment of conception. Human life was sacred, a fertilised ovum was human life and so abortion was always wrong.

But real human life is messy. A married mother with children whom I know had the emotional and psychological trauma of a stillbirth and several miscarriages. She conceived again and her embryo was diagnosed with a fatal foetal abnormality.

Would this mother's dilemma have dented my absolutism in voting to bring in the Eight Amendment to the Irish Constitution in 1983, which recognised the equal right to life of the pregnant woman and the unborn? I doubt it. I probably would have countered that hard cases make poor law; argued that she might have learned more

2

by continuing with the pregnancy; and that guilt over the abortion would make her bereavement more difficult.

However, statistically God aborts far more fertilised ova than human beings do, making God the world's number one killer of 'babies' in the womb. If God does it, why can't humans? If it is a sin for humans, is not God the greatest sinner of them all, the greatest mass murderer in history?

Would it not make more sense for pro-lifers to protest outside churches that their God should slaughter countless innocents on a biblical scale throughout human history, rather than outside abortion clinics, who perform a smidgen of abortions in comparison to the Creator?

Leaving my priestly path was the hardest – and best – thing I have ever done. It involved rethinking everything I had learned, everything I believed, everything I had thought was true.

My RTE Radio One documentary *From Belief to Unbelief*, first broadcast in 2012, was cathartic for me. I spent some 24-hour stints working on it in the bowels of Montrose and didn't notice the time passing. By the final cut, I cried, all those years later, listening to my vocational crisis, my life's lesson, and the key turning point of my life.

But a 40-minute documentary is constrained by time. In this book, I get into the nitty gritty of my journey from wanting to be a priest to knowing I had to leave to be me. This book shows my struggle and how I succeeded in extracting myself from the labyrinth of religious thinking.

I worry that, even today, millions of children are being taught religious myth as scientific fact. Religion is being reborn anew each day in new generations of malleable minds. It warped my thinking, feelings and choices. Child abuse is not limited to the sexual and physical. It also concerns abuses of the mind.

If we are to grasp how a religious human being can strap explosives around their body and cause mayhem, carnage and death to others, fly planes into skyscrapers, behead fellow humans, ban unbaptised babies being buried in consecrated grounds, deny abortion and ordination to women, or describe fellow humans as intrinsically disordered, we would do well to examine ourselves and for me to begin with myself.

Socrates said: 'The unexamined life is not worth living.' So, let's begin.

## *Chapter 1*

# 'Many souls will be saved'

#2

Faith is caught not taught, as believers say, without realising that so too is a virus. Having caught faith as a child, I was taught what was right and wrong. Founded by God, the Catholic Church had infallibly determined its teachings on things like Heaven, Hell, salvation, damnation, masturbation, pre-marital sex, contraception, marriage, divorce, abortion, homosexuality, vocation, celibacy and women's ordination.

Who was I, a fallible individual, to question its authoritative teachings based on scripture, tradition and the magisterium of the Church? Aged 17 at secondary school I was slapped in the face by my religion teacher for asking a question. And I was at that time a committed Christian!

But let's go back, younger; way younger.

My father's first wife, Joan, had died in 1958 soon after giving birth to their third child Arthur. The baby died too.

Their other two sons, Paul and David, were aged only six and three. Just over a year after Joan's death, at the ordination to the priesthood of his brother John in Rome, my father proposed to my mother.

A photograph of my mother Pauline taken at Lourdes just four years earlier shows her, then in her early thirties, dressed as a 'Child of Mary' like the Virgin Mary, complete with veil and cape, beside two other women, similarly attired. Behind the three women is a statue of the Blessed Mother with a halo around her head.

A swift six months after their engagement, Arthur, aged forty-two, married Pauline, aged thirty-six, my uncle Father John officiating. A year and a half into the marriage, my sister was born. I followed a year later, in 1962, when Pope John XXIII convened the Second Vatican Council and the Beatles signed their first music contract. The Cuban missile crisis erupted. Kennedy faced down Khrushchev and the world feared nuclear Armageddon.

For Paul, the bombs had been going off ever since the death of his mother. Three weeks after running away for the last time in his mid-teens, he came home; dishevelled, cold and hungry. But he did not spend that night there; nor any other night. The story of the Prodigal Son would not be re-enacted. He was banished, that evening, from his home forever. My mother made sure of that. Either he was going or she was going, and the latter was never likely.

I determined – out of fear – that I would be a 'good boy'. I dreaded meeting with her disapproval, being cast off by her like Paul was, expelled from home like Adam and Eve. If you crossed her, you lost. Love became shot through with fear. I loved her – she was my mother – yet I was terrified of her too.

6

My father had to arrange for his brother and my namesake Uncle Joe Armstrong to take Paul. Later that year, my father had a heart attack – a stroke and a heart attack before he was forty-nine.

Paul would live with Uncle Joe and his wife and son for the next two years before joining the army. He only returned to our house once during the next four years and that was to paint a ceiling.

I recall an incident when I was a young child. I had been naughty and my mother insisted I join her kneeling before the picture of the Sacred Heart of Jesus. It hung in pride of place over the fireplace in the small back living room of our end-of-terrace house in Donnycarney, Dublin. At the centre of the picture beat a radiant heart, dripping blood. The top of the heart had a cross on fire. A crown of thorns surrounded the heart like a belt. Jesus suffered for us.

His large, all-seeing eyes followed you throughout the room, reading your mind and knowing your every sin. A panel in the corner of the picture declared: 'I will bless the house in which the image of My Sacred Heart shall be exposed and honoured.'

My mother beseeched the Sacred Heart to make me a good boy, blessing herself repeatedly and joining her hands with fervour. Her hands were clenched, her head bowed, then she craned her head upwards with each new entreaty. Jesus gazed down upon us from the chimney breast. Even as a young boy I was unconvinced by my mother's unquestioning devotion.

Yet despite my embarrassment at my mother's piety, I was susceptible to the belief that she had a hotline to an omniscient God. On another occasion when I'd misbehaved, she knew immediately – as any adult would

7

have known – whatever misdemeanour I'd done, even though she hadn't witnessed the unremarkable incident.

'How did you know that?' I asked, awestruck by her seeming access to divine omniscience.

'Holy God told me.'

Her lie made a deep impression on my young mind. The myth of God was taking root in me. It was catching.

## #3

I have recounted how my brother Paul was banished from home when he was only 16, and I was just five. And David?

One day my mother wailed in pain, accusing David: 'He slammed the door on my hand!'

'It was an accident!' cried David.

'He did it on purpose!' she insisted.

'It was an accident!' David pleaded.

I do not know whether or not it was an accident and probably my father didn't know either. He felt trapped between his second wife and the sons of his first marriage and he ordered David out to what we called 'the passage', the narrow pathway that had linked the front and back gardens of our house. Now it was enclosed with a pitched roof, a door at either end. I heard the door slam from the kitchen to the passage, then David's thrashing and cries of pain, which seemed to last for ages.

Another time I remember my dad ordering David, who was seven years older than me, to strip in the living room, while I was there. I can't recall if he was beaten but I know I felt embarrassed for my brother, naked in front of me.

Neither the expulsion of Paul nor the violence and humiliation visited upon David deterred my parents' dutiful exercise of their religion. I recall in 1970, when I was eight, a likeable, elderly Christian Brother quizzing pupils about our families' religious practice.

'Hands up, boys, who goes to mass every Sunday?'

Every hand shot up.

'Hands up if your mammy goes to mass every day.'

Several hands shot up, including mine.

'Hands up if you have a relative a priest.'

Several hands ascended. He asked us to elaborate.

'Sir, my Uncle John is a priest in South Africa,' I answered with pride.

'Isn't that fabulous, boys?'

'Yessir!' resounded the class.

I used to hate going home from school on washing day. The tension was palpable. My mother would concede she would be 'up to high do'. Maybe it was before she was prescribed diazepam. She had to pull the washing machine out from the wall so she could feed the clothes through the wringer at the back. The tiny kitchen would look like a warzone, with clothes on the table, on the floor, in the machine and sticking out of the wringer.

My mother, like the washing, was strung out. She was in the trenches, fighting to the death with the soiled clothes. If it was raining, she couldn't hang out the wet clothes. If it was dry and they were on the line, she would watch the clouds like a prowling enemy, darting out to take in the washing at the first drop.

A boy my own age used to call to see if I'd like to come out to play. I liked him, but my mother didn't approve of him. She felt he was 'common'. I didn't want to cross her, so I discouraged my friend's visits and he stopped calling; a lost chance for friendship. I used to play with other boys on our street. One boy told me his dad was an engineer.

'He's not an engineer,' my mother told me scornfully. 'He's a mechanic.'

I didn't know what either job was, if there was any difference between them or why it mattered. But it mattered to my mother.

David, like Paul before him, disappeared from home aged 16 or 17, probably in 1972 (possibly 1971). I was about ten (maybe nine). I didn't know where my brother had gone or what caused his departure. There was a vague sense that he might be in London; or maybe Spain. We had no contact details for him so we didn't know if he was alive or dead.

After he had left, I was prohibited from entering David's bedroom. In fact, his bedroom was kept locked. It was strange growing up in a small three-bedroomed house with one bedroom permanently locked. David's disappearance, and the fact that he, like Paul before him, was rarely spoken about, intrigued and perplexed me. Whenever I asked about him, I was fobbed off.

I sensed my father's anguish but I had to resign myself to not knowing where David was or why he had vanished. My mother acted as if it was perfectly natural for young siblings to disappear and never come back.

'Once I turn against someone, that's it,' my mother once said to me.

Home felt unsafe for this five-year-old, witnessing Paul's banishment; this 10-year-old grappling with David's permanent, unexplained disappearance and the implacable conspiracy of silence. My father saying nothing. My mother pretending this was normal. I wanted to understand. I

10

craved security; that I wouldn't be next, falling foul of my mother's steely-stated incapacity to forgive and its terrifying consequences seen through the eyes of a young boy.

## #4

On a weekday evening, hundreds of men and boys, including my dad and me, were walking to our parish church for a men's retreat. It was the parish mission at Our Lady of Consolation, Donnycarney. A massive church built in 1969, it was packed to the gills. A Redemptorist priest commanded our attention.

'Men, raise your hands up high.'

We did.

'Do you renounce Satan?'

'I do!' thundered the men.

'And all his works?'

'I do!'

'And all his empty promises?'

'I do!'

I felt excited to be part of this, among ordinary Catholic men, tough manly men like my dad, professing our religion. Even to this day, I know it hurts some people who are dear to me that I am no longer a believer. It can feel like betraying the tribe, with its shared myths, rituals and beliefs. One elderly dear friend, who was like a father to me, wept in the past few years while expressing the hope that one day I would return to the faith.

During Lent, we gave up chocolate and sweets and we'd say the family rosary every night.

# IN MY GUT, I DON'T BELIEVE

'The family that prays together stays together,' my mother would say, missing the irony of my banished and vanished brothers Paul and David.

My father would kneel bent over; his face buried in the seat of his rocking chair. He'd yawn loudly and rattle through the mysteries, fusing syllables. 'HailMaryFullof gracetheLordiswithDee, BlessedartDouamongstwomen ... '

Each May, we erected a Marian altar at the top of the stairs, a tiny grotto with a plaster statue of the Blessed Virgin Mary, wallflowers from the garden and a candle. Around it we would recite the Hail Holy Queen, Mother of Mercy, our life, our sweetness and our hope, praying as poor banished children of Eve, sending up our sighs, mourning and weeping in this valley of tears.

When I learned that Santa didn't exist, my immediate thought, in light of the parental deception, was that God didn't either. And yet, when the whole world around you seemed to believe in God, you find yourself believing too.

One day when I was in the living room, the Sacred Heart overseeing all, lost in the unselfconscious world of my boyhood, I practised saying mass, mimicking the words and gestures of a priest. Suddenly, I became aware of being watched in my reverie by my father and mother. I'd forgotten they were in the room.

'We might have a priest in the family,' said my father.

I was mortified; unintentionally having revealed my priestly ambition at so tender an age.

Some years later, while I was in primary school, I was seated at my desk, writing in a crowded classroom. A Christian Brother came up behind me, leant over my right shoulder and fondled me, his hand on the outside of my trousers. It was the first time ever I'd been touched

12

sexually. Even as a young boy, I knew he shouldn't be doing this and that he knew it too because he covered his abuse by pretending to be helping me with an exercise in my copybook.

I told no one. In 1970s Ireland, who would believe a pupil against a Christian Brother? Corporal punishment was rife in Irish schools. We were often slapped with leather straps, for little reason. The sting on the palms of the hands after you were biffed was awful. Your hand would feel raw and glow red and you'd bristle with pain. Some Brothers sewed a coin into the end of their leather strap to make it even more painful. Others used rulers and canes.

I witnessed one twelve-year-old boy being brutally beaten by another Christian Brother. His sole offence was not understanding a lesson. I had so wanted to leave the classroom and go and get somebody to stop the boy's battering. But I lacked the courage or confidence to do so. Next day that Brother sought to justify his excesses on the grounds that the boy now understood what he hadn't grasped the previous day. What would they do to me if I accused a Christian Brother, a member of their order, of sexually abusing me?

The sexual abuse had a profound effect on me. Powerless over my abuser's authority, I resigned myself to the single-instance violation. I felt an inexplicable shame at having been sexually abused by him. I wondered, of all the boys in the class, 'Why me? Why did he single me out?' His abuse undermined my boyhood confidence in my masculinity and my emerging sexual identity. I worried, 'What is it about me that he saw or identified that he felt he could just do this and get away with it?' I felt confused and isolated and there was nobody I could talk to.

## #5

I would soon detect the foul breath of another particular Christian Brother. In my last year at primary school I went, like tens of thousands of schoolchildren before and since, to the Gaeltacht – an Irish-speaking area – for a month to improve my Irish.

In that short time, one Christian Brother became known by students for his interest in young boys. He had access to our bedrooms at night and I felt vulnerable that he was prowling around at lights out. If it took only a few weeks for us boys to suspect his sexual proclivities, it is difficult to imagine that the Brothers were not aware of them too.

I shared a bedroom with four other boys, all of us aged about twelve. The others were in two bunk beds at the other end of the room but I was in a single bed near the door. One night, that particular Christian Brother came into our bedroom after lights out.

'I hope you have taken off your underpants,' he said to me, as I lay in bed, light filtering in from the nearby open door.

'No, Brother.' If I lied and he checked I didn't know what he would do.

'That's unhealthy. Get out of bed and take them off.'

'Can I do it in bed?'

'No. Get out.'

He could have let me remove them under the sheets. But he wanted to watch me strip naked in front of him. There was nothing I could do. Isolated from the others in the

14

bedroom, I felt violated, forced as a young boy to be nude before him for his sick sexual thrill. I worried that he would fondle me like the other Christian Brother had.

I got out of bed, turned my back to him, took off my pyjamas, removed my underpants and put my pyjamas back on. I can still sense him, inches from me, invading my personal space. I can hear and smell his noxious breath as he stands at close quarters behind me; sating his devious sexual desire watching a prepubescent boy naked at his behest.

When I got back into bed and he left the room I cried, reduced for a second time to an object of sexual desire by a Christian Brother.

*

Sometime after my return home from the Gaeltacht, I'd another nocturnal visit from an adult while I lay in bed: my mother.

'Keep your hands joined like this on the pillow. Like you're praying. Sinning alone is a mortal sin.'

She didn't explain what sinning alone was; but I guessed it meant touching my genitals.

I was taught at home and school to obey Church teaching without question. Nobody I knew questioned the faith. Freethinking was a sin. The Church had asked and answered every question under the sun over two millennia. Obedience demanded submission of the mind and will to God.

Sex was sinful and only permissible within marriage and only then for the procreation of children. Even marital sex was not removed from the stain of sin and mothers had needed to be 'churched' after giving birth. Sin came into the world through sex. Babies were born with the stain of

15

original sin and needed to be baptised. Only a Virgin Mother could lead to the birth of our Saviour, a God–man born without the stain of Adam. Masturbation, sex outside marriage, homosexuality…all were mortal sins.

All this induced in me a sense that sex was dirty and sordid. It was something forbidden, shameful and secret. A Christian Brother, dedicated to God, could grope you. Another could force you to strip. And my pious mother reinforced the Church's official message to operate from the neck up.

And so, when the more natural thing for teenagers to do is to explore their sexuality, I found myself repressing mine. Aged 18, I chose the seemingly asexual vocation of the priesthood. So deeply had I repressed my sexuality that following the entrance psychological tests the Superior felt I should do a medical. A scholastic drove me to the surgery where an elderly doctor listened to my heartbeat.

'What a good boy,' he said. Then: 'Lie down and open your trousers please.'

He pulled my briefs to beneath the testicles and stimulated the penis.

'Excuse me – I had to check.'

In the Catholic Church, you need to have a penis to be a priest. No penis, no priest. Moreover, the man must be potent, the ecclesial authorities assured of his erectile functionality. If you have erectile dysfunction rendering you incapable of penetrative sex, you cannot be validly ordained. Male organ present and potent, but never, at least in theory, to be used for one of its primary functions, one has fulfilled the sine qua non of becoming a Catholic priest.

Women and eunuchs need not apply.

16

## #6

'All happy families are alike: each unhappy family is unhappy in its own way,' wrote Tolstoy, his first words in *Anna Karenina*.

'There's no point talking to her,' my father once said to me after I emerged frustrated from an attempt to engage my mother in a rational conversation. 'You can't reason with her,' he continued. 'Nobody can.'

I was sad that my father's marriage had brought him to that conclusion.

Often when my mother was talking 'at' my father, he would surreptitiously turn down his hearing aid or, if he was watching television, turn up his long-cabled stethoscope-like device to hear the television better. She never seemed to notice. I'd often seen people's eyes glaze over while my mother spoke 'at' them in meaningless meandering soliloquies. And yet others remember her fondly as 'holding court' in their home. She was a different person to different people. She reminded me of Eleanor Rigby, with not just one face but many that she kept in a jar by the door.

My relationship with her was the most complex one of my life. I loved her and I feared her. Flesh of her flesh, I was her favourite. She mollycoddled and suffocated me. She manipulated me. There was a strong unhealthy bond between us. She undermined me, controlled me, left me doubting my perceptions, feelings, thoughts and memories. I couldn't breathe with her suffocating 'love'.

I would tell her something that I knew had happened and she would say it hadn't happened. I'd tell her my thoughts and she'd say I was mistaken. I'd share a feeling and she'd ignore it or say it was 'wrong'. She had me doubting my eyes, ears, touch, taste, smell and memory. Instead of encouraging me to think for myself, she gnawed away at my perceptions, understanding, judgements and decision making; crippling my confidence in myself.

One day in my mid-to-late teens my dad began to open up to me. We were alone in the living room, just him and me.

'Joseph,' he said.

I knew by his awkwardness, anguished face and the considered intention in his voice that this was a conversation he had wanted to have with me for a long time; one he had been waiting for me to be old enough to receive like a man.

'What?' I asked, apprehensively, knowing it was something about my mother.

He stood at the edge of his personal parental precipice, sighed and spoke. 'Joseph…the things that woman did.'

I knew in every bone and sinew of my body the tension I had felt at home from my earliest childhood. My father torn between his sons Paul and David and his second wife, my mother, Pauline. My mother's hysteria, my parents' fights, my mother's accusations against my brothers, my father beating them. Paul often running away from home and, that last time, my mother, steely-eyed, bitter and angry, looking out the kitchen window towards the garages and sheds that filled the back gardens and the concrete lane behind our house and saying to me devoid of compassion: 'I know he's around here. He's doing this to get at me. He won't win.'

And then those words that seared my soul and scared me, intended as a warning to me: 'Joseph, once I turn

18

against anyone, that's it. I hope you never turn out like those two brats.'

And Paul banished from the house forever the same day that he had returned, warning me that her threats were real. And David, vanished, his whereabouts still unknown.

I remembered all that and I feared hearing worse now from my father. I was on a precipice of my own, unsure whether to welcome my father's instigated confidence or defend my mother, fearing what he was about to reveal would irreparably damage whatever relationship I had with her.

'What things?' I asked, my tone askew, liking the man-to-man moment, yet defensive of my mother and protecting myself from having to deal with whatever he wanted to tell me.

My father hesitated, wrong-footed by my attitude.

'I'll … tell you another time,' he uttered, his courage gone.

And then I said something that I regretted: 'If you don't tell me now, I never want to know.'

He said nothing more.

When he died, I had a recurring nightmare. My father was about to speak to me, to tell me what he had waited and wanted to tell me, and each dream ended with the silence of the grave.

My relationship with my mother convinced me that happiness wouldn't lie in the arms, mind or heart of a woman. My dad wasn't happily married. His marriage was a lonely façade. Our family wasn't happy. Women, marriage and family didn't feel to me like the path to fulfilment. Priesthood seemed a better, wiser choice.

19

## #7

In my last years at secondary school I pondered that, if God existed and intervened in human history, then the Gospel should change our lives. But during the consecration at mass people looked bored. If we believed the bread and wine became the body and blood of Christ, Second Person of the Holy Trinity, would anyone waste their time watching telly or playing golf?

As a student member of the Society of St Vincent de Paul, we visited old folks once a week, kept them company and disbursed a small allowance from the charity to each. We visited a hospital, running errands for patients. But this seemed to me to fall short of the radical response of the first disciples of Jesus who had left wife, family, work and possessions to follow Christ.

In the late 1970s and early 1980s in Dublin, as around the world, the charismatic renewal was taking off. Prayer groups were sprouting up in parishes and schools. There were 'Camp Jesus' youth jamborees, all-night vigils, and thousands of laity and clergy attended charismatic conferences. People spoke of a new outpouring of the Holy Spirit, that the gifts of the Spirit in the Acts of the Apostles were being seen anew. There were 'Life in the Spirit' seminars, with people 'baptised in the Holy Spirit'. If Jesus healed the sick two thousand years ago, it made sense that miracles would still happen today; and there were reports of priests, nuns and others with the 'gift of healing'.

I began attending a charismatic prayer meeting at our school. About twenty adults and teenagers gathered, male and female, singing lively songs and raising hands aloft in prayer. Some strummed guitars. Enthusiasts, they seemed to believe the faith, compared to the monotonous responses at parish masses. Here prayer was spontaneous, with people whispering – or shouting – 'Praise you Jesus! Glory to you God!'

There were people 'praying in tongues', saying foreign-sounding made-up words in gradual or whirling crescendo, with people standing arms outstretched in dramatic gestures of prayer, culminating with 'Praise you God!' or 'Alleluia!'. I asked a priest about speaking in tongues and he said to babble like a baby. I tried it, choosing gibberish sounds. I felt self-conscious, but then it became liberating, like singing aloud at a concert or football match. Like a mantra, it helped you bypass the brain, a useful skill when it comes to religion. A pal told me I looked cool standing six-foot-two tall, with arms and palms extended in prayer. Context is everything!

It was a friendly welcoming space. I felt accepted and that I belonged. It helped that girls attended. There was lots of hugging. As someone put it: 'If it moves, hug it; and if it doesn't move, hug it until it moves.' I was comforted by scriptural passages like: 'Come to me all ye who labour and are overburdened and I shall give you rest. Shoulder my yoke and learn from me, for my yoke is easy and my burden is light.'

I went with a school friend, Colm Kenny, for an all-night vigil at a priest's house. The priest and perhaps twenty young people stayed all night. People were prayed over individually. When my turn came, I knelt and felt the heat of many hands being laid on my head, shoulders, back and legs. They prayed, 'Praise you Jesus!' and in tongues. Someone broke into song; the noise grew louder and I realised I was crying.

I cried my eyes out and, after they'd finished praying over me, I continued crying for ages.

'What's wrong?' asked Colm.

'I haven't got a clue.'

I don't know to this day what caused it. Maybe it was a release of pent-up sadness, loneliness or anguish. Perhaps I was overwhelmed by the intimacy of being touched by so many people and receiving their collective attention. Possibly it was because I felt accepted and acceptable, that it was OK to cry, and I was allowed to feel whatever I was feeling deep down.

The vigil had a profound effect on me. When I returned home next day, neither of my parents asked me about the night. They didn't seem interested. There were people within the charismatic renewal, relative strangers, who knew me far better than anyone in my family.

I came to hate going home. My mother was, as ever, unpredictable. I never knew what she would be like when I walked in the door, what mask she'd be wearing. I felt stifled and unable to be myself or to grow there. It was for me a place of tension and pretence. I could not relax there. As soon as I turned on to our street heading home, my heart sank. I needed to get out and find a place where I could grow.

### #8

On 29 June 1979, aged 17, I wrote a letter to my Uncle John, the priest in South Africa at whose ordination my parents had become engaged.

I was fond of Uncle John. He had a big heart and a deep, booming voice. He was tall, broad and manly. He had joined a religious order – I think the Carmelites – but he left and joined the Irish army during the Second World War. He contracted tuberculosis and spent about eleven years in hospital, 'gathering cobwebs in a bed' as he told me. All those years, he had prayed 'Lord, make me your priest,' which seemed a hopeless prayer.

Eventually, he had surgery, I think removing a lung, leaving him with one part-functioning lung but it was enough for him to leave hospital. On his visits to our home he would stand at the open front door at night 'recharging his batteries' as he put it, inhaling and exhaling deeply.

Before being discharged from hospital, he wrote to Archbishop McCann of Cape Town, telling him he wanted to be a priest. McCann told him to report to the Beda College in Rome. Ordained in 1959, he worked as a priest for 23 years in South Africa until his death in February 1982.

Uncle John's faith story and the seeming efficacy of his prayer made a deep impression on me. Our affection was mutual. He once kissed me on the lips. There was nothing seedy, unseemly or furtive about it. He did it openly in the presence of my mother and father; a spontaneous, unexpected, gesture of his fondness for me. He paid for my driving lessons before I entered the Marist Fathers and he gave me his copy of the *Jerome Biblical Commentary*, a massive tome.

My letter to him in June 1979 is embarrassing, revealing my innocence and gullibility as a 17-year-old believer. In my RTE radio documentary, *From Belief to Unbelief*, my son John – named after my uncle – reads from this letter; my son then being the same age as I'd been when I'd written it.

*Dear Uncle John,*

*I would like this to be the first letter you receive from Ireland after the postal strike. The first thing I want to tell you, and it's the only thing that's really important, is that I joined a charismatic prayer meeting. And really Uncle John, it's great!*

*Christ's love is flowing more and more in Ireland through the charismatic renewal. Pockets of Christians are opening up all over our city. Only last night we heard news of a new prayer meeting in Sean McDermott Street. Only weeks ago, another in the Mater Hospital. This, along with the many little-known parish prayer meetings like Edenmore and Donnycarney, and the bigger ones like the Airport and Eustace Street.*

*Only in the last few months have we seen the increased numbers of 'dove' badges – which are seen worn by all sorts of people. Mass that was boring and dead is now joyful and alive. The Risen Christ is seen so often.*

*Four weeks ago, I joined our parish meeting, and I've been going for months to the one in our school. We have one charismatic priest in our parish but only last night another priest turned up from our parish. I pray that he will get over his initial discomfort. Please, Uncle John, pray for him too. And for all others that are starting to know not about Christ but to actually know Him. Please, if you have a minute, pray for me too.*

*At present in our parish we are about 100. In Dundalk it started at fifty. Now it is 1,000! Last weekend there was a major gathering at Knock. Many witnessed to Healing. One, who was so far gone physically, had returned an invalid to Ireland to die and he witnessed to healing. Another was cured of multiple sclerosis. Our own charismatic priest tells of a man cured of a 20-year-old ankle disorder. And mental healing spreads like fire!*

*To those of us within the renewal it's back to the excitement lost and forgotten for centuries. The excitement of the realisation of the*

*Risen Christ! Whatever happened to the Church between then and now?*

*You know it feels like we're just continuing on another chapter of the Acts of the Apostles. As if there has been no time-lapse at all. The Fruits of the Spirit are flowing. God is Alive. Jesus is Lord! Isn't it wonderful? Oh! Sure, I always knew with my head that Jesus was God but now it's with my heart. I hope I'm not being hypocritical. The enthusiasm, the excitement seems false it's so long been absent. Let's praise God night and day.*

*God bless you, praise God and write soon.*

Phew!

### #9

Before dawn on 29 September 1979, one million people – a number equal to the entire population of Dublin and about one third of the Republic's population at the time – gathered in the Phoenix Park for the first ever papal visit to Ireland. If sometimes I'd felt embarrassed because of my faith, this gargantuan assembly leant legitimacy to Catholicism, making it more socially acceptable to be a committed believer. When the Aer Lingus jet with Pope John Paul II on board flew overhead, the hair on my neck stood on end.

The Pope had arrived in Ireland. The Brits had the Queen: we had the Pope. He kissed Irish soil when he stepped off the plane. (Later it was said the Pope kissed the ground and walked on women.)

I also made it to Galway for the papal youth mass. When the Pope said, 'Young people of Ireland, I love you!' tens of thousands of young people clapped and cheered in jubilation for ten minutes and we sang 'He's got the whole

25

world in his hands.' And we didn't mean God. We meant the Pope. He was our superstar.

Eventually, the popular singing priest Father Michael Cleary interrupted our spontaneous cheering and singing, saying the Pope had to get on with the mass.

Bishop Eamon Casey was on the podium too. Cleary and Casey were probably the most prominent clerics in Ireland at the time. Both had clandestine relationships and had fathered children which, when it came to light in 1992 and 1993, caused scandal and anguish for the faithful, the clerics' duplicity sparking disaffection and doubt in the laity who felt betrayed by the clerical Church. By then, I'd become convinced of the need for a married clergy and I was struck by the innocence of many laity. I knew many wonderful priests who had been forced to leave their priestly ministry because the Church elevated the man-made law of celibacy over what it claimed to be the God-given vocation to the priesthood.

But back to those innocent days – for me and for Ireland – of the papal visit. I had begun to attend a charismatic prayer meeting held in St Doolagh's Retreat House in north Dublin run by the Marist Fathers. I was impressed by a charismatic Marist priest based there, Father Larry Duffy, who was such a powerful preacher that he was nicknamed 'the laser beam'. Earnest and genuine in his faith, he prayed for hours every day and his slender frame suggested he fasted too.

I believed that this man had a direct link to God, like the prophets of old. I was so influenced by him that I began to imitate his mannerisms, like other young people might copy a pop idol or a sports star.

I had been mortified as a young boy when I'd been caught unawares mimicking the words and gestures of a priest saying mass and when my father had said: 'We might have a priest in the family.'

But now, aged 17 or 18, it was time to decide what I wanted to do with my life. Money didn't appeal to me – buying a house, taking out a mortgage, getting into the rat race. I wanted to do something meaningful. I wanted the excitement and adventure of following Christ. I wanted to spend my life addressing the real needs of others, helping them too to find meaning in their lives.

The Marist Fathers seemed to me to be the place where it was all happening. The congregation was open to what I thought the Holy Spirit was doing anew in our day. I liked that the Marists did various ministries – retreats, parishes, foreign missions and schools – and so I wouldn't need to decide yet what work I would do as a priest. I heard that their seminary was vibrant with many young men like me testing their vocations. And Father Larry Duffy, my hero, was the Marist vocations director.

During an all-night vigil I told him I wanted to be a priest.

'Praise be God!' he said.

He asked me about my family and I told him I'd an uncle a priest in South Africa and two cousins training to be priests. He explained that if I joined, I could see if I liked it and that the Marists would be looking at me to see if I was suitable. He said there would be entrance tests but he was sure I'd be grand and meanwhile I could take a trip out to the seminary. There was an open day for new entrants coming up soon.

I wanted to be a priest more than anything else in the world. Father Duffy placed his hands on my head and prayed that 'Many souls will be saved by your ministry.'

## #10

Seated in the front room at home, I told my mother what she had long suspected, that I wanted to be a priest.

'You know not marrying will be a sacrifice,' she said.

'Yes.'

'Your dad and I don't, you know, do it often but it's pleasurable.'

I was astounded by her candidness, her raising the topic of sex, the unexpected disclosure about her occasional sex life, and her first ever acknowledgement to me that sex could be positive.

I couldn't tell from her response whether or not she supported my decision but it was one of the rare, semi-normal adult conversations we'd ever had, despite her cryptic ambiguity.

My father was pleased with the news and he recounted, 'Once Good Pope John was asked if becoming Pope was the happiest day of his life. The Pope said no. The happiest day of his life was the day he was ordained a priest.'

My dad was relieved too that he wouldn't have to fund my third-level education from what remained of his modest retirement lump sum. I would be financially independent of my parents: the Marists would feed, clothe and educate me. It is an amazing boon to realise that you will never want for food, shelter, education or healthcare. The vow of poverty can be appealing and liberating.

28

I got the bus to Mount St Mary's, Milltown, the Marist Fathers' House of Formation. I had to ask the bus conductor where to get off and handed him the leaflet headed 'Open Day for Young Men' with the address on it.

'Are you joining?' he asked.

'I hope so.'

'You're very young.'

I walked through those gates feeling in my gut that this was the place where I would grow. And it was. My daft religious beliefs had brought me to this place. From the get-go, I loved the buzz and vitality in the community and I was confident that this would be the making of me. Community life would often be challenging, occasionally intimate, generally vibrant, sometimes boring but it was shot through with meaning and significance. We felt we were doing something good and worthwhile and that our lives had a great purpose. This would become my home, my fraternal family and where I belonged. We were idealistic and wanted to do great things with our lives. Of course, there would be rows, tensions and fallings out too.

After my first glimpse on that open day of the Marist community in Milltown, I wrote my letter of application. The Provincial replied in April 1980 praying that someday I would praise the Lord from their altars.

I wrote to my Uncle John who replied on 19 May 1980 from Durbanville, South Africa.

*'Moladh go deó le Dia! Praised be to God! This is the good news I was hoping for. Thanks be to the good God. Now I know I will have someone coming after me and I rejoice in it. How happy your Dad and Mam must be. May God make you a holy and devoted priest. I thought it might have been Clonliffe. Nevertheless, that is your choice and may God direct you.*

*I hope to be over in July please God so we will see you safely across the Monastic threshold. We had an old priest in the old days who was one of the first to join that congregation in Ireland. He always wanted to go to the foreign missions but they sent him teaching instead. So he joined the Carmelites. I was with him in his last moments – lived and died a saint.*

*God bless you Joe and grant to you many great graces. Love to all, John'*

I did the entrance psychological tests and medical and in a telephone call with Father John Hannan, Superior at Mount St Mary's, he confirmed I'd been accepted into the novitiate beginning on 23 September 1980.

His subsequent letter said I had all that was needed with God's help to be a very good Marist. He was happy that I was willing to give my life to the Lord Jesus.

He enclosed a list of requisites which included my parents' marriage certificate. Yes, in 1980 it still remained – as had been the case since the 11th century and confirmed in the 1917 *Code of Canon Law* (Canon 984) – an impediment to ordination to the priesthood to have been born out of wedlock, a prohibition only removed as recently as 1983.

## *Chapter 2*

# A new family

### #11

There were as many as twenty novices in our novitiate; seventeen from Ireland, two from England and one from Germany – numbers unimaginable today.

The 'formation staff' comprised Superior and Novice Master Father John Hannan, who had a background in psychology and management. He would later become Superior General of the congregation. He was assisted by Father Denis Green, then in his 60s, whom I grew to love. Decades later, when he was in his 90s, he helped me to make my RTE documentary. I've always thought of him as one of the youngest men I ever knew – creative and ever open to new ideas.

Father Peter Allen was a handsome Englishman who had the distinguished air of a Benedictine abbot. He had a beautiful speaking voice and he was an expert on liturgy and spirituality: he regaled us with stories of spiritual quest and adventure. Finally, German Father Bernd Kordes had an astute ability to listen one-to-one. His focus was

31

relationships: he facilitated group exercises helping novices forge lifelong friendships.

We were told to respect the *clausura*, the separation between the scholasticate and the novitiate. Scholastics, students who had completed their novitiate, studied philosophy and theology. They slept in the middle wing of the sprawling seminary, sat on the right in the chapel, had their own common room and dined together in the refectory. Novices lived in the new wing, prayed on the left at chapel, ate with fellow novices, and had a novitiate common room.

In 1980, there were some forty men living in Mount St Mary's, including priests, scholastics and novices. When I did my RTE documentary *From Belief to Unbelief* in 2012, there was only a handful of mostly elderly priests, no seminarians and the chapel lay silent.

Lectures were held in a drab, high-ceilinged room, with old wooden sash windows. I remember Denis's first lecture. He rubbed his eyes so hard with thick-veined hands that I wondered if his eyes might squish out. He was like a Shakespearean actor, employing dramatic variations of voice, volume and pace; still one moment, he moved about the classroom the next, with dramatic hand gestures, facial expressions and effective eye contact.

'Brothers, do you want to know the purpose of your novitiate? To know yourself. Make that your aim this year. We want you to enter into yourselves, attain a manly self-possession. Contemporary man seeks truth and they will see through any hypocrisy.'

John Hannan distributed jobs between us, like librarian, 'infirmarian', coordinators of external and internal manual labour, guest master, sacristan, master of ceremonies,

32

manager of the *'poustinia'* (a self-contained wing for retreats), security and lock-up, house maintenance, and Monitor, whose task was to foster unity within the novitiate community and to liaise with the formation staff.

We prayed about three hours a day: an hour's personal prayer, plus mass and the Divine Office at morning, noon, evening and night. There were also weekly prayer meetings. We had four silent week-long retreats over the one-year novitiate.

I loved the close bonds we were forming. I felt lucky, freed from the rat race to explore the meaning of life, get to know myself, learn how to love as Christ did, prepare myself to serve the real needs of people, and train to be a holy priest.

If at home I'd felt isolated, here in novitiate I was included and belonged. We shared a common purpose. My confrères listened to me and I listened to them.

Shortly into the novitiate, on a religious feast day, alcohol was produced.

'I don't drink,' I told Father Peter Allen. 'I'm cautious of it. Two of my uncles were alcoholics.'

'I respect your choice,' he said, sipping his wine.

'It's not for life. I intend to drink. Maybe by Christmas.'

A few days later, alcohol was again produced. I had a beer. Peter Allen saw me.

'I decided not to wait!' I grinned.

'Good for you! Given you'd decided, I wondered what you were waiting for.'

Conversations were stimulating. Strong characters abounded. Great 'dirty' jokes were told. Priests and students challenged our religious ideas and pieties. The Church was criticised constructively. Theology, even in novitiate, involved questioning many things, although not everything.

Self-knowledge was essential: humility was knowing yourself as you were. Psychology was valued and personal motivation was explored. We were on the path to a healthy, realistic self-knowledge, an insightful understanding of ourselves for personal growth.

After Compline each night, the community gathered around the statue of the Blessed Virgin Mary in the dark vestibule lit by a solitary blue votive light. We sang the *Salve Regina*. I loved this: my brothers' faces lit by the flickering light; the chapel's aromas of polish, candle wax and incense; the ancient lulling Latin melody with its plaintive air; the intimacy with the imagined Mary, compassionate and all-accepting mother.

But then came that feeling of loneliness as we retired alone, each to his solitary room.

## #12

In a long letter in early October, 1980, my mother wrote: 'The tears haven't flowed as I anticipated.' She adjudged my room 'beautiful', which it wasn't, and 'so tastefully furnished'. In fact, it had a basic short single bed, a cheap table, simple shelving for books, storage space for clothes and a sink. She said a friend of mine 'shed the tears that were spared to Mum – how she will miss you!' (Perhaps another exaggeration.) Enclosing a card from another friend, mother wrote: 'I know that you won't be offended at me opening it.' I was.

In contrast, my dad's letter was short, wry and level-headed. He had left school at twelve so his spelling wasn't great.

*Dear Joseph Glad to get you letter to day, am glad to hear you are Settleing in in the V.I.P. suite. We have not started to miss you yet. I say about next week we will God Bless Dad*

A few weeks into the novitiate, a fellow novice came to my room perplexed.

'This place is getting to me, Joseph. There's too much religion! If it wasn't for you and a few others I'd be outta here.'

'You'd a girlfriend, didn't you, before you entered?' I asked.

'Yeah, I miss that an' all,' he sighed. 'Oi, I could do with a good shag!'

He said one of the priests had told him that celibacy was harder for the sexually experienced.

'It's unnatural, Joseph, a house full of men. Then again, sex isn't all it's cracked up to be. My dad said to me that he often has to be celibate too. Marriage isn't sex on tap.'

Sexually repressed and inexperienced – apart from, and partly due to, the long-ago child abuse of fondling and being forced to strip by Christian Brothers – I'd never before talked to a friend so freely about sex.

In my journal, I wrote that Milltown was *'the best place for me'*. It was. I was exploring the meaning of life. I was getting to know myself. But behind my choice lay a self-limiting lack of confidence in myself, a fear that I couldn't cope outside of religious life, that no woman would ever want to marry me and that shorn of my religious identity I would be lost.

35

# IN MY GUT, I DON'T BELIEVE

We had a wonderful Christmas at Mount St Mary's and, for the first time since entering in September, we returned home on 26 December for a few days. My mother had an obsessive–compulsive need to 'give'. Insisting I take money she proffered, I declined, saying I would have to hand it in to the bursar.

'You don't need to give everything in.'

'I do. Everything we get, we give to the Marists. Everything we need, we get from the Marists. That's the deal.'

'You don't need to tell them.'

Parental tensions persisted over the Christmas. Tactfully, I raised the possibility of marriage counselling.

'Tommyrot,' said my mother. 'I know marriages that broke up after counselling.'

I yearned to understand my childhood and the tension I'd felt in my gut from my earliest memories; parental rows, Paul banished, David vanished, his whereabouts still unknown. Talking had never worked. So I asked my mother to write to me reminding me of family holidays, pet dogs and, as I put it, 'stuff about Paul and David'.

Eventually, I received this: *David was very fortunate in getting a very nice clerical position as junior clerk in the clerical department of Grangegorman.*

It isn't easy to grasp what delights a boy aged 15 or 16 might enjoy as a clerk in a depressing mental institution.

*'After two years he resigned and packed his bag for London and the big smoke. Be that as it may, he chose, apparently, to break away from his roots, and, as a friend of mine said to me, "For Heaven's sake, don't be worrying, he is just like so many more. If he wasn't doing alright he would have shown up on your doorstep long ago."*

36

*Anyway, he was an adult at twenty-and-a-half years of age so he was well able to look after himself.'*

Serpentine-slippery words: after two years he would have been at most 18, not 20-plus. My brother Paul believes David left Ireland in 1972 aged 17.

*'In my heart,'* she continued, *'I must confess I am not worried about him for the simple reason that common sense tells me there is nothing to worry about.'*

This from a woman terrified of thunder or every time I got on my bicycle.

*'Having said that, I must also confess, that having reared him, I am interested to know how he is getting along, and whether he is married or what. One just doesn't rear children and write them off as if they never existed, although I would nearly bet, that, at times, one could be nearly forgiven for doing so.'*

She concealed more than she revealed.

## #13

On 4 November 1980, Ronald Reagan was elected US President. In Ireland, the controversial Health (Family Planning) Act, 1979, came into operation. It allowed contraceptives to be available in Ireland for the first time but only with a medical prescription, 'for the purpose, bona fide, of family planning or for adequate medical reasons'.

Taoiseach Charles J. Haughey declared it 'an Irish solution to an Irish problem'.

My 18-year-old piety was shocked by seeming dissent by some within the seminary. I was discovering that the Catholic Church wasn't a monolith. Critiques by priests and students included:

'Why should the Church impose celibacy on people with AIDS when it's hard enough for *us* to live the vow of celibacy?'

'The Church is preoccupied with sex – Jesus rarely mentioned it. It should be less bothered by what consenting adults do between the sheets.'

'The Billings method of contraception is Vatican roulette.'

'Once a man is consecrated a bishop two things happen – he'll never want for a hot dinner and he'll never hear the truth spoken to his face again.'

'If John XXIII opened the windows of the Vatican, John Paul II is slamming them shut again.'

But in our teenage innocence, some novices were upset by these criticisms.

'But what are we to believe?' asked a novice, angered by what he saw as disloyalty to the Pope.

'Well, I know what I mean when I recite the creed,' said author and theologian Father Seán Fagan, 'but I doubt if the Pope interprets it the same way that I do.'

'But that's so confusing!' replied my fellow novice.

'Confusion is a good thing,' responded Seán. 'That's how we learn. We need a critical, intelligent faith. The Church accepts today things it condemned before and it condemns today previous orthodoxies of the Church.'

Seán was one of several widely-respected Irish priests silenced by the Vatican around 2012. He died on 15 July 2016.

*

During the four week-long silent retreats we weren't permitted to speak, watch television, listen to music or radio, or read, apart from 'spiritual' reading. Our first retreat focused on 'purgation' and concluded with a general confession of a lifetime of 'sin'!

The retreat director, Father Hannan, preached, 'What is the ultimate meaning of your life? You belong to God. The world will be poorer if you don't fulfil His plan for you. To refuse to serve God, to disobey Him, is a disorder.'

That hook would keep me in religious life for nine years. If God was calling me to the priesthood and I walked away, I would be unhappy, like the rich young man in the Gospel who declined Jesus's call and went away sad.

During the retreat, I went to Father Hannan for 'spiritual direction'.

'I'm struggling with celibacy,' I said.

I had long sought to suppress any sexual urges, having been taught at home, in school and at church that they were sinful. I wondered if admitting to sexual desire would disqualify me from the priesthood.

'Joseph, there is a great work of God taking place in you,' he responded. 'You are growing in self-awareness. You are sexual. We all are. I want you to go to your room and be thankful for your genitalia. God made you; and all that God made is good. Throw aside the pride about failures in perfect continence. Satan's work is to discourage. The holiest people struggle with God.'

I felt encouraged by this. I had grown up thinking of priests as asexual, never imagining they experienced sexual desire or succumbed to solitary pleasure. I had been honest with Father Hannan and he had accepted me.

During the retreat, the novitiate dined in its common room. When most novices had finished eating, every noise was accentuated. I bit into an apple. No matter how hard I tried, each bite was amplified. Tension built, a novitiate held its breath – and the grand silence transmogrified into laughter!

I made my general confession, laying my life bare. After absolution, the confessor said, 'You've made a marvellous confession.'

I had been my honest self before my Novice Master and confessor during the retreat. Both accepted me as I was, and encouraged me to proceed towards my cherished dream of becoming a priest.

After the retreat's final ceremony at which we had made our general confessions, we emerged jubilant and noisily from the chapel as if high on sanctifying grace.

Father Fagan told us the joke about two priests seated side-by-side in an aircraft. The pilot announces the plane is about to crash. They hear each other's confession. Then the pilot announces they won't crash after all. Mortified by his confession, one priest says: 'Funny how you exaggerate in an emergency!'

My dad wrote to me on 18 November 1980, after our silent retreat, saying he supposed I felt a relief that I could talk again, adding: 'Any chance of getting Mammy on the next one?'

## #14

Novitiate life continued apace. We weren't generally allowed visitors during novitiate but an exception was made for my Uncle John in November 1980 before his return to South Africa. He concelebrated mass for the novitiate. I hoped my fellow novices would like him. I was a bit embarrassed that he preached for 20 minutes but afterwards a confrère spoke warmly of him and loved my Uncle John's expression urging us to enjoy the novitiate and 'Lap it up!'

One evening, I happened to knock on a confrère's door. Inside were three novices, the lights dimmed, the curtains drawn – a whiff of subterfuge.

'Come in, Joe!'

'What's going on?'

'We've got a cassette of *The Life of Brian*!'

Monty Python's 1979 film was considered blasphemous in Ireland. But the audio tape worked its comic genius on us. I nearly died laughing.

Occasionally, we had a '*congé*', when we were allowed to leave Milltown, each with pocket money of about seven pounds.

Sometimes a few of us cycled to Dún Laoghaire, walked the pier and had a pint. Or we would borrow a house car and drive to Wicklow and go hillwalking. Or we would go into town to see a movie. One confrère loved to dress in his best clothes and walk up and down Grafton Street savouring the sight of girls.

When a priest died, dozens of Marist Fathers concelebrated the mass.

'It's impressive to see so many turn up,' I said to Father Brian Keenan, a much-loved and popular priest.

Pursing his lips and winking, he retorted, 'Not always. When one bastard died who had taught us in Milltown, half the priests turned up to make sure he was dead!'

I had not considered that earlier regimes were different to ours.

'Some made life Hell for us,' said Brian. 'And our theological training was abysmal. All we did was regurgitate

41

Latin texts which we didn't understand. It was, literally, ordained ignorance!'

We were growing into adulthood in Milltown.

'Remember those psychological tests before we joined?' asked a novice. 'That thinly veiled picture of an erect penis and we had to write down what we saw? I thought, no way am I putting that down – they'll think I'm a pervert. Today, I'd just write down what I saw. We came in too young Joe!'

Lectures on celibacy began. Father Denis Green said, 'Brothers, priests of my generation were taught that sex was wrong. Our human formation was deficient. Nowadays, we see sexuality as an integral part of the human personality – it is part of our relationship with God. Rejecting our affectivity or thinking poorly of marriage isn't an option for priests.'

I had been taught that celibacy was a higher calling than marriage. If both were equal, I wondered why be celibate? I wanted to be a priest but I also yearned for intimacy, affection and an exclusive relationship.

'Some priests seem crushed – not enriched – by celibacy,' observed a novice.

'Some men were ordained who shouldn't have been. Others might have been put in ministries for which they were unsuited,' replied Denis.

I was struck by his admission that some men were ordained who shouldn't have been. Were priests called by God or was the Church just a human club, with men alone deciding who was ordained?

Denis continued: 'If Rome were to permit priests to marry in the future, as members of a religious congregation we would still not be allowed to marry. Secular priests promise celibacy to their bishop. But we make a vow of celibacy to God for life.'

That too was news to me. There was much debate about a married priesthood and I was dismayed to hear that, if the rule changed, I would still be stuck with celibacy.

The Superior Father Hannan said that priests must love but not genitally. We were not to repress the sexual but 'if you are turned on by someone, don't tell that person. And if you can't resist the sexual urge, get out of there. Either terminate the relationship or give it space so you remain faithful to your vows.'

'I still need human love and friendship,' he continued. 'Our community life is vital to help us live the vow of celibacy. Friendships in community are important. Non-exclusive, non-genital spiritual friendships are good for celibates, so long as the relationship remains open and honest. There are risks. When you're nineteen, a sexual attraction can occur.'

'Are you saying we could fall in love with one another?' asked a novice.

'Yes,' said Father Hannan.

'Men loving men?' retorted the novice. 'I can't imagine that.'

Father Hannan responded: 'Well maybe it won't happen for you. But Freud taught us that relatively few people are exclusively heterosexual or homosexual. Most people are somewhere along the spectrum. Even if this is theoretical to you now, before long it won't be.'

## #15

The Superior told us he was required to ensure that we knew the facts of life. Embarrassed, he delivered his lecture.

Afterwards, a novice asked, 'Is masturbation against the vow of celibacy?'

'Yes,' said Father Hannan.

An awkward silence descended.

Father Bernd Kordes posed questions for our private consideration.

'Do you feel frightened of commitment?'

'Yes,' I wrote. 'I wonder how well I know myself. And whether the Church is really worth committing to.'

'Do you have a sense of belonging here?'

'Yes, but less than before.'

'Do you feel your sexuality is making sense?'

'I don't know,' I recorded honestly. 'I'm only waking up to it. If I was as sexually aware before I joined as I am now, I doubt if I would have entered. I wonder if the Church accepts students too early and they remain trapped in adolescence for the rest of their lives.'

The question we faced was whether to apply for first profession at the end of novitiate. First profession seemed the definitive end to any hope I had of sexual intimacy in my life, a profound decision to make when I would be only 19. I talked to Father John Hannan in his office.

'I really don't know if I can commit to a life of celibacy.'

'Joseph, none of us know our future. We can only live in the present. We can't be celibate without the grace of God. Jesus won't ask anything of you that you won't be able to do, with His help.'

'I want to be a priest but I want intimacy too.'

'That's normal. We are human but with God's help we don't need to act out our desires. We sacrifice our sexual urges for the sake of building up the Kingdom of God. We're called to transcend sexual desire but be thankful for it too. We can't sacrifice what we're not aware of.'

He continued: 'In no way does your sexual awakening make you unsuitable for the priesthood. There is no perversion in you. You passed the psychological tests and we are confident that you will make a good priest.'

Again, I was close to tears by the Superior's acceptance of me.

'I worried I would be unsuitable for the priesthood,' I said.

'On the contrary, Joseph, you show yourself to be very open and honest. You lay your soul before me. Nothing you have told me bars you from the priesthood. Your self-knowledge for someone your age is remarkable. You will be Superior here one day.'

That conversation happened close to Christmas. When we returned to Milltown after our few days at home, to my surprise I discovered that Father Hannan had made me Monitor. I was encouraged by his confidence in me.

On Valentine's Day, 1981, 48 young people perished in a fire at the Stardust nightclub in north Dublin, near where I'd lived. Taoiseach Charles Haughey wept at the scene. My mother rang to assure me that my sister was safe. Dumbfounded by such tragedy so close to home, I shared the widespread anger when reports alleged that some fire doors had been locked.

That same month my naïve, still only 18-year-old self, wrote: 'On a congé in Howth, I was so at peace with the

Lord that even when I walked into a cowpat, I praised Jesus.'

Yikes! Nowadays I'd write, 'I was so calm in myself that even when I walked on a cowpat it didn't bother me.'

Language aside, my critical thinking faculty was functioning. I had come to regard religious relics, scapulars and miraculous medals as superstitious nonsense. I cast an increasingly critical eye on the institutional Church. And, despite being in the Society of Mary, I wasn't much persuaded by many Catholic devotions to Mary, some of which seemed to me more akin to worshipping a female deity.

In early March 1981, one of my closest friends beckoned me to his room.

'Joe, I'm leaving.'

I was bereft and tried to change his mind.

'I'm sorry, Joe. This is the right decision for me. I will miss you.'

We hugged and then prayed together and, after we'd finished, I saw he had been crying. I wanted to cry too, but couldn't.

'I cried watching Jesus of Nazareth,' he said. 'The scene where Peter left his boat, never again to be a fisherman. He looked back at it, broken-hearted.'

A page pinned to his wall read: *'The novitiate is a lonely place.'*

I left his room in a sudden vortex of my own doubts. He left Milltown shortly afterwards. The Superior gathered the shaken novices into the common room. We sat close together, shell-shocked to have lost our confrère, the first of our band of brothers to leave.

'The first one is always the worst,' said Father Hannan.

The next day, a second novice left.

## #16

The departure of my friend from the novitiate in March 1981, and of a second novice the next day, precipitated existential questions.

*'I thought religion would satisfy my every need,'* I journaled. From my sexual awakening, I realised that it wouldn't.

So convinced had I been that I only needed 'God', I had, two years earlier, stopped studying. From one of the highest achievers in my school in the Intermediate Certificate, I got a pedestrian Leaving Cert.

My mother hadn't known I wasn't studying. When she returned from the next parent–teacher meeting, she said nothing. All my life, she had received good feedback from teachers and had come home glowing. Not this time.

Silence persisted for days. Either teachers hadn't been honest or mother decided to say nothing. Then, out of the blue, she came to my bedroom.

'I have never been so humiliated in my life!' she spat, handing me a letter reinforcing her response. There was no discussion about what I was thinking or doing and how it might damage me. It was all about her.

Whereas many teenagers underperform because they have discovered sex, drugs and rock 'n' roll, my adolescent fix was religion and the highs and hugs of charismatic renewal.

I chose to sabotage my Leaving Certificate lest, if I did well, I might abandon my religious path. Also, despite high scores in the Intermediate Certificate, I lacked confidence in myself academically; and my crazy adolescent thinking went that it was better to do badly than be mediocre.

More positively, I observed the calm of a clever friend of mine at school minutes before one of the Intermediate Certificate exams. Seeing his equanimity, I wanted to define myself less by academic achievement and enjoy a more balanced life. He embodied a person at ease with himself, which may have been more educational for me than had I studied for the Leaving Certificate.

Remembering all this in novitiate, I journaled: *'I'm such a docile twit. I've thrown my chances away.'*

Docile foolishness apart, at only 18 I had hardly thrown my chances away. Freed of my religious fix, I could have left and taken my chance in the world. However, I was not free of religious thinking and still clung to my hope, encapsulated by Father Larry Duffy's prayer, that many souls would be saved through my ministry.

*'Why am I staying?'* I journaled. *'I'm afraid that by leaving I'd be rejecting God and go to Hell.'* While this may seem silly, consider this from Luke's Gospel: 'Nobody who puts his hand to the plough and abandons God's work is fit for the Kingdom of Heaven' (Luke 9:62). Many religious believers fear damnation. That is why millions of Catholics used to attend weekly confession, lest they died in a state of 'mortal sin'.

*'I'd feel ashamed, leaving,'* I journaled. *'So many people gave me such nice gifts and good wishes. I'd be embarrassed. I was so convinced priesthood was right for me.'*

Leaving wouldn't only involve changing job, career and home. My identity as a person and my philosophical worldview were inextricably interwoven with my desire to be a priest.

I journaled: *'I'd be afraid that I'm not mature enough to form a lasting relationship.'* At 18, I wasn't; but few people would be at that age.

I decided it was better to stay in Milltown and to give my vocation at least three years, although my choice of language suggests an element of calculation. I journaled: *'It would look better if I left after three years.'* Look better to whom? Other people? My superego? Between an imagined, jealous and threatening deity, and real or imagined other people, I caught myself in a bind.

Besides, I loved this vibrant and intellectually stimulating community; its concern for what mattered in life; its values of compassion, justice and love. And I was drawn by my literary interest to the poetry and promise of parts of the Bible, such as that God would do far more within us than we could conceive of or imagine (Ephesians 3:20).

Moreover, while two novices had left, three female friends of mine had entered convents during my novitiate, and two scholastics at Milltown had been ordained priests.

Having a son of the parish ordained was still a big deal in the 1980s, especially in rural Ireland. Following his ordination, my confrère Father Paddy Stanley said his first mass in his home parish of Castledermot. Bunting in the Vatican's yellow and white festooned the streets and a brass band led a parade through the village of happy townsfolk.

In contrast, a senior priest in Milltown told us the true story of an Italian who had left the priesthood immediately after ordination, to widespread consternation. He had been seeing a psychotherapist who had advised him to proceed with ordination 'to get it out of his system' and then leave; which he promptly did.

The holy oil hardly dry on his hands, he legged it!

#17

A family day was planned for April 1981; the only one, thankfully, of the novitiate. Before it, I received a letter from my mother deliberating, in copious detail, on the merits, or otherwise, of bringing a picnic bag for lunch into the chapel or whether leaving it in the car would be better.

I was exasperated reading it; and I despaired of the chasm between us when she said to me before a presentation that day, 'Is there anything you want me to ask?' She couldn't understand that this was my new family, where I could be myself, ask questions and, on most things, speak my mind.

However, there was one area within novitiate that we could not discuss. Nationalist feelings ran high among some novices when IRA hunger striker Bobby Sands was elected Member of Parliament for Fermanagh and South Tyrone on 9 April. He had been on hunger strike for forty-one days. It was a non-violent protest and it ignited my Irish nationalism. But we were banned from discussing it in the novitiate, probably because three of our confrères were English; although one English confrère was happy to talk about it and favoured a united Ireland.

The Superior spoke to us about the vow of obedience. After presenting us with the relevant Vatican Council documents, and scriptural passages employed to support it, he said: 'Obedience is listening to God's will. We do not ignore our personal judgement but we submit our mind and will to God's will, the Church, and the call of the Superior. Obedience requires sacrifice.'

Bobby Sands died on 5 May, 1981. Nine more hunger strikers and sixty-one others died due to sectarian strife during that seven-month protest. But in a seminary on the island where the maelstrom was happening, we were forbidden to discuss it.

I was angry about this prohibition and wondered if I might find the vow of obedience even harder than celibacy. How could suppression of discussion and debate be good? I now consider submission of the mind to anyone a dereliction of adult responsibility.

Novitiate life had its comic moments. During an intense, heated community meeting on our food wastage, emotions skyrocketed until a novice pricked the tension with: 'Imagine getting emotional about carrots!'

We exploded into laughter.

In late May, the novitiate got the ferry across the Irish Sea to visit the Marian shrine of Walsingham in England. We travelled in a clapped-out minibus with extraordinary play in the steering wheel. On the English motorways, we swayed from side to side, alarming other road users.

Even to my innocent eyes, Walsingham was a strange place. At a pub frequented by camp Anglican vicars, a clergyman asked a fellow novice, 'What are you into?'

'Elephants!' my confrère replied, beating a hasty retreat.

A third hunger striker died while we were in Walsingham, and we learned that Charles Haughey had dissolved the Government. The election, the first of three in two years, was held on 11 June – the first poll I was old enough to vote in.

Back in Milltown, our third silent retreat began. Led by Father Peter Allen, it focused on suffering. My mood at the start of the retreat was of anger for no obvious reason.

Doubts resurfaced and my journal records thoughts about leaving. But by the third day, happiness, contentment and joy abounded. A spontaneous and authentic smile oozed forth from deep within.

I enjoyed cutting the lawns. Rather than focusing on getting the job done, I lived in the present. When we were finished, four of us got two wheelbarrows, a novice in each, and we had a silent wheelbarrow race!

That evening, while Peter led us through relaxation exercises – in his words 'breathing in the presence of the Lord' – I remained joyful and couldn't stop smiling.

*'It's as if some healing is going on within me,'* I journaled. *'The thought of getting a job in the world and staying at that work for the rest of my life appals me. Within religious life, I'll be changed continually, which should keep my mind broad, adaptable and always learning.'*

It wasn't just me: everyone looked serene. One night, after Compline, a novice broke the silence and whispered to me: 'We should all become enclosed monks!'

'Why?' I asked.

He said: 'Everyone is so happy!'

Next day, I sat outdoors on sweet-smelling hay, the sunny sky above, the potatoes we had planted earlier in the year doing well. I heard a scholastic playing his guitar and singing. I was peaceful, happy and self-aware. I walked barefoot through the potato furrows, the clay soft beneath my feet, oozing soil between my toes.

When I had entered novitiate, I had thought: 'Who wants girls, money or independence once you've got Jesus?' But, by the end of the third silent retreat, I had an awakening appreciation of what I would be giving up.

'Yes, now I feel I can be a priest,' I mused, sensing the sacrifice, and that faith alone was needed.

## #18

On 30 June 1981, aged 19, I wrote to my father. While the letter was sentimental, its essence was important and I'm glad I wrote it.

*Dear Dad,*

*I've survived the first three retreats. This was my favourite. I relaxed into it. I missed you Dad during the solitude of retreat. I prayed for you.*

*September is fast approaching and, if it's God's will, I'll be professed into the Society of Mary. I hope that the Lord will spare yourself and Mum for my ordination to the priesthood, if I choose to remain. I keep in mind and heart Uncle John in South Africa.*

*Sorry for not appreciating you while I lived at home. I ask your forgiveness Dad for not being to you what I ought to have been and what you deserved me to be as your son. Dad, I love you.*

*Thank you, Dad, for being my father. For all the years when you worked so hard to support the family and the holidays we enjoyed together. Above all Dad, many thanks for the faith yourself and Mum passed on to me. Without it, I would not have spent these nine months where I am. No movement or figure could have put into me the wealth I received from my home.*

*May God's grace be yours Dad. May Mary wrap her mantle around you. And may Peace be yours.*

*Your son, Joseph*

I reflected in my journal: *'My father, I know, deeply resents my mother for the unbelievable things she did. But what things?'* My mother's mother died when she was only two. She never knew her mother.

53

On 14 July, my father sent me a cherished letter.

*Dear Joseph*

*Was delighted – to get – you letter You will have to forgive me for not writeing more often. writing letters is not one of my strong points*

*Well Joseph I have the house to myself – a present Mamnie is gone to the dentist so I thought it would be a good time to try – and – get on paper what I have in my mindy to me that is very hard work. I have your letter in front of me I but I – cannot read it because my eyes – are – giving me some trouble. I will be going to see about them on Friday*

*Joseph we miss you very much at home, but we never miss you in our prayers. Well Joseph what – can I say to you – after getting you Lovely letter except you havene nothing – to worry about being a good Son You – and Mamme or I have no worries about you the Man – above will look after you with the help of our Prayers we mever forget you in the Rosary Don't forget David in Yours.*

*I am still waiting on another Banger I should have one this Month are you getting much driving yourself. I will say bye bye for the present as the writers cramp has started I hope you – can Read this letter alright because the way my Eyesare I – cannot Red iit back*

*From Your Loving Father*

*P.S. Is the writing any better than Uncle John*

What struck me most in that treasured letter was 'Don't forget David', my half-brother, still missing after seven (or nine) years. It felt like a bequest.

Just five days later, I received a lucid letter from my mother.

*My Beloved Joseph,*

*... Dad is not really well at all at the moment. I'm not too happy to leave him on his own for long periods. His eyesight has deteriorated over the last few weeks and he is complaining of headaches and dizziness. The doctor has arranged for him to see a consultant ... He*

*also has an appointment with his ophthalmic surgeon to have an eye test and see if he needs a change of spectacles.*

*He seems to be rather depressed in himself and the doctor says he is to take it easy. We go out for walks, and he is alright, but I would not be happy for him to go out alone until things settle down a bit. Hopefully, with a change of specs, he will be O.K. No harm to say a few extra prayers…*

*My love, Mammy*

Her phrase 'not really well at all' had me worried. I told the Superior, who said to keep him advised. I wrote home, explaining the summer Rule of Life in novitiate had begun – *'We're told what to do but not when to do it'* – and it was easier to receive phone calls.

Within novitiate, the focus turned to first profession, when we would take vows of celibacy, obedience and poverty. Father Hannan told us: 'You need to prepare, know the obligations they impose, and have the right sort of maturity to proceed.'

## #19

We began a module on the vow of poverty. The Second Vatican Council saw the vow as witnessing to the love of Christ above everything else. Our treasure lay in Heaven, not here on earth. Poverty sought to awaken the consciences of other people. We were not to be concerned with appearing to be poor; neither were we to judge the rich. We were not to collude with social injustice. The purpose of the vow was the conversion of hearts – starting with ourselves.

By being poor, we would be one with Christ. We would challenge the view that a person's worth was determined by their material wealth. The vow of poverty promoted fraternity and community. It challenged us to curb the pursuit of ease and comfort; and to discern whether or not to accept all that was offered to us. It aimed to help us to purify our love. It was to help us to be one with the poor, sharing their cares. It involved us being dependent.

The Vatican Council called us to a life without luxuries, affectation or vanity; and being poor not only in spirit but in fact. We were to experience poverty even in what we needed for our sustenance. We were to be seen to be poor; and obliged to pool our goods and share with the poor. We were never to have everything we wanted but were permitted to have what we needed. We were prohibited from accumulating possessions. Poverty was not for poverty's sake but to proclaim the Gospel.

Anything we received we were required to give to the congregation and anything we needed we got from the congregation: shelter, warmth, clothes, food, pocket money, holidays, books, personal items, money for work or study, education, and security for illness and old age.

We novices were idealists. At least some of us felt we were not living the vow of poverty as radically as we should. Jesus had said to sell everything and follow him. But within religious life we had everything we needed and more. Mount St Mary's was in a lovely part of Dublin, with playing fields, walkways and gardens. We ate well. We were educated and we were financially secure for life. We didn't need to worry about funding healthcare or providing for pensions. Everything we needed would be given to us by the Marists.

Lots of people could live happily with that kind of poverty. In fact, my lifestyle had improved since entering the seminary. We had a three-course dinner every day. Although we were personally poor, having only a few pounds' pocket money per month, and I didn't like having to ask the bursar if I needed to buy something, it felt like we were millionaires. We lived in large buildings and the Marists had several houses in Ireland and scores more around the world. We ran private schools, catering for the rich. The real concerns of people, like the fear of losing their job or home, were alien to us. Our vow of poverty seemed a bit of a sham.

The Superior set us an essay on our personal view of poverty. With the wisdom of an adolescent, I wrote that we should have nothing of our own, like bikes, towels, bed clothes or books. All these should instead be shared. I questioned whether we should have expensive pens. I admitted that watches, while they could be seen as luxuries, were needed.

I posited that breakfast should be simple, just bread and tea or coffee, with no expensive cereals. I pondered the excesses of marmalade and jam. I felt soup was an unnecessary luxury at dinner time. Sauces, gravies and mustard betokened excesses that should be excised from our diet. And why have dessert? I envisaged a student house of inexpensive typewriters, with all of us sharing one collective good dictionary. Televisions should be black and white rather than colour. We shouldn't accumulate personal possessions or gifts – I was thinking of chess and other board games.

We should be frugal in our use of furniture polish, washing up liquid and shampoo. Did we really need two cars for forty-five people? Did I need all seven of my shirts? I pondered the extravagance of shoelaces. I questioned the need for toilet rolls and wondered if better use could have been made of old newspapers.

Father John Hannan explained to us that the vow of poverty did not require that we be destitute. What we needed, we asked for and received. Need was determined through openness with our spiritual director and Superior. We were meant to live a frugal lifestyle. We shouldn't accumulate stuff. Rather than being attached to our possessions, we should be willing to lend things to others. We should work hard and strive for social justice. We were to be men of conscience.

## #20

The calm and happiness of the third novitiate retreat deserted me. Faced, aged 19, with the vow of obedience, I wondered if I might be running away from having to take responsibility for my life, by letting other people make decisions for me. With obedience, if something didn't work out, I could always blame someone else.

I still felt the vow of poverty was a bit of a sham, for we were not materially poor.

Committing to a life of celibacy, I increasingly longed for physical and emotional intimacy. Never having had a relationship before, I didn't know what two people who loved one another shared, apart from sex. What might it feel like, I wondered, to open oneself up emotionally to another human being in an exclusive relationship?

I had no confidence that any woman would ever want to marry me. Uninspired by my parents' marriage typified by hurt, pretence and their inability to communicate, married life wasn't attractive. I worried that I wouldn't be able to cope with it and thought my lack of confidence had partly motivated me to enter religious life.

The honeymoon period of the novitiate was over and some relationships were under strain. My immaturity and self-doubt resurged and my teenage angst spiked. I felt isolated, lonely and of no consequence. I hadn't yet learned to accept and be comfortable within myself.

I wondered should I leave or take a year out and get more life experience before committing to religious life and priesthood. I was honest and discussed everything with the Superior.

'You're going through a semi-adolescent crisis, which you'll soon get over,' said Father Hannan. 'Look, I don't honestly know if you have a vocation or not but you'll face the same challenges outside as you do here. God is filling you with His love but not the way you thought He would.'

'I wonder if I was mesmerised by Larry Duffy,' I said of the charismatic priest whom I had so admired and sought to emulate.

'I can't say,' said Father Hannan. 'You were certainly influenced by him. But you have a strong influence on others in the novitiate. You're a strong person and I don't think you realise that yet. You have the capacity of a strong leader. You can speak with decisiveness but you must first be educated so that you can lead well. You're a much more attractive figure than you think.'

Having discussed my adolescent crisis of self-doubt with him, he said: 'You'll always have mini-complexes – all of us do. The saints had them too. You have this "all or nothing" thing. God has a vocation lined out for you. You must live it. Growth is slow, long and painful. You're not yet ready for marriage. You're looking for Utopia.'

I mentioned the possibility of leaving for a year, adding: 'I may need to leave this place to pray!'

'There can be value in leaving for a year,' Father Hannan replied. 'But I don't find it too credible that you need to leave here to pray. It's the commitment here that takes the glamour off it.'

He was right about that.

'I'm frightened of obedience,' I said.

'I'm frightened of it too,' he responded, with candour.

The silence rested between us for a while. His honesty had elicited within me a sense of our fraternity. Despite his authority over me, we were confrères.

I told him I doubted my previous religious experiences.

'God works where we're at,' he said. 'He won't work last year's ways in us now. You are right to question past religious experiences but God did work then, though not the same way as now.'

But by such reasoning one could question every seeming religious experience, adjudge each previous one deficient, hasten towards a more authentic encounter, which in turn would be questionable tomorrow. A never-ending cycle could ensue, without ever having experienced anything of substance that was real, authentic or true.

However, Father Hannan seemed to validate that God had somehow been involved in what I had previously regarded as possible religious experiences. Moreover, his belief that God's action was still taking place in me, albeit in new ways, was comforting and reassuring. He was my Superior and Novice Master: I was just a novice.

'I daydream a lot in prayer,' I added.

'We'll always daydream in prayer. You will until you're ninety!'

Again, that sense of my acceptability and our fraternal bond.

I was encouraged. Having once again been vulnerable and presented my unvarnished self to him, the Superior expressed no reason for me to leave.

## #21

In July 1981, novices attended a charismatic youth jamboree in Artane, close to my home. A neighbour saw me and rang my sister, who arrived and told me Dad's health had deteriorated that morning.

I went home immediately. My father was in bed, looking better than I expected. He was able to chat and sit up. I had in my pocket the rosary beads he had given me when I joined the Marists. We used it to pray together, his holding them for one decade and me taking them for the next. There was a tangible shared sense of finality.

An ambulance arrived and he was taken to Mercers Hospital. I spoke to a nurse, worried that they mightn't realise how unwell he was because he looked all right.

'Mr Armstrong, we realise your father's condition is serious.'

That night when I returned to Milltown, I updated the Superior but shrugged off confrères' queries. Alone in the chapel, I cried my eyes out and thought of the letter that I had written to him so recently and his treasured reply.

Father Hannan told me I could visit my father as often as I liked, despite the normal seclusion of novitiate.

# IN MY GUT, I DON'T BELIEVE

It was a difficult time. Fear erupted every time the phone rang. Once, while hitching a lift to the hospital, Charles Mitchel picked me up. He was the first ever newscaster on RTE television in 1961 and he had cried announcing the death of US President Kennedy.

'You looked desolate. I couldn't pass you by.'

I wasn't certain it was him.

'You sound like Charles Mitchel.'

'That's because I am.'

I visited my dad frequently during those weeks. He shared chocolate, biscuits and sweets with me. One day, as we both sat on the side of his bed, he said he had a headache. His words were slurred. Unable to cope that day with his decline, I left shortly afterwards.

Next morning, my school friend and fellow novice John told me my mother had phoned.

'Your dad took a bad turn during the night. Come on, I'll drive you in.'

My father was lying in bed. When the nurse told him I had arrived, he tried to rise from the pillow and talk. He rose but fell back, letting out a loud, bellowing groan. Horrible words arose in my mind describing that sound which I thought I could never express. Dad's face was sunken on one side. When a doctor opened his eyes, his pupils were like pinpricks. He had taken a massive stroke.

I was distraught to see and hear my father, once strong and physically powerful, this manly man who had lugged Guinness barrels about and worked on their trucks, barges and cranes, struck down. Outside in the corridor, I wept.

A neighbour told me to stop and be strong for my mother. Although she meant well, I resented her intervention. I needed to express my distress, not bury it.

62

Back in the ward, my mother took my father's stroke disarmingly well. She joked with him about the garden and the dog. He smiled, showing he understood. My Uncle Joe and I sat beside him. Dad became restless and tried moving his arm. He manoeuvred his hand to his right eye and tried to open his eyelid but couldn't. Uncle Joe did it for him. Dad smiled. I held his hand and he tightened his grip. But by later that day, we lost more of him: he could no longer indicate even if he could hear us, or whether he knew we were there. At one point, tears fell from his eyes.

With no change in my father's condition, I returned to Milltown that night. Recently ordained Father Paddy Stanley came to my room.

'Talk to me,' he said.

I couldn't speak.

'Get it out.'

Here was the permission denied me earlier.

'Come on,' he persisted.

I spoke aloud those horrible words conceived earlier: 'He brayed like a donkey.'

As I write this, aged 56, those words still have not lost their power to upset me.

'Good man,' whispered Paddy.

Father Denis Green arrived in my room and sat beside me. I lay my head on his shoulder and cried. A confrère arrived with tea and toast. I learned prayers had been said at mass and Evening Prayer and the community had gathered to say the rosary for us. Next day, when I came back from the hospital, my room had been tidied, the bed made, my shirt had been washed and ironed, and an unsigned card lay on my pillow: 'We are with you, Joe, at this difficult time.'

I don't know who did these kindnesses but I was buoyed up by them. The support of the community deepened my sense of belonging and wanting to remain, all my life, in the Society of Mary.

## #22

*D*on't forget David,' my father wrote to me in his cherished letter weeks before his massive stroke in 1981. As he lay dying in Mercers Hospital that August, it became my bounden duty to find my brother.

David left home probably in 1972, when I was about ten. Fobbed off whenever I had asked about him, we assumed he was in London.

I rang dozens of people named David Armstrong in various phone books. I rang the BBC, the Irish embassy in London, the Department of Foreign Affairs in Dublin and the Garda, who in turn spoke to Scotland Yard. He wasn't on any records held by either police force.

Officers from the Metropolitan Police went to his last known London address. All present were interviewed. Someone remembered the name from 'about ten years back'. The police said a BBC broadcast would only be considered if my brother was my dad's only relative. I contacted the missing persons services of the Red Cross and Salvation Army. They took David's details and told me they would contact me if they heard anything. Clutching at straws, I telephoned Jacinta, a neighbour from home then living in London who knew David. She promised she would keep her eyes peeled for him.

Someone suggested he went to Spain but the Spanish embassy told me no visa was issued to him between 1973 and 1977, dates based on my mother's misleading letter. Previously I recounted how, trying to solve the mystery of my missing brother, I had asked my mother to write to me 'stuff about Paul and David'.

My mother's subsequent letter lied by evasion: *'David was very fortunate in getting a very nice clerical position as junior clerk in the clerical department of Grangegorman. After two years he resigned and packed his bag for London and the big smoke. Be that as it may, he chose, apparently, to break away from his roots...'*

Now, as my father lay dying and knowing I was trying to find David, I asked her yet again to tell me anything about my brother that might help me trace him. Despite the imminent death of our father, she still withheld the truth.

I hardly knew Paul. Eleven years my senior, my mother had laid down her ultimatum about her elder stepson to our father when I was only five. Ejected from home, Uncle Joe took Paul in. I saw him only once in the next four years when he was brought back to paint a ceiling. Paul joined the Irish army and we went to his passing out parade. He married and, as a virtual stranger to me, I was asked, aged 14, to be godfather to his daughter.

I was getting to know Paul at the hospital and I liked him. I told him I was trying to find David.

'Do you know that he's gay?'

I was flabbergasted.

'Does Mammy know this?'

'Of course, brother! No doubting that!'

I thought of my mother's words 'married or what' in her serpentine letter to me: *'I must also confess, that having reared him, I am interested to know how he is getting along, and whether he is married or what.'*

65

My mother's deception, reiterated at my father's deathbed, pierced through me like a lance, lacerating further the hacked umbilical cord. I imploded with anger and knew I could never trust her again.

The Church, of which my mother was always so uncritical a member, teaches in its Catechism (1994, #2357) that homosexual acts are 'acts of grave depravity', 'intrinsically disordered', 'contrary to the natural law' and 'under no circumstances can they be approved'. All homosexuals are 'called to chastity' and, if they are Christians, to 'unite to the sacrifice of the Lord's Cross' for the trials of their 'condition'.

I could only imagine how my unquestioningly obedient Catholic mother had reacted when she discovered her stepson was gay. Same-sex sexual activity was not decriminalised in Ireland until 1993, so for my mother her stepson was not only engaging in gravely sinful depravity but committing criminal activity too.

Mother did not do shame well. I recall her reaction to her only ever negative school report about me, the silence for days and eventually her selfish, 'I have never been so humiliated in my life!' Yes, it was all about her.

Imagine her response to David. I recall ongoing family tension. All I know is that David packed his bags and left home aged, at most, 17; at some point arrived in London; and chose not to inform us of changes of address nor to contact home again.

Knowing his sexuality, I contacted a London-based gay newspaper. They interviewed me and published an article on a distraught young man trying to find his brother as their father lay dying in hospital.

## #23

The Superior had encouraged me to take temporary vows for three years but now we discussed the possibility of my postponing first profession given my father's terminal illness, my visits to his bedside, my attempts to find David, and the many contacts with my family – countering the normal seclusion and solitude of novitiate. On balance, we agreed it was better to proceed with first profession, taking an initial commitment of promises for one year.

Soon afterwards, the Superior, my mother, Uncle John – who had returned from South Africa because of my father's illness – and I, were sitting in a family room in Mercers Hospital.

'Will this affect Joseph's profession?' my mother asked Father Hannan.

I had never known whether my mother was pleased or displeased by my entering the Marists. Years later, she told me 'people' expected me to leave and look after her when my father died. I feared being sucked back under her influence, manipulation and control.

'That's Joseph's decision,' the Superior replied.

Relief, freedom and dignity filled me by his firm response to her, respecting my choice.

The final silent retreat began, to conclude with our first profession on Saturday 12 September 1981. On the Tuesday of the retreat, as I sat in the chapel just before Evening Prayer, the Superior came up to me.

'We need to go to the hospital.'

He drove me in. After a few hours, the nurse told me Dad had stabilised and Father Hannan drove me back to Milltown.

Next day, Wednesday 9 September, Evening Prayer had already begun so it caused more of a stir when Father Denis Green called me from chapel. I was worn out and sensed that this was it, determined that I wouldn't come back to Milltown until Dad had died.

My mother, sister, brother and Uncle John were already there. Only David was absent. Other relatives, and patients well enough to leave their beds, joined us around my father's death bed. Denis administered the Last Rites. The hospital chaplain handed Uncle John the Blessed Sacrament, who held the host over my father's head.

No doubt as part of the natural physiology of his death throes but nevertheless for the first time since taking his massive stroke, my father opened his eyes. His pupils were no longer pinpricks as they had been since his stroke. Now the pupils were wide, brown and beautiful. I mumbled prayers and we all prayed the rosary aloud.

It seemed he had breathed his last and a nurse ushered us aside to check his pulse.

'He is alive,' she pronounced, and in a comic moment amidst sorrow, we all traipsed back around his bed again for yet more rosaries.

Uncle John held a crucifix above Dad's head. Its corpus broke off, falling on my father's broken body, my uncle left holding the figureless cross – to believers, a symbol of the Resurrection. Dad died. I felt numb and did not cry; and, watching a relative cry, I wondered why, since it was so obvious that he was dying. I had shed most of my tears the day he took the massive stroke.

68

My father, a member of the Third Order of Saint Francis, was laid out in the Franciscan habit. His removal and requiem mass were in Church Street. Entering the Franciscan chapel, walking behind his coffin, now my tears flowed freely, triggered by the full-voiced singing of the choir above me. I was overwhelmed by the music, the moment, and the gathering of so many who had come to support us. Perhaps forty Marist Fathers and Franciscan priests, each clad in alb and stole, concelebrated my father's requiem mass.

As the cortege entered Mount Jerome cemetery, from the backseat of the mourning car I saw a friend walking outside close to me. She was someone whom I felt I might have had a future with outside the Marists. But such was the support I felt from my fellow Marists, that I thought I could never leave them now. I had found where I belonged. I would repay their love with my life.

The next day, 12 September 1981, I made my first profession. The Superior called each of the remaining seventeen of the original twenty novices by name.

In turn, each novice knelt on the sanctuary making his first profession. I promised to live for one year the vows of chastity, poverty and obedience, according to the rule of the Society of Mary.

'I ask you, Reverend Father, to receive these promises of mine as a sign of my desire to commit myself wholly to the Lord and to His Church in the life of this religious community.'

And then I said the prayer considered most intimate to Marists: *'Strengthen, O God, the work of your hand. Mary, most loving Mother, I am yours; by your powerful intercession secure my everlasting welfare. Amen.'*

Near the end of the ceremony, I heard the Provincial announce: 'Yesterday, one of the newly professed buried his father.'

This public recognition of my bereavement was appropriate. But I was numb. It took me a moment to process that he was talking about me.

## *Chapter 3*

# Love and desire

### #24

Together with most of the newly professed Marists, I spent the next two years from autumn 1981 studying philosophy at the Milltown Institute of Theology and Philosophy in Dublin. Our English and German confrères returned to their provinces accompanied by some Irish confrères to swell their student communities.

I am sad that the Milltown Institute closed permanently in 2015. In the 1980s, it was a highly regarded, thriving third-level institution offering pontifical degrees and diplomas in philosophy and theology. Jesuit-led, it comprised a consortium of religious orders, pooling lecturers and seminarians. There were also many nuns and some lay people taking courses in philosophy, theology and spirituality.

It was here that Taoiseach, Garret FitzGerald, gave a speech within days (possibly on the eve) of signing the Anglo-Irish Agreement with British Prime Minister Margaret Thatcher on 15 November 1985 at Hillsborough

Castle. Here too Jesuit priest Jorge Mario Bergoglio spent a few weeks in 1980 studying English – the future Pope Francis.

I thought of it as an intellectually honest institute. The 1980s saw the silencing of leading international theologians, most notably Hans Küng, who, days before the dawn of the new decade, on 18 December 1979, lost his licence to teach as a Roman Catholic theologian. I sensed the tightrope our lecturers walked between academic integrity and the party line. I think several of them feared that they too could be silenced.

Although some women took the same degrees as seminarians, the Milltown Institute was not permitted to award them pontifical degrees. Not only were women excluded from the Catholic priesthood, but their academic achievement went unrewarded too.

Like any college, it had a few lecturers ill-suited to teaching. It was said of one that he had died but went on teaching; and rumoured that he would give a lecture to an empty classroom, not noticing that nobody was there. He would fix his eyes on the wall behind us and murder us with monotone, his voice his weapon of choice.

But most lecturers were interesting, engaging and challenging. They opened our minds to philosophise and theologise for ourselves. In my first two years of philosophy – the love of wisdom from the Greek *philos sophia* – we studied epistemology, logic, ethics, metaphysics, the philosophy of the human person, the phenomenology of religion, the history of philosophy and the philosophy of God. Electives included psychology and the development of the human person, and biography, which I loved.

I was fascinated by atheistic existentialism, and relished Camus's *The Stranger*, astonished by its independence of thought and its violation of cultural expectation. I also loved theistic existentialist Martin Buber's *I and Thou* for its insights into relationships.

Some seminarians took a degree, others a diploma. The former were awarded a baccalaureate in philosophy after two years and then proceeded to a three-year Bachelor of Divinity. Some were ordained deacons during their final year of theology and ordained priests upon its completion. Others took a year's pastoral work before ordination. The path to the priesthood could take anything from six to 14 years; the Jesuits usually taking the longest.

My priestly path took nine years to the cusp of ordination: a year's novitiate; the two-year Baccalaureate in Philosophy at Milltown, a three-year Bachelor of Arts in English and History at University College Dublin (UCD); and a three-year Bachelor of Divinity degree at Milltown. These could have been followed by a pastoral year or teacher training or both.

*

'I'm glad you're in my life,' Father John Hannan said to me one day in his office after I'd started philosophy at the Milltown Institute.

I dismissed this as psychobabble. I couldn't accept a compliment.

'You respond well to love,' he continued. 'You have a great hunger for love and a desire for intimacy.'

He had said something similar in novitiate, and I wondered if he was hinting I'd never survive in religious life.

'I imagine you regret that you didn't have more experience in the love line before you entered.'

'Yes, I do.'

'You have always been very open with me. Your knowledge of yourself for your age remains remarkable. It's a great blessing. I want you to buy yourself a decent journal. I'll give you the money for it. Keep writing your journal, like you did last year. Write down the warm, compassionate, sensual part of you. If you feel angry, write it down. I know your moods and your pain by reading it. It will be of great interest to you in later life and help you through life as crises occur. And never get rid of it. You might be tempted one day to burn it all. But keep it always.

'Joseph, you're a much stronger person than you think you are. When you arrived in novitiate last September you were a boy. Now, you're a young man.'

## #25

In a letter dated 17 November 1981, two months after my father's death, my mother wrote to me: 'I love you very much. I think about you all the time. It is seldom, if ever, that you are out of my thoughts.'

My 19-year-old self found this obsessive and oppressive. I didn't want to be entangled in my mother's thinking at almost every moment.

She urged me to write to someone I hardly knew whose brother was ill. I felt she was trying to control me, conjuring an image of me, promoting it abroad, and expecting me to conform to it. She had even enclosed a stamp.

She also told me about a relative who had had a hysterectomy, adding, *just in case you are not sure what that is, it is an operation for the removal of the womb'*. She then spent a page and a half telling me how 'she' would get there, the visiting hours, what bus to take, and at which stop 'she' would get off.

*'If you would like to ring the hospital and tell them who you are, and ask them to tell her that you are making the enquiry for her it would, perhaps, be rather nice of you. Don't you like the way I put that?'*

No, I didn't. I found it manipulative; trying to get me to conform to her stereotype of me.

In another letter a fortnight later she addressed me as *'My Beloved Joseph'* and signed off, *'Love my dearest Joseph from your loving Mum'*. She wrote, *'I am praying for you all the time and lighting lamps for your old exams that are coming up, so don't worry about anything.'*

I saw no causative connection between her prayers, lamp-lighting and the outcome of my exams. Was this the faith I was sacrificing my life to propagate?

The Christmas after my father's death, my mother suggested things were tight for her financially and I felt under pressure from her to leave the Marists and return home.

Years later – I don't recall when – she said, 'When your father died, people expected you would leave to look after me.'

I wondered who these 'people' were or if it was just herself. Indeed, I was appalled at the prospect of returning home: it was hard enough resisting her manipulation while living in Milltown.

But I didn't know if she had enough to live on. So I spoke to my Auntie Sadie and Uncle Paddy and they assured me that my mother was well-provided for. She had two good pensions, her mortgage was fully paid off and my sister lived at home and had a well-paid job.

I asked Sadie and Paddy about the early years of my parents' marriage.

'Arthur told us that Pauline used to hide food,' said Auntie Sadie. 'He didn't know what to do. He was torn between his new wife and his sons. He didn't have an easy life, your dad.'

I also spoke to Aunty Mary and Aunty Peggy – my brothers' aunts. They told me they were so concerned about the treatment of Paul and David that they felt obliged to raise it with my parents. After that, both aunts were ostracised and not seen again in our home for many years.

Soon after my father's death, my journal records *'volcanic eruptions about my family's history'* leading to *'anguished upheaval'* for me, further straining my complex relationship with my mother. I was beginning to see my early childhood from the perspective of my father and my brothers.

I felt I had backed the wrong horse in so often siding with my mother during family tensions. Her calculated deception – concealing that David was gay even while I tried to find my missing brother as our father lay dying – had hacked asunder the umbilical cord. I hated and distrusted her, yet loved her as my mother. I was bone of her bone, flesh of her flesh.

I felt guilty for hating her and ashamed of feeling as I did about her. It was an emotional vortex of love and hate, guilt and shame, and fear that my feelings were unacceptable and incompatible with my studying for the priesthood.

While searching for David in August 1981, I had telephoned Jacinta, a friend living in London, who had known David. It seemed a long shot in a city of more than

76

six million people, but she had promised to keep an eye out for him.

In early March 1982, she walked into a flower shop.

'David!' she said to the florist.

'Yes,' replied the man behind the counter.

'It's Jacinta.'

'Jacinta!' he gasped.

She asked: 'Are you in touch with home?'

'Of course,' he lied.

'Then you know that your father is dead?'

That night, for the first time in perhaps a decade, David phoned home.

## #26

You'll never guess who's just been on the phone!' teased my sister, her voice jubilant at the other end of the line.

'No, who?'

'David!'

Our missing brother David flew home on a Friday in early March 1982. My brother Paul is convinced that David left Ireland in 1972, so this was our first sight of him in a decade. He was 27, I was 19. I hadn't seen him since I was nine. And he was rarely at home in the years before he disappeared.

My mother, sister, brothers and I visited Dad's grave. It is also the grave of my brothers' mother, Joan, and baby brother Arthur, named after my father. I still can't fathom that my life was contingent upon the death of my father's first wife. Without her dying, and all the grief and pain her absence caused in the lives of my father and brothers, neither I, my sister nor my children would exist.

David treated us all to dinner in a hotel. No expense was spared. At the end of the meal, he asked for the cheeseboard, tested the temperature of the cheese, and sent it back – saying it had only just been taken from the fridge. There was no ill-feeling involved. When he asked for another bottle of wine, the waiter said it was late and he was sorry but he couldn't oblige. Smiling, David put a £20 note in the waiter's breast pocket: the wine arrived.

He ordered two taxis to take us back to Donnycarney. My mother, sister and I took the first, while David and Paul travelled in the second.

'Don't bring up the past!' Paul warned him on their way home.

I wish he hadn't. I found the whole weekend exasperating. Anytime I sought to steer the conversation beyond the superficial, a conspiracy of silence descended. Nothing of substance was mentioned, discussed or examined. No question was answered. Everything stayed hidden, unexpressed. Missing for so long, his departure and disappearance were ignored. However, that conversation was never going to happen with my mother in the room.

That extraordinary and anticlimactic weekend ended with David flying back to London and, as far as I know, he never returned to Ireland again.

*

The previous month, on 9 February, 1982, six months to the day after my father's death, the Superior knocked on my bedroom door.

'Sad news, Joseph. Your Uncle John has died.'

'Fuck,' I said.

78

Uncle John wanted to be buried in South Africa, where he had served as a priest for 23 years. I couldn't attend his funeral and mourned him alone.

He played a significant role in my life. Born on Christmas Eve 1913, he was ordained priest in Rome, on 14 March 1959, aged 45, the occasion that led to my parents' engagement. His visits home punctuated my childhood. His 'recharging the batteries'; breathing deeply into his post-tubercular lungs. His inspiring faith journey – eleven years in hospital praying, 'Lord, make me your priest'. His booming voice. His paying for my driving lessons. His *Jerome Biblical Commentary*. His kiss of affection in front of my parents. His rosaries by my father's deathbed.

After my father's death, Uncle John, Uncle Joe, Aunty Cora and I spent a day together visiting people in Knockananna, Tinahely, Rathnagrew (pronounced Ran-a-gr-eye) and Hacketstown in counties Wicklow and Carlow. We had lunch at the Downshire House Hotel in Blessington, where Uncle John and I both ordered trout. I watched him eat every morsel, including the head.

'The best part,' he said.

I have a vague memory of doing likewise and vowing never to repeat it.

For health reasons, Uncle John wasn't meant to drink alcohol. But he did so that day. Later, I wondered if he knew his time was up. We called into people's houses unannounced, some of whom neither Joe, Cora nor I knew and, after accepting a whiskey in every home, Uncle John fell asleep, leaving us to make small talk with strangers.

Our increasingly inebriated odyssey culminated at Jim and Ita Ellis's home near Hacketstown, where we played cards – Newmarket – into the early hours. It was great fun.

I remember declining drinks, saying, 'I've had enough, thanks,' – and my Uncle Joe looking aghast: 'But that was ages ago! You'll have another one!'

After a magical day together, Uncle Joe drove home, doubtless over the limit; but those were more innocent days. I was privileged to be with my Uncle Joe the night before he died on 14 December 2016.

I was struck in recent years to find a handwritten 1959 letter from Uncle John to my mother, dated two months after his ordination, four months before my parents' marriage and three years before my birth. He wrote: *Who knows but you may have a son a priest yourself. It's all in the hands of God and all we can do is to give the little ones good example.*

## #27

My mother's deception about my brother David threw me into turmoil. I couldn't trust her. Moreover, anything she said was distorted by the prism of her mind, filtered by her version of reality.

Following David's anticlimactic visit home, a decade after his disappearance, I wrote to him in London on 9 April 1982, saying I loved my mother but didn't know who or what to believe anymore.

He didn't reply until 1 July: *Dear Joseph, Sorry I've taken so long to reply to your letter. I'm not sure what you really want to know, but I will tell you anything you want to ask about when I see you which will be some time in August. I'll phone before I come. David*

But he didn't come back to Ireland.

80

My Uncle Jack – my mother's eldest brother – was very religious. A teetotaller bachelor in his 60s, regarded within the wider family as an intellectual, he travelled around by vintage bicycle and often tried to get us to speak Irish. He had a shock of grey hair, its thick mass due, my mother swore, to his lifelong habit of massaging olive oil into his scalp every night. It might also have accounted for his bachelorhood.

He wrote to me after Easter 1982, enclosing my Uncle John's ordination card, entitled *Beati qui audiunt Verbum Dei* (Blessed are those who hear the Word of God).

*'Yes, Joseph,'* Jack penned, *'your mother at Festival periods especially can be depressed or in low-gear, yet, the Father of All gives to each the necessary comforting grace to weather-off each storm on life's waves.'*

I was intrigued by this glimpse of how another significant person in my mother's life viewed her. His words also show the ubiquitous religious air I breathed as a child and young man. Faith was a given, as sure as gravity.

Meanwhile, I was growing in self-knowledge. By mid-June, I wrote in my journal, *'Much within others that I used to regard as degenerate or base, I am discovering within myself. I can no longer condemn any man.'* From which I decode that my idealistic 20-year-old self, struggling with celibacy and racked by Catholic guilt, was losing the battle of id versus superego and succumbing to sexual desire through solitary pleasure.

My religious upbringing and the ideal of chastity clashed with my sexual desires, which I could no longer suppress. Isolation, loneliness and abstinence fought with my desire for affection, intimacy and an exclusive relationship.

It has, for me, been a lifelong journey to extricate myself from my childhood-ingrained Catholic guilt. I envy children who did not have it drummed into them from the cradle that sex was evil, that Adam's sin caused all our woe, and that humanity could only be redeemed by a God–man born of a Virgin Mother, an ontological conundrum begot by a sexual contradiction.

*

My pastoral work in the summer of 1982 was in a Legion of Mary shelter for homeless men in nationalist West Belfast. While I couldn't identify with the conservative Catholicism of rote rosaries and devotions in the hostel, I liked the staff and residents.

Located near the peace line on Divis Street, it was a stone's throw – tested by both sides – from the loyalist Shankill Road. It stood opposite Divis Flats, on the top of which perched a British Army observation post.

Despite the political and security tensions, as RUC armoured vehicles rumbled by and British Army helicopters chuntered overhead, I felt at ease in Belfast. I wondered if it was because my paternal grandfather hailed from there.

As a boy, I'd often heard my dad speak of a famous Antrim footballer, his cousin, Kevin Armstrong. I had assumed my dad was exaggerating. But when I enquired about him in Belfast, he was acclaimed. In fact, six years later, in 1988, Kevin received the Gaelic Athletic Association All-Time All-Star Award in Football.

Belfast is a small city and, a day after my enquiry, the great man himself visited me. He and his family welcomed me to their home and showed me around Belfast and County Antrim.

I was in Belfast for the Twelfth of July, the Unionist celebration of the 1690 Battle of the Boyne. Catholics told me how much they hated the Twelfth, when many kept their heads down or travelled to the 'Free State' to escape.

An enormous bonfire, visible from the hostel, was prepared on the Shankill, with the papal flag and Irish tricolour at the top of it, for triumphant incineration by loyalists. I attended the parade in Belfast city centre but kept my mouth closed lest my southern accent drew unwelcome attention.

In fact, Pope Innocent XI backed Protestant King William of Orange in the Battle of the Boyne. A painting by Dutch artist Pieter van der Meulen, acquired unseen by the Unionist Stormont Government in 1933, caused consternation for some unionists when it was discovered that it portrayed the Pope blessing King William. Indeed, the Pope had a *Te Deum* sung in the Vatican to celebrate William's victory at the Battle of the Boyne.

## #28

In late July, 1982, my mother and I flew to Lourdes, the Marian shrine in France where, some 25 years earlier in her mid-30s, that photograph was taken of her with two women, all three dressed like the Virgin Mary, with cape and veil.

As our plane descended, I had severe earache. At the reception of the hotel, distressed, in pain and barely able to hear, I was dismayed to discover the hotel had assumed we were Mr and Mrs Armstrong and allotted us only one room with a double bed. Despite my Oedipal horror-ignited

83

protestation in broken French, the hotel's only concession was a room with two single beds.

I could not sleep in the same room as my mother. When she finally got into bed, I got up, dressed and went to reception. No, they still did not have another room nor could they transfer me to another hotel and I didn't have enough money to go elsewhere.

I stayed up all night and, as there wasn't a decent chair in the lobby, I spent most of the night sitting on the stairs. This was the last place on the planet I wanted to be. The next day they cleared out a tiny storeroom and moved a narrow bed into it – my quarters until the ghastly pilgrimage ended.

I was appalled by the tacky religious merchandise in Lourdes; the myriad statues of the Blessed Virgin Mary, miraculous medals, bottled 'holy water', rosary beads and devotional scapulars. A middle-aged Dublin woman we befriended regarded the traders as 'bad minded', suspiciously eyeing each pilgrim as a potential trinket thief.

I couldn't identify with the conservative Catholicism of Lourdes, with its tens of thousands of pious pilgrims carrying candles in the open-air torchlight procession singing the Lourdes hymn: 'Immaculate Mary, your praises we sing. You reign now in Heaven with Jesus our King. Ave, Ave, Ave, Maria! Ave, Ave, Ave, Maria!'

Nor their walking the life-size Stations of the Cross muttering, 'We adore you, O Christ, and we praise you, because, by your holy cross, you have redeemed the world.'

Nor the one-minute naked dip in the cold baths, about which French writer Émile Zola, following his visits to Lourdes in 1891 and 1892, wrote: 'The miracle being that anyone emerges from this filthy water alive.'

I regarded the old crutches displayed near the grotto, supposed evidence of miracles past, as manipulative and bogus. Not for a moment did I believe that the Virgin Mary appeared to Bernadette Soubirous in 1858. Undeniable, however, was its undoubted commercial success, with tens of millions visiting the Pyrenees shrine since then. Religious myth-making transformed this barren mountainside into a perennial cash cow.

'You treated me with contempt in Lourdes,' said my mother after we returned to Ireland.

I don't remember the specifics of my alleged offences but the love which I had once felt for her was gone or buried deep. I found it impossible to talk to her. When I didn't speak, there was tension. When she insisted and I spoke and she didn't like what I said, she'd say, 'If only your father could hear the things you say to me.'

Like my father before me, who had told me there was no point talking to her, I sought refuge in the garden for the remainder of my holidays. I unearthed a jungle of weeds from where my dad used to grow vegetables. I dug, raked and sprayed it, in preparation for planting a lawn on my next visit home.

Conflicted by my feelings for my mother, with relief I returned to the seminary in September 1982. I renewed my religious profession within the Marist Fathers, taking vows for a further two years.

Beginning my second year reading philosophy at the Milltown Institute in October 1982, there were as many as 140 seminarians enrolled, an unimaginable number in the 21st century; when so many religious houses and seminaries have closed and congregations prepare for extinction. In the 1980s, the Milltown Institute was just one of several Dublin colleges for training priests. Others included Clonliffe College, which closed as a seminary in 2000, and All Hallows, which closed in 2016.

The closure of all three – and many more once thriving seminaries around Ireland – bears architectural testimony to the profound cultural changes of my generation. Whole swathes of Irish society have outgrown the myths they once lived by. Yet in State-funded schools, we continue the intellectual and emotional abuse of children by putting religious beliefs into their impressionable, trusting and malleable minds.

Moreover, while denouncing parents who sexually or physically abuse children, many remain unaware of the lifelong consequences of parents abusing children's minds, emotions and sexuality with crazy religious myths.

#### #29

Our Superior Father John Hannan had warned us in novitiate that celibates needed human love and friendship: 'Non-exclusive, non-genital spiritual friendships are good for celibates, so long as the relationship remains open and honest. There are risks. When you're nineteen, a sexual attraction can occur.'

'Are you saying we could fall in love with one another?' asked a novice.

'Yes,' he had said. 'Freud taught us that relatively few people are exclusively heterosexual or homosexual. Most people are somewhere along the spectrum. Even if this is theoretical to you now, before long it won't be.'

In winter 1982, it happened to me. My journal of that autumn shows an earnest 20-year-old struggling with religious endeavour: *'disappointed with meditation'*; *'Meditation difficult'*; *'Distracted a fair bit. Ended by thanking God for the day…not very successful.'*

I visited my father's grave on All Souls Day – I may still have been having the recurring dream of his being about to tell me something important but culminating with the silence of the grave. I wrote to the Salvation Army missing persons office letting them know that we had found my brother David.

I had a new spiritual director, an honourable Marist. On 5 November, after making my confession to him, we discussed my occasional *'atheistic tendencies and views'*. However, I remember being underwhelmed by his argument that I could doubt God 'but that doesn't alter his existence'. Applied to the proverbial flying pink elephant, doubting the airborne proboscidean doesn't 'alter his existence' either: he still doesn't exist and no sensible adult stakes his life on belief in Dumbo.

My new pastoral work was to befriend two long-term inmates in Arbour Hill prison. I found it intimidating walking into the austere building, its massive steel doors clanging shut – locked behind me. We had privileged access to the men, meeting them alone in their cells. Unlike the 'string them up' brigade, I realised that I was no better than these prisoners, just luckier.

Although I have in recent years won awards for public speaking, I was far from that in my early years in Milltown. Faced with a packed congregation during novitiate, my legs used to shake dramatically, my mouth dried, my lungs clamped and I blushed like a beacon. The problem remained two years later. I journaled in November 1982:

*'On Saturday at Eucharistic adoration I'd a near heart attack prior to reading.'*

An entry for 24 November reads: *'Almost vomiting with nerves about driving test.'*.

But the mood changes with an entry of 30 November. *'Lord, praised be your name, now and forever.'* My pastoral work at the prison had gone well the previous night, I passed my driving test and I thanked God for *'the pleasure and the company and the companionship of home on Sunday'*. For sure, this could not refer to my mother. And so I deduce that a confrère had accompanied me. *'And then Saturday. Alleluia, Amen,'* effuses the journal. *'Thank you Lord. I praise you for the beauty and the treasure of my precious hours and moments spent in deep intimacy.'*

Lest the reader think I had just lost my virginity, I had not. Far from it. The intimacy in question was the first budding of a short-lived six-month on–off affective and emotional crush; but something nevertheless more real than cultivating a relationship with an imagined pink elephant.

My journal records my *'inner certainty, stability and delight'* and my awareness of *'beauty and love'*.

When you take twenty virile young men, most of them aged between 17 and 19, and leave them together for years in a seminary, sexuality will inevitably manifest. I was on a diet of celibacy and loneliness. I had a need for affectivity that was not being met. I desired an exclusive relationship which wasn't permitted in a Church that valued celibacy above the priesthood. And in this emotional barrenness, I got a glimpse of what my life could be like, freed from isolation and religious constraint.

On 1 December 1982, I recorded: *'I've read over 100 pages, indeed closer to 120 pages, of* An Experience of Celibacy *by Keith Clarke since bedtime last night.'* That recently published book, which had just arrived in the Milltown library, was a big hit among seminarians.

I was experiencing my loneliness. My desire for sexual pleasure was heightened. I craved an emotionally interdependent, physically expressive relationship. I realised that these normal yearnings could not be fulfilled while committed to the vow of celibacy. On 5 December, I felt the solution was *'praying and presenting myself to God at such a time as tonight when I want so much to touch another'.*

Humbled, I prayed that my celibacy could *'testify to the primacy of the love of God in my life'.* But all I felt was a lonely burning desire.

## #30

A lot of hugging went on in the Marists. We hugged confrères at the sign of peace at mass. We hugged when we returned to Milltown. Maybe it was an extension of the charismatic maxim to hug everything that moves and if it didn't move, hug it until it moved.

And there I was, a naïve 20-year-old seminarian, hugging my confrère one night, who had visited my home two weeks earlier, and I was aroused and I wondered if he was too. Though I reflected and questioned, I did not feel guilty about anything. It felt like an authentic overflow from our friendship. He had been sharing some upsets and concerns, I listened patiently, and it terminated in the embrace. *'There's a lot in the above. Don't just gloss over it,'* I recorded in my journal.

*'He is beautiful physically, is comfortable to be with, likes me and being with me,'* I journaled. *'I am sexually responsive in his presence. My desires in his presence. My fantasies. This is me. I'm convinced I'm "normal". That one was ironed out in noviciate with JH* [the Superior Father John Hannan]. *It is now a question of being more sexually self-conscious.'*

This was a new experience for me. I needed to accept myself and integrate this into my sexual identity. It involved pain and mortification for me. *'In light of my commitment, I must refrain and restrain.'*

*'It is probably not right for me to indicate to him how I respond to him,'* I journaled, as it would *'make our relationship too high-powered…when the "crush", for want of a better word for it, goes away. I do not know if it is what people call "falling in love". I know it is quite normal to fall in love with men or women.'*

Telling him, I reckoned, *'would help neither of us. But the impulse is strong and greatly absorbing. I sometimes wonder how I can refrain from at least telling him; though I suspect he is aware or has clues to how I may feel.'* I wondered if he felt the same.

I wrote, *'He is beautiful and I long for him,'* adding, *'I felt I had to write that as I do feel it. I find it hard to have written it. It is, quite evidently, bluntly honest and uncensored.'*

I felt I could write it because *'intellectually I have accepted it and see it as "normal" yet at a gut, non-cerebral, level there's something in me that cries out it's sick, maybe perverted, dreadful and enough to disqualify me for priestly ministry.'*

The Superior had told me during novitiate to, *'Lie in bed Joe and thank God for your body, your penis.'* He had said this to me before making me Monitor after Christmas in novitiate, adding: *'I'm convinced there is no perversion there.'*

*'I too am convinced,'* I reflected. *'Yet the fear is present. The fear generated by non-acceptance. The fear I may always carry with me.*

*Maybe this too is just part of me. In conclusion, I feel most men could write the above but may have neither the self-honesty or daring self-acceptance to say it.'*

I discussed everything with my spiritual director on 16 December 1982, holding nothing back. I brought my journal and read the pertinent parts of it to him. *'I said nothing other than what was in the diary. It was and is the whole truth,'* I journaled.

My director said he was struck by my sense of balance with it all, that it was good to become aware of, and accept, my sexual self and that later, as a priest, I wouldn't have time to do so. He also said, and this surprised me, that as a priest I could fall in love with men, women and children. I have fallen for men and women, but never for children.

He suggested that I should not tell my confrère about my feelings for him and that if he discussed it with me 'a white lie might be the order of the day'; and to avoid the occasion of being together too much, particularly at night-time.

In chapel the next day, I was overcome with loneliness and despair at the prospect that never in my life as a priest could I have an exclusive intimate relationship. *'Am I to believe despite all? Sacrifice my life in the hope that someone out there may be consoled by my priesthood while I am beyond consolation?'*

I felt avoided by my confrère and suspected he had been talking to his spiritual director too. I also felt distant from him. I wrote: *'It seems that once I named what was physiologically going on in me, the attraction ceased.'*

This foreshadowed a period of disillusionment for me with religious life and with life itself.

## #31

*T*hanks be to God I got out of that hellhole,' I journaled on 3 January 1983, upon my return to Milltown, having spent some days after Christmas at home with my mother. I regarded the house in which I grew up as *'a den of hate, resentment, secrecy'*; from which Paul had been banished, David had vanished for a decade, my father had died with resentments untold, and I had escaped hoping to lead a meaningful life.

*'I am abhorred by myself often these days,'* I wrote, finding myself seething with anger, disaffected with relationships, overeating and succumbing to solitary pleasures. *'But this is me,'* I reflected, taking solace from Leonard Cohen's song 'Suzanne', which spoke to me of the wisdom of finding beauty and hope even in our failures.

On 7 January, I recorded my *'terror to go to bed'*, my superego losing the battle against the id. It was difficult for my idealistic celibate self to come to terms with my cravings, urges and appetite for food and sex. And yet, making my confession, I did not feel contrite. My spiritual director counselled it didn't matter that I didn't feel guilty.

He said: 'It's the sacrament of celebration of God's forgiveness in Jesus. Feelings are a distraction.'

Two days later, I journaled: *'An earlier me is shocked by my present self.'* But I also wrote: *'My present "me" feels I am more real than ever before.'*

I sought a new understanding of celibacy by reading *The Sexual Celibate* by Donald Goergen. My spiritual director advised that, after completing it, to study the spirituality of celibacy. He consoled me: 'Don't be vexed at not yet being master of yourself – you're not yet old enough to be.'

But my confidence in myself and in my ability to sustain relationships was at a low ebb. Tense, disheartened and unsettled, community life became a burden and several relationships were strained. For example, historian Father Donal Kerr, with whom I normally got on well in community, asked: 'Do you not love me anymore?'

He meant fraternal love – nothing inappropriate was intended.

Another journal entry reads: *'I stared angrily at* [named confrère] *the other day at Morning Office as he did his usual stint of shouting down his side of the chapel and dictating a rapid recitation. I wish to God he'd leave.'*

Cycling for miles alone in the Wicklow hills was my favourite healthy escape for my mind, mood and body. During a 90-minute prayer in the chapel on 16 January, I silently, *'thanked God for day spent on hills'.*

But the *'crucifixion of community'* continued. I tried my best to be helpful to a confrère, whom I felt was isolated within the community, and he responded by cutting me to the quick with cynicism, attacking my motivation for talking to him. I broke down, flummoxed by how nasty he was to me.

Days later I drew a picture in my journal of a man with a closed plastic bag over his head, doubtless an image for myself at that time. The eyes are sad. The lips are a focal point of attention, like I'm trying to show myself that I was sexual and suffocating. I was basing my life on religious faith, in the hope of reward in this world and the next, but forfeiting the one and only life I could be sure of in the here and now. It was a period, as I journaled, of *'weariness, uncertainty, confusion'.*

I was saddened when a popular confrère left in February 1983. We were thirty-eight students in Mount St Mary's after I had entered in September 1980. Now, two and a half years later, almost a third had gone.

But my gloom lifted in late February 1983 – I thought my confrère had fallen in love with me.

## #32

Happiness returned in late February 1983 after my confrères and I did a weekend of journaling at a retreat centre.

*'This period of my life is like a chance for me,'* I journaled. I saw it as a time for personal growth, leading towards autonomy and authenticity. I was thankful for my friendships. And I was encouraged by my aggregate score in philosophy. After the slough of despond since December, I grew again in quiet confidence.

The weekend was typified by my *'unguarded joviality'*. I shared a room with my confrère and enjoyed his company. I wasn't used to sharing a bedroom with anyone. I liked our mutual freedom to strip and get into our separate beds and talk.

Celibates don't normally have anyone to chat with in bed. At some point, probably the next morning, I saw him erect. He had pulled his duvet back, maybe to get up or, I wondered, perhaps to show me. Or just to be himself in that moment without any need for concealment. Celibates are rarely seen by others with an erection.

I recorded in my journal: *'I am ever awakening to my sexuality and the varied and various manifestations of it.'*

I returned revived and cheerful from the weekend, journaling: *'I am learning the poetry of each day.'* My improved mood seemed also to banish my religious doubt, since I wrote: *'I believe in God and my heart extols him.'* Borrowing the title of C.S. Lewis's book, I declared myself *'surprised by joy'*.

In truth, what sparked my positive mood was a belief that it might just be possible, after all, to fulfil my affectivity needs within religious life. I thought spiritual friendship could do the trick.

Aelred of Rievaulx, a twelfth-century Cistercian monk and abbot, had, in his book *Spiritual Friendship*, praised the value of friendship for a monk. He wrote that, without friendship, we were no better than a beast, and that spiritual friendship filled us with love. Aelred held that we could entrust our hearts and its secrets to our friend.

*'Why not entrust myself into the arms and heart of another?'* I wrote. *'Why not let him know I delight in him and discover myself in him? Why not trust and be!'*

My confrère shared with me an erotic dream he had dreamt about me. He had discussed it with the Superior. He asked me if there was anything sexual in my relationship with him and if I was seeking something beyond what he conceived of our relationship. I found the question ironic given the dream he had just shared with me.

I said no. But as most people are somewhere on the spectrum between gay and straight, I wondered if he had not yet come to terms with what I presumed to be the homosexual part of himself. I journaled: *'If his experience has been similar to mine, and at times I feel it must be, then he's probably this moment regarding me with the same wonderings as I presently regard him.'*

The *'crucifixion of community'* of the previous weeks gave way to feeling blessed by my friendships and confrères, consolidating my belief that I could be fulfilled as a priest. I found myself sought after. One time I sensed my confrère was jealous when he saw me talking to my best friend at the Milltown Institute.

For months, I had been grappling with the problem posed by Ibsen's play *A Doll's House*, at the end of which the lead female character, Nora, leaves her husband to make her own way in the world. Grappling with the vow of celibacy in light of my complicated sexual awareness, I had journaled on 1 December 1982 that the play explored *'the problem of incomplete knowledge or maturity at the time of a commitment and how people change'*.

I had taken my vows before I was old enough to appreciate the importance and value of sex.

But by 8 March 1983, I saw myself as *'a fuller person before my God'* and that I was *'walking steadily on sound and level ground, the battle over for a while'*. I was becoming more integrated, growing as a person. Looking back over the rocky road I had climbed, I felt it had been worthwhile. I was at ease with myself and others.

I recalled the Gospel story in Luke 13:8 where the gardener advises the owner: 'Leave the fig tree another year and see if it bears fruit.'

*'It has!'* I journaled. Remaining in the Marists was bearing fruit. I was beginning to love myself in a healthy way.

But that night a dramatic dream awoke me with a jolt at 4 a.m.: *'I am being projected forward towards a man standing still and wearing black clothes.'*

I was being catapulted towards priesthood, stagnation and death.

## #33

The Superior, Father John Hannan, met me in his office in March 1983 and I told him that I would like to read psychology that autumn at university with a view to becoming a priest–counsellor or psychotherapist. People often opened up to me and shared their inner self and private life. I seemed to have a facility for listening to people at their core, and others had remarked upon this to me.

Father Hannan said he had it in mind that I might go to Mater Dei to train to be a religious education teacher.

I hated the idea. Not only did I not want to teach, but I would miss out on the opportunity of going to a secular university where I wanted my religious identity and thinking to be challenged.

He said he was merely proposing it as an option and observed: 'Psychology wouldn't be of great value to those who leave, although I do not believe you will leave.'

'If I left, I'd prefer to be a psychologist than a teacher,' I said.

'Would you take honours psychology?'

'I'd hope so. My aggregate for first-year philosophy was first class.'

He was impressed.

'If you take honours psychology and then do a two-year diploma you could join the Irish Psychological Society and you would be well set up,' he said, adding, 'You would make a good counsellor.'

I was thrilled. We also spoke openly about my confrère. The Superior said it was a good relationship and good to have a special friendship. And then he had more great news for me.

'The formation staff have chosen you to go to Rome this summer,' he beamed.

The General House was looking for someone to assist the archivist for six weeks. My time in Rome would coincide with an international gathering of Marist seminarians. I would be able to join them for some of their sessions and take a full part in their cultural and tourist programme. It sounded fabulous.

'There is a lot being invested in you so you'd better be ordained!' said the Superior, smiling. 'I want you to stop seeing me as your superego. I like you. I don't have to Christianise my relationship with you as I have to do with some other confrères.'

I was privileged, excited and encouraged by this sign of the formation staff's faith in me.

*

The night after Father Hannan had told me the good news about Rome, I walked into the refectory. It was twilight. The curtains were open in the large dimly-lit room and there, by the sink, two confrères stood close together in a sexual embrace. Startled from their intimacy by my arrival, they disengaged; and one of them left the refectory without a word.

I too had my moment of acute embarrassment around this time during my crush on my confrère. One night I sat in the dark in a pew near the back of the chapel in Mount St Mary's. Believing that I was alone, I prayed audibly. I can't remember my precise words but they might have been something like: 'I thank you Lord for my friendship with my confrère, for my love for him and his beauty, and that it's OK to feel attracted to him.'

Next thing, I heard movement from the front of the chapel and a confrère stood up. He had been lying prostate on the sanctuary in silence all along. He must have heard my every word and now he walked down the aisle, his footsteps echoing on the polished parquet floor. He passed by me, transfixed in the pew, without looking at me or saying anything, and exited by the door at the back of the chapel. I was mortified!

That humiliation aside, March 1983 was a time of affirmation, contentment and gratitude. If once I had felt trapped – fearing that I had burned my bridges academically and professionally – now I felt free. I was more at home within the Marists and within myself. I accepted myself and I was accepted by the Society of Mary as I was, without pretence or deception.

'This has been a very rich time for me,' I told my spiritual director. As ever, I was fully open with him about everything in my life, including my acute embarrassment at having been heard in the chapel.

'You are a model *dirigé*,' he responded. 'The reason you were proposed for Rome was that you will give yourself entirely to it and it will be good for you.'

On my 21st birthday card, the Superior wrote: 'God has truly chosen you.'

#34

*D*are to be me before God and man,' my 21-year-old self journaled on 21 April 1983; a challenge (minus the

99

god bit) for me today too, in my late 50s, as I write this.

A couple of days later, at spiritual direction, I felt *'battle sore and weary, buffeted and bashed'.*

'The struggle continues,' said my director, after I had confessed my 'sins', chief among them, I'm guessing at this remove, playing with myself; and my anguish at the guilt of hating my mother. I was cold and distant from her, the new norm in our relationship. It wasn't getting any better. I was uncomfortable talking about it.

'The area of common ground,' my spiritual director observed, 'is dwindling all the time. It's not just a problem of relationship but it involves your very self too.'

*

My infatuation for my confrère reached its zenith twelve nights later in his room. Possibly after sharing my angst about my mother, we had extended, naïve hugging, then he stripped naked and got into bed. Let's allow the journal take up the actual account:

*I desired him greatly. I wanted to touch him and was glad he turned on the light before he was beneath his continental quilt. Already in my pyjamas, I lay beside him: he beneath the quilt, I, to his left, above it. We did not touch. But desire was flowing between us. We dared to look at each other. Our eyes, our faces, were so very close. I barely dared look in his eyes.*

*Making to go, though I not for a moment wished to, he said: 'Wait just a while.' I interpreted all as invitation.*

Despite the melodramatic Mills and Boon tone of all that, what transpired was nothing more than a few short kisses between two human beings desperately longing for affection and intimacy in an all-male celibate world.

I wanted to be a priest but I had never wanted to be celibate. It was a cruel unnatural man-made part of the package. Saint Peter, the first Pope, was married. And for more than half of the Church's history there was a married clergy. Today there are tens of thousands of priests who are prohibited from exercising their priesthood because they fell in love and got married – the Church elevating what it admits to be the man-made rule of compulsory celibacy over what it claims to be the God-given vocation to the priesthood.

It was, as far as I can remember, my first time ever to kiss anyone on the lips, male or female; apart from the time my Uncle John had kissed me chastely, affectionately and briefly in the company of my parents.

I am not gay and I don't think that my confrère was either; but I yearned for intimacy. I journaled that if he had stripped naked in front of me again, I wasn't sure if I might *'feel powerless to resist him'*. Had he done so I feared I might *'collapse in his embrace'*. Observing my desire, I concluded my journal entry: *'Seemingly, all flesh, this day.'*

Struck by a sense of powerlessness over my passions, I tried to pray and found solace in the classic spiritual text *The Imitation of Christ*, Book III, chapter 55: *'O Lord , while I delight in your law, and see Your commands as holy, yet in my body I sin, obeying my senses. So, while I have the will to do good, I am powerless to do so.'*

I wondered whether I could live a celibate life. At spiritual direction two days later, on 7 May, I told my director everything and let him read my journal.

He said desire must not be suppressed but neither should it be acted upon. He suggested I go for a short walk with my confrère in daylight hours, acknowledge the intimacy enjoyed but that we should not repeat it lest it led us to 'very serious sin'. We were not to visit one another's rooms at night nor spend an inordinate amount of time together. I was to apply myself more to study and prayer and spread myself more in the community.

My spiritual director said that this was a good experience for me. Many would never encounter it and be the poorer for it. He did not at all see it as standing against me for religious life. Rather, it was necessary that celibacy became more real for me. I was being tugged in opposing directions: between a glimpse of what marriage could be like and the lonely life of a celibate.

## #35

Desolation, sadness and tears arose between my spiritual direction of 7 May 1983 and my departure for Rome on 16 June. It was an existential realisation of the death to self that would be required were I to continue in religious life.

Humbled by the strength of my desire for tactile love, I was struck dumb, unable to continue to read aloud, by an antiphon at Evening Prayer. We were exhorted to seek heavenly things, not those of the earth.

But Heaven – an afterlife – might not exist; whereas flesh and blood were real. You could see, touch and kiss a beloved. I also reacted against another line of Vespers, warning us not to love 'anything' in the world. This prayer was cruel and heartless.

I cried, sadness overcoming me, at the self-destruction awaiting me within religious life. I found neither joy nor liberation in celibacy. If this was dying to self, I didn't want it. Self-annihilation had no tangible benefit. It was barren. I didn't want a life of loneliness over intimacy, isolation over affection, abandoning human love for faith in an intangible, possibly non-existent, deity.

I couldn't understand how any human could choose celibacy, forsaking the comfort of hands to hold, lips to kiss, flesh to worship and embrace. My affectivity and sexual needs could never be met in the celibate priesthood or religious life.

On 2 June, I woke with a swollen tummy and I had sweated profusely. My eyes looked yellow, I'd wobbly legs, and I had a headache. I went to the doctor.

'You're tense. What's going on?'

'I'm in the middle of my final philosophy exams, I'm heading off to Rome in two weeks and I've been finding celibacy pretty tough.'

'I have no idea why you've chosen your career,' said the doctor. 'As I see it, you haven't lived unless you've slept with a woman. You know that saying: "Plant a tree, write a book and father a child." I think you're throwing your life away.'

I told my spiritual director on 10 June that I'd been to the doctor and he had said I was stressed.

'Understandably so,' said my director.

I told him what the doctor had said about sleeping with a woman and throwing my life away.

'He had no right to say that to you,' he said.

I disagreed. My doctor had every right to speak his mind to me and I'm glad he did. I did not want to be insulated from the real views of anyone about my life choice, least of all an intelligent physician. I got the impression that my director might complain to the doctor but I may be wrong and I do not know if he did.

I completed the final exam in my Baccalaureate in Philosophy on 13 June and redeemed myself academically. At a party afterwards, a classmate, Eugene, led us in a rousing rendition of A Root Chy Cha, each graduate joining with gusto in the silly dance, our thumbs up, shoulders back, knees together, bottoms and tongues out.

At the party, a beautiful, intelligent married woman in our class, Maureen, whom I admired and respected, said that I had looked sad in recent weeks. I was astonished by some women's ability to hone in on a man's spirit in travail. I envied her husband.

Relations with my mother were as bad as ever. My journal records a *'horrid night at home'* around this time but I don't remember what transpired. On the eve of my departure for Rome, I spent another day with my mother. I needed willpower of steel. She played the martyr, but I was numb, unmoved by her performance.

On Bloomsday, 16 June, I began my journey to Rome, boarding the boat to England. In London, I met up with a female friend who said, 'Sex is the security of waking up and somebody being there.'

Exhausted and wrecked, I got the tube to Heathrow airport. I watched two lovers, male and female, wrapped around each other, tears streaming down their faces. I didn't know if they had just been reunited or if one was about to board a plane, leaving each other bereft. The image of that couple burned into me. It was like a scene from a film, except they were not acting. Their tears were real; their love intense, authentic and true.

That hug encapsulated what I needed and yearned for in life.

## #36

I arrived in Rome on 17 June 1983 and was collected at the airport by Father Tony Ward, archivist at the Marist Fathers General House, my boss for the next six weeks.

A witty, black-bearded Englishman, outside the gusty airport his arms fought a losing battle to control long strands of windswept hair, cultivated to cover his bald patch.

'My sister tells me the game is up!' he laughed.

I liked his self-deprecating humour. The vibe was good.

Days later, sad and lonely from recent weeks, struggling with celibacy and *'many questions and doubts'* about the faith, I wondered about the worth and effectiveness of religious life. *'Will the Society of Mary exist in X years?'* I journaled. And, if Jesus was true God and true man, I wanted to know *'how much was he like me'*.

I enjoyed working with Tony in the archives, especially his mischievous humour. After a few days, he declared: 'Let's be perfectly frank about your singing. How do you feel about working in silence?'

I looked at him quizzically.

'Was I singing?'

'Yes, Brother. Yesterday, I produced a radio but you missed the subtlety of my approach.'

I sunbathed on the roof of the General House and found it sensuous. Some days, as there was nobody else up there and no buildings overlooking it, I slipped off my swimming togs for an all-over tan.

Over a cup of tea, Tony impersonated a *'very proper and polite'* recently arrived man in the community whom I hadn't seen yet. I laughed when, five minutes later, the stranger walked in – the exact embodiment of his lampooned caricature.

Tony took me to see sights like the Vatican and Spanish Steps. The streets and cafes of Rome were filled with loving couples, laughing, holding hands, enjoying life. I could see what I was missing.

*'There is a magic for me in Rome. Just being here; the joy of it,'* I journaled on 24 June.

I found it hard to sleep that night. I'd spotted two provocative pamphlets in the archives which potentially undermined the point of being a priest: *Église sans prêtres* (Church without priests) and *Prêtre: pour quoi faire?* (Priest: to do what?')

And I wondered if I'd ever earn my own living and go with a woman. I journaled: *'Desire for sexual activity. Will I ever sleep with a woman? How much has the Church yet to change? What part can or will I play in the Church? Is faith and God talk trash? And what would the Superior General have thought if he had gone up to the roof and seen me starkers today?'*

At the end of June, ten scholastics from Canada, Belgium, Ireland, Italy, Mexico, South East Asia, Spain and the USA arrived in the General House for a month-long international gathering on Marist history and spirituality. I spent less time in the archives, attended some seminars and joined in on their cultural and tourist activities. It was an excellent way to stay in Rome and I felt privileged to be there.

On 5 July, Tony told me he was fond of me and that the rest of the community liked me too. We had a drink and chatted in his room for over three hours. We talked about ourselves and about Marist things – the crisis within the Society of Mary about vocations, Marists leaving the priesthood and the future of the congregation and the Church.

The Superior General, Father Bernie Ryan, a very likeable and humble man, had been away until then but arrived back in Rome on 6 July. For Marists, he was next in line to the Pope. He welcomed me and later called me by my name. I had a sense that he wondered if we realised what we were letting ourselves in for.

I talked at dinner with an Assistant General. He told me that 25 per cent of Marist priests in Spain had left and a bulging seminary had shrunk to just one seminarian. I was shocked.

The next day we went to Assisi, home of Saint Francis. In the intimate Portiuncula chapel within the Basilica of St Mary of the Angels, out of the blue I saw a beloved English confrère. He was an extraordinary, bubbly, happy character, who had entered the year before me. He had been the life and soul of Milltown, a great singer, actor and enthusiast; a central character in the life of our community.

But today he was unusually pensive, his high spirits restrained.

He said: 'Joe, I'm leaving. Everything that was meaningful for me is gone.'

Numbness and sadness oozed within me. I was gutted. Yet another beautiful patch in the quilt of community life, that had so attracted me to the Marists, was being torn away.

## #37

A tear fell as I watched, from my bedroom window in Assisi, swallows soar and dive outside, so close I could almost touch them. I was sad that my English confrère was leaving the Marists after five years.

He visited my room, we prayed Vespers together, and he said that he had come to realise that he had to make the painful decision to leave.

On 7 July 1983, I wrote in my journal: *The possibility of the dissolution of the Society of Mary is real. Indeed, maybe even of the Church herself.'*

Next day we had mass at St Francis's tomb. I found it hard to look at my English confrère. My world was threatened. At the intercessions I prayed aloud: 'Lord, Saint Francis rebuilt a tottering Church. We pray for the Church today, that you may give us the strength to rebuild it.'

I lit a candle in the tomb, praying for faith, convinced that neither I, nor the Church, actually believed. I climbed the hill with my English confrère where Saint Francis used to pray. Even a year before, he hadn't imagined that he would leave.

For me, the whole project lost its meaning if my confrères left. I had joined a community to learn how to love. But if the community left one by one, what was the point of my life choice?

I remembered the Superior General, Father Bernie Ryan, had conducted a formal visitation of the Irish Province. Addressing the community in Milltown he had asked: 'How realistic is this highly affective community? What is it being formed for?'

The Assistant General who had accompanied the General said that everyone who had gone through a similar set-up in the USA during the 1960s had left. Outside of their formation community, their affectivity needs were not being met.

History would prove their questions and comparison prescient. Most of the thirty-eight students in Mount St Marys in 1980 would leave, including seventeen of the twenty novices of my novitiate; several after many years in the religious life and priesthood.

On 10 July, back at the General House in Rome, in the chapel *'I cried as the Society of Mary, belief, Church, Milltown seems to collapse around me.'* I had a sense of *'the destitution of religious life'*, by which I meant its ultimate emotional barrenness and the growing possibility that it, and the faith, was built on a lie.

The general archivist Tony Ward and I were already firm friends. He invited me to consider studying in Rome so I could return. His friendship helped my faltering faith in the possibility of community. Nevertheless, on 14 July I recorded my sense of *'the uselessness of prayer'*.

On 16 July, we had mass in the catacombs. A beautiful Italian girl stood beside me. I sensed a strong vibe between us – our standing close together, our body language, our smiles – and, at some point, she took my hand and held it.

It all happened so naturally. I imagined she had no idea I was a seminarian.

That night, I dream I am on a train. I try to find a way to get off the train but there doesn't seem to be any way out. *'No. I must just wait.'*

As is the way with dreams, I'm then on a bus, get off the bus, rush for a train to get me to a ferry. I forget a bag on the bus. I rush back but the bus is gone.

*'I seek directions. Which way did the bus go? Then, I am amazed. From out of the crowd comes a beautiful girl. She feels for my hand. It all happens so naturally. I respond with sensitivity, trust and welcome. Now we're just holding hands and walking together. I feel so very good. Was it as easy as this? All this time I've dreamt of something like this happening to me.'*

Our dreams can offer us solutions to waking problems. Looking back, it is clear that I wanted to get off the train to the priesthood. I wanted to cast off the religious myths I lived by. I wanted to hold the hand of a woman, to marry and have a family. The dream told me it was easier than I realised; literally and metaphorically, within my grasp. But it also reveals my sense of being trapped: *'No. I must just wait.'*

I dashed around between public modes of transport – bus, train, ferry – collective carriers of meaning, like religion. For years, I missed the meaning of the dream and rushed back on board that train from which I could find no way out. *'I seek directions'* from others, whom I thought knew me better than I knew myself.

But it was only when I got off the bus that I could be myself, direct myself and find what I needed: *'Then, I am amazed. From out of the crowd comes a beautiful girl. She feels for my hand. It all happens so naturally.'*

## #38

*I wanted to get out of the FMS General House as soon as possible,'* I journaled on 18 July 1983.

The international gathering in Rome of student priests from the Marist Fathers had visited the headquarters of the Marist Brothers (FMS), a separate religious congregation of teaching brothers founded by Marist Father, Marcellin Champagnat, in France in 1817.

The building was a massive marble monstrosity, which I felt was an affront to the vow of poverty. Inside, I perused printed comic strip materials of Champagnat, aimed at children. It smacked to me of a manufactured myth, the cult of the founder. Perhaps it paid off too – he would be canonised sixteen years later, on 18 April 1999.

I think underlying my distaste and unease was an unarticulated sense that Christianity did the same for Jesus, and that I, like so many others, had fallen for it. There is no infancy narrative nor any resurrection sighting in the original version of Mark, the earliest canonical Gospel. These were added later, many years after the 'events' they purport to record.

My mother and her letters had long induced in me exasperation and anger. After the visit to the Marist Brothers, my journal records: *'Ripping mother's letters'*. I don't remember the contents of her letters to me in Rome but I imagine destroying them gave me some sense of liberation from her.

One of the priests who happened to be in the General House at the time didn't inspire me. Once, when he was asked to do something, he retorted at full voice and in all seriousness in the refectory: 'But I wanted to do my nails today!'

Another time he said, 'Look at the rubbish they're ordaining. I won't be happy until they've all left!'

I didn't know who he was referring to but his view undermined the belief that it was God who called to the priesthood. I also wondered if he was talking about Milltown, but I can't be sure.

On 22 July, Father Jean Coste (1926–1994), the preeminent historian of the Marist Fathers, presented a seminar to us on the history and spirituality of the Society of Mary. I asked him if he was personally optimistic about the future of the congregation.

His response was guarded. He was optimistic for Marist spirituality but he couldn't express confidence in the survival of the Marist Fathers *per se* – a telling admission by the then leading expert on all things Marist.

Next day, Father Roger Wilhelm, an Assistant General from France, was visibly upset on the bus on our way back from a visit to the Vatican museum. I asked him what was wrong. He was sad because he had just heard of the departure from the Marists, after six years, of one of the few German scholastics.

After six weeks in Rome, on 31 July, I started a three-week low-budget Interrail trip; visiting Florence, Bologna, Venice, Yugoslavia, Austria, Hungary, West Germany, France, Denmark, Sweden and Norway. I travelled with a friend from college and a confrère from Milltown who told me the Superior had said to him: 'Make sure Joe has a good time.'

We had very little money and we slept in train stations, on trains or in Marist houses. Six years before the fall of the

Berlin Wall, prices were incredibly cheap in Yugoslavia and Hungary. In Pula, in modern day Croatia, we bought bread, grapes, cheese, chocolate and a large tomato for 190 Yugoslav dinars, the equivalent then of about £1.50 Irish pounds.

To enter Hungary – behind the Iron Curtain – we had to disembark at the last train station in Austria and walk across the border at dusk, where our papers were checked. It was scary seeing dark silhouettes of armed soldiers with German shepherds patrolling the border. We arrived by foot at a tiny Hungarian train station. Unlit, and unable to see or find a light, we settled down on the floor for the night. Only in the morning did we realise how dirty it was, with insects crawling about where we had been sleeping.

In Budapest we got chatting to an English-speaking Hungarian Catholic called Pál. He showed us around the city and invited us to stay with his parents that night, a considerable improvement on our previous night's lodgings. We repaid his kindness next day by taking him out for a four-course meal in a restaurant. The total bill for three people was the equivalent of only five Irish pounds.

Our Interrail culminated in Oslo, Norway, where we were welcomed by the Marist community. Confrères took us to visit Vigeland Park with its scores of magnificent bronze and granite sculptures celebrating humanity. I loved the nude figures and their interconnectedness in the circle of life, all in relationship, young and old, male and female, parents and children.

My European odyssey ended on 21 August, when I arrived back in Dublin, where an unexpected and deeply traumatic experience of obedience awaited me.

## #39

The Superior at Mount St Mary's in 1983 was and remains a good and conscientious man of unassailable integrity. However, to err is human, and he made a mistake that affected me.

It concerned two conversations we'd had in March and June 1983. On 10 March I told him I didn't want to be a teacher and that I'd like to study psychology with a view to becoming a counsellor.

'If you take honours psychology and then do a two-year diploma you could join the Irish Psychological Society and you would be well set up. You would make a good counsellor,' he had said.

But when I got back from Rome at the end of July, he told me I couldn't do psychology.

'I made a mistake,' he said. 'I thought you had a teaching subject. I apologise. Yes, and it was a serious enough mistake. I don't think you're suited for psychology.'

I couldn't fathom his shift. What I wanted to work at as a priest had been summarily dismissed.

Twenty-three years later, in 2006, Dr Joyce Senior of the School of Education, University College Dublin, asked me to consider becoming an educational psychologist after she read my essay *How to Motivate 10 Zoo*. She also asked if she could use it with her Higher Diploma students.

We had been taught in novitiate that obedience was listening to God's will. We were not to ignore our personal judgement but we were to submit our mind and will to 'God's will, the Church, and the call of the Superior'.

But was it 'God's will' when the Superior said I'd make a good counsellor or 'God's will' when he said I wasn't suited for psychology? How could 'God's will' fluctuate like that? The vow of obedience seemed to me nothing more than the whim of a fallible man.

When I had told my Uncle John that I was joining the Marist Fathers, his reply to me of 19 May 1980 contained a caution: *'We had an old priest in the old days who was one of the first to join that congregation in Ireland. He always wanted to go to the foreign missions but they sent him teaching instead. So he joined the Carmelites. I was with him in his last moments – lived and died a saint.'*

I had never wanted to teach as a Marist. I'd never contemplated joining the Christian Brothers because I couldn't see the point in taking on the sacrifice of celibacy, poverty and obedience to teach. Nor was there any shortage of lay teachers.

I knew Marists whose lives had been blighted by teaching, broken men sent teaching who were not suited to it. Now I, too, was being forced into teaching against my will.

I was apoplectic with rage.

'I've never felt angrier in my life,' I told the Superior. We had been taught to express how we felt.

'Well I'm angry with you! Over that Interrail. You went on that holiday with more money than any priest in the Province! You took what you hadn't used in your budget. That's just like having a savings account!'

I was staggered. Father Denis Green had written to me suggesting I have a holiday after Rome. The Superior had told me he was anxious that I would have a holiday after my work there and he had told a confrère to be sure I had a good time on the Interrail.

115

He had personally granted me permission to go and now he was blaming me for a decision he had made. Asked on 7 June if he was happy about the proposed Interrail trip, he had said: 'I am. When I say go, I say go with all my heart.'

I had asked him if I could take the £60 allowance that I hadn't used due to my frugal living during the year.

'I don't know how justified that is,' he had said. 'I don't know if we'll continue the budget system next year. That's like having a savings account.'

'I hadn't thought of that,' I said.

'No, this is something that must be looked into for next year. But as things stand, that's OK,' he decided.

He had forgotten that conversation. But I had recorded it in my journal and showed it to him. He read it as I fumed in his office. We were like two angry tigers in the same cage.

'And you can leave over this if you like, I'll not stop you!' said the Superior. 'You can walk out this door but I'll not come after you.'

I wouldn't have dreamt of leaving over this. I knew right was on my side.

With his characteristic integrity, honesty, self-knowledge, and humility, he would later tell me that this had been the biggest mistake he had made in his time as Superior. Which, in the grand scheme of things, shows he did an excellent job. He was rightly known as the conscience of the Province, and he would later, deservedly, be elevated to Superior General of the Marist Fathers.

116

## #40

Father Bernie Ryan, Superior General of the Marist Fathers in the mid-1980s, wrote a personal letter to me after my time in Rome in 1983: *'You are a charming young man, Joe. I pray you will feel encouraged to continue the pilgrim path of faith within the Marists. You have much to contribute. I'm thankful you have chosen to journey with us.'*

I was touched and appreciated the General taking the time to write to me but I did not feel encouraged.

Before Rome, my experience of loneliness and desire left me unable to understand why anyone would choose the vow of celibacy. But I lacked confidence in my ability to initiate and sustain a committed intimate relationship. Such was my poor self-esteem that I didn't believe any woman would ever want to spend her life with me.

After Rome, I became depressed following the Superior's mistake about my university subjects and future work as a priest. I doubted God had anything to do with the vow of obedience. Rather, I felt the 'will of God' was only obeying what, at that time, seemed to me to be the whim of an honourable but fallible man.

That autumn, I began a Bachelor of Arts (BA) degree in English and History at University College Dublin. Glad to be in a secular environment, I wore lay clothes; a small lapel cross the only visible hint I was a student priest.

On 24 October, I visited my mother. I went upstairs to my old bedroom and she followed me. I didn't know why but suddenly I was crying. She hugged me and I was glad she was alive.

'What have you got to tell me?' she asked.

'Nothing.'

'Is it the fellahs in the seminary?'

'No,' I replied. As ever, she misread everything.

My eyes kept filling. I didn't know where this unexpected emotion was coming from or why it was manifesting in the presence of my mother, from whom I remained alienated.

'As your father told you, you're always welcome to come home,' she said.

It was the first time she had ever said it. However, I knew that returning home to live under her domain would be psychologically damaging for me, a retrograde, self-destructive trap from which I might never escape.

Back in Milltown, on 29 October I journaled: *'Feel cheated by God. I could walk out of here and it wouldn't matter a damn.'* I felt *'misled, deceived by God'* and by *'belief itself'* and by *'the lie'* of community life.

I wondered how confrères, family and friends would react if I left. I journaled: *'I feel a fake.'* Even more disturbing for me was my sense that *'the very thing I stand for'* was also phoney.

Given that human values seemed inextricably tied up with religion, I feared that life without religion would be immoral, unethical and rudderless. I joined the Marists to do good. I journaled: *'I feel if I left here, I wouldn't give a shit about anything or anybody.'* In my depression, I added: *'Or is that not the case already?'*

'What have you got to tell me?' my director asked me at the start of a marathon two-and-a-half-hour spiritual direction. He had chosen the same words as my mother.

I told him everything, as I always did: how my whole belief system and my faith were on the rocks, disillusioned by the priesthood, community life and the Church.

'It would not be good for you to leave now, in these circumstances,' he counselled, adding: 'I'm pleased with your progress over the last year.'

'What progress?' I asked, my eyes wet, my stomach tense, my mind a sea of mud.

'Truth,' he replied.

He expressed concern about my receptivity to his counsel and suggested if I could live my life forgiving and loving, that's challenge enough for any man. Indeed, so why bother adding the encumbrances of celibacy, obedience and faith in a silent God?

I journaled: *He pretty much told me I'd be daft and foolish to leave. This encouraged me no end.'*

The following day, I attended mass as an atheist, unbelieving at the consecration. I could not pray. I read the bible too as an atheist. It was just a book, black hieroglyphics on a page.

But again, faith – or was it fear? – kicked in when I read Luke 9:62: 'No one who puts his hand to the plough and looks back is fit for the Kingdom of God.'

## #41

*For some inexplicable reason I am driven sick for love of my confrère. I want to adore him. I want to touch him. I love him.'* So reads a journal entry on 2 November 1983. It was 'inexplicable' because my intense but short-lived crush on my confrère, which we had been warned about in novitiate could easily happen to us, had sizzled out months beforehand.

I hadn't a clue about relationships. And within religious life I had no opportunity to explore my sexuality. It isn't normal or healthy to take adolescent boys in their late teens, isolate them from women, impose celibacy upon them as a condition of the priesthood, and infect their minds with nonsense about sex and sin.

Christianity is built on the big lie that humanity could only be 'saved' by a God–man conceived in the womb of the 'Virgin Mary' by the 'Holy Spirit', without her having had sexual intercourse with a man, and so avoiding the transmission of the 'stain' of 'original sin', like a sexual virus, to Jesus.

Most of the twenty novices who had joined the Marist Fathers with me three years earlier had been aged just eighteen. Three were as young as 17. I suspect most of us who entered the seminary had never had sexual intercourse. I certainly hadn't. I once heard the Superior say that religious who had had an intimate sexual relationship found celibacy much harder. They knew what they were missing.

*'How I long,'* I wrote on 7 November *'for intimate sexual contact with a lover. Is this to be denied me forever? Am I to deny it to me? Or, as a priest, will I sin and lie with a woman? Would I lie with one now? Will I before my university career is over? Will I before this day is gone?'*

Next day, I journaled: *'And again last night. But this time worse, much worse. I'd a four-hour private orgy. I simply refused to control myself.'*

You can impose man-made religious doctrines on people but nature, desire and the sexual impulse will, indeed must, emerge.

I didn't run off to confession or spiritual direction but the Gospel of Luke 9:23 rang a chord: 'Whoever wants to be my disciple must deny himself and take up his cross every day and follow me.'

120

I prayed: *'God, be with me today. Help me deny my lust.'*

And a phrase from Matthew 16:25 resonated for me after a gloomy prayer meeting on 10 November: 'Whoever loses his life for my sake will save it.'

Mount St Mary's had its tensions and cliques. On 14 November, I journaled: *'Mass today was a symbol of division for me. Also, it was pretty dead.'* Next day, I journaled: *'I've done my three years. I want so desperately to believe…and reality. I'm left with me.'*

But faith fought back with, 'Lord, to whom else shall we go?' (John 6:68)

On 1 December, I journaled: *'Can it be that I am no longer master of my own fate? Am I no longer free to disbelieve? Have I been trapped by God?'* Could I not choose *'my dime of happiness'*? Could I only be happy by submission to God? *'And yet why no peace? Why tension in my intestine? And what of my body and my carnal resistance?'*

Days later I had a scary dream. *'We're in the House of Horror. Mirrors, mad men, Dracula, continuous battles, all eerie, discomforting. There's loud laughter. Men, old and mad, with huge heads gaping at us. Eventually, I go into one room and very easily escape through the window. It's easy to climb down the wall.'*

The ease with which I escape reminds me of my dream on 16 July in Rome, where a girl takes my hand: *'It all happens so naturally. Was it as easy as this all this time?'*

Perhaps there's a lesson there: what we desire but consider impossible may be far easier to attain than we realise.

When I had visited London alone as an 18-year-old during my novitiate, I had felt lost in the sea of identities of the millions of people in the bustling capital city. I felt the need to wear a lapel cross to secure for myself some sense of personal identity in the madding crowd.

I remembered one occasion when a confrère challenged me to take off the cross, suggesting I was hiding behind it.

On 18 December, seven weeks since my last spiritual direction, more than ten weeks since my last confession, having given up on my nightly battles for chastity, and in a state of anger, unbelief and nascent independence, I took off my lapel cross, placed it under the heel of my shoe and, ensuring I could never wear it again, I crushed it.

## #42

The Marist community sang mass at the Central Mental Hospital on Christmas morning 1983. Then, five of us drove to the Hellfire Club for a walk, to work up an appetite for a fine festive dinner back in Milltown. We had a prayer meeting, relaxed in the common room, said Evening Prayer, followed by private prayer, then TV and bed. I summed it up in my journal: *'Good – very good – with community. Felt this is my place. I belong here.'*

In contrast, I was tense and felt alienated at home after Christmas, where there was bad feeling and rows.

My emotional barrenness at home was epitomised on New Year's Eve. I had stayed there to ring in the New Year with my mother; but at midnight she went across the road to a neighbour, where she remained until 1.15 a.m. I was left alone with a bottle of brandy, a drink I hadn't tried before nor hardly ever since: my first hours of 1984 were spent puking my guts up.

With great relief, I returned to Mount St Mary's in early January and was greeted by confrères with heartfelt hugs, handshakes and smiles. I felt accepted and loved. I was glad to be back in community.

'You look very happy,' said Father Donal Kerr to me, as I smiled my way down the stairs to mass on 3 January.

On 15 January, the Superior asked me if I could trust him again, after the mistake he had made the previous summer about my subject choices for university, with its lifelong consequences for my future work. It was big of him to say that. I don't remember how I replied.

I was enjoying UCD. On 21 January, I journaled that I had 'a *sense of confidence*' in myself, '*that perhaps it wasn't a fluke that I did well in my last essay; but that I've a flair for it; for English and for writing. I always hoped I might.*'

I realised that writing wasn't '*an image I must keep up*'. Rather, I saw it as: '*God's gift. Originality, self-creation. Daring to be me, clearly, boldly, for God's sake, on the page. Avoiding at all costs spoof. Being clear myself first and, being clear, to entertain, to record, to enlighten, to share, to dare, to assert, to enjoy, to run wild, to adore. That this may contribute to God's little kingdom being worked out in me.*'

I loved English literature. The Old English poem *The Seafarer* appealed to me. I relished Chaucer's unmasking of the motivations and relationships of the pilgrims in *The Canterbury Tales*. I devoured *King Lear*, the self-destruction of a great man by his own folly. I marvelled at *Paradise Lost*, appreciating the lecturer's observation that Satan had all the best lines.

I loved Pope's *The Rape of the Lock*, Johnson's *The Vanity of Human Wishes*, and Gray's *Elegy Written in a Country Churchyard*. I cried reading Tennyson's *In Memoriam* and laughed at comic moments of religious hypocrisy in Sterne's *Tristram Shandy*.

I identified with Arnold's receding sea of faith in *Dover Beach;* with Yeats's *Second Coming* – things falling apart, the centre not holding; and with Stephen Dedalus's *'non serviam'* – I will not serve – in Joyce's *A Portrait of the Artist as a Young Man.*

And I enjoyed history and got on well with my tutor Liam de Paor. When I told him that I'd have to miss a tutorial he said I'd be missed.

Assistant General Roger Wilhelm, whom I'd met in Rome, was in Milltown and asked me if I'd like to return. I said I would. My friend, general archivist Tony Ward, was sending me advance copies of Marist publications. I was excited at the possibility of returning to Rome to research Marist spirituality. I journaled: *'With all this talk about us dying out, it could be of use to the congregation.'*

Something – I don't remember what – in the Irish Marist newsletter of late January 1984 *'gladdened my heart',* encouraging me to journal: *'The congregation is renewing itself. It will change. It must. It shall. The Lord isn't playing games with us. We are men with a mission.'*

But my subconscious was not fooled by my sense of a rejuvenated Marist mission. On 21 February, I dreamt that I had forgotten a girl's name. She was insulted and left. A tear came down my left cheek.

I had forgotten that I wanted the love of a girl; and celibacy would never be life-giving for me. I had forgotten that I wanted to make my own decisions; and not obey those of honourable but fallible men making their decisions for my life. And I had forgotten why I'd crushed my lapel cross: to stop hiding behind it. And so, with what I thought was calm, I prepared to leave religious life.

## #43

It's a bombshell!' said my spiritual director when I told him on 14 March 1984 that I was thinking of not renewing my vows. Before final profession, we each took temporary vows for periods of one to three years. My vows would expire that September.

I had been calm. I wanted to make my own decisions and experience life without the shield of my religious identity. I was tired and weary of my incessant vocational questioning. And I journaled: *Is there really any chance or hope of reviving the Society of Mary?'*

I knew priests, including Father Peter Allen whom I admired, who had taken time out and returned later and progressed to ordination. *'On my side of things, it doesn't have to be final. Would I be readmitted if I applied?'*

I was getting on well with girls at UCD, I was the right age and I wanted to shed the barrier of celibacy. At a recent party, I'd danced with a girl, just danced with her, but she was so sexy. I was missing out on this.

I journaled: *'Why not take some years out now, having the freedom of most fellahs my age? If I leave for some years and, at a later date, rejoin, give it a second try, the few years out can only be to my advantage.'*

I felt it was better to depart in first Arts than later: *'Leaving after UCD is scabby.'* I hoped I could work that summer to earn my university fees for the following year.

*'I feel quite calm about the real possibility of my not renewing profession,'* I journaled. But when I verbalised all that to my spiritual director, the calm departed. My eyes moistened and I was shaking.

'You're very upset,' he said. 'You sound like you have resigned yourself to leaving. It would not be a free decision.'

He was wrong but I presumed he was wiser than me. And he dismissed my concern about the Marists paying for my degree if I continued in the Society while unsure of my future within it.

'You have things to work out that are infinitely more important than the expenses of your degree to the Marists,' he reassured me, 'whether that takes a year or two years.'

He moved closer to me, to the edge of his chair.

'Vocation is that unknown,' he said. 'Only rarely is it confirmed by the Church – at final profession and ordination. For the rest, everything depends upon inner conviction.'

'I missed out by entering so young,' I said. 'I haven't given up on the priesthood. I may well come back. I may eventually *like* to come back.'

'And what if you were not readmitted?'

'A lot hinges on that,' I replied. 'If I thought I wouldn't be, then I should surely leave now! If I am readmitted – if I choose to reapply – the experience out can only have been good. Anyway, when would the ideal circumstances present themselves to make a "free" decision? It's never as clear-cut to leave as it is to enter. Joining, you make a clean option for a new life. But leaving, you're enmeshed in both lives.'

'Is there a girl?' he asked.

'There is no particular girl but I resent the general restriction. Celibacy, I experience, as shackles – not gift.'

My faith in the vow of obedience was undermined by the Superior's mistake about my subject choices at university. As for the vow of 'poverty', I would be poorer outside the Marists than within it. Moreover, while the experience of community in novitiate had been good, each of us now seemed to be going his separate way.

I doubted my previous religious experiences and everyone else's too. Although still a believer, I journaled that I didn't know *what it is to pray. My leaving is not a flight from God. God calls me to myself. To my destiny. Not to a construct, a discipline, a shape imposed upon me.'*

I was attracted to lay life and to the *'experience of most other fellahs – their future not mapped out for five years' time'.* I was willing *'to jump into that tide. That it may bring me where it will.'* I needed time out to experience life. *'It's like an opportunity for me. A chance, once gone, cannot be relived.'*

He said: 'I suggest you do a retreat, the sooner the better – you'll agree?'

Later that day, I journaled: *'I must follow this thing through. Otherwise, I may as well forget all about inner workings within me.'*

But I agreed to do a retreat.

## #44

I told my sister on 23 March 1984 that I was thinking of leaving the Marists.

'You might as well scourge us as them,' she said, adding that I was to make my decision without complicating things by worrying about coming home. 'It just means I couldn't have records blaring if you're studying.'

'Don't mention it to Mother,' I said, encouraged by my sister's response.

127

'No, not a word. How long have you been thinking of it?'

'This last year,' I confided.

I began my retreat the following day at Avila, a Carmelite house in Dublin.

Raw, emotional and intense, that I agreed to do this retreat revealed my uncertainty about leaving. I doubted my doubt. Leaving was risky, freedom was frightening. Afraid of making a mistake, I feared change. Trusting what I had called my *'inner workings'* seemed a dangerous bet, especially as it involved leaving the security of religious life.

If I had been confident in myself, I would have dismissed my spiritual director's contention that I had resigned myself to leaving, and his personal view that it wouldn't be a 'free' decision.

I lost my inner battle the moment I consented to doing the retreat. By agreeing, I had already raised the white flag of surrender, like an alcoholic holing up in a brewery to quit the booze.

At the start of the week, my emerging self was in the ascendancy: *'I don't really believe an angel appeared to Mary.'*

*'I thought priests made a sacrifice of their lives – but we religious are just as selfish as everybody else.'*

*'The challenge was to be a man living the Word made flesh, a man missionary and faithful – mine has not been this experience.'*

*'I need to stand on my own two feet without the crutch of religious life.'*

*'I see no oneness of mind and heart. No two of them have the same purpose in life!'*

*'"Priesthood", "religious life", "popes" and "bishops", "obedience" (pah!) and the "Divine Will of God". Celibacy and whorehouses and little boys!'*

I knew I wasn't the only one to be abused as a boy.

*'I have longed that Isaiah 43 – "I have called you by name" – may be addressed to me. I do not believe it is.'*

*'I will not bow and grovel. I will choose and make my own choices: not make choices my own!'*

*'You haven't lived if you haven't slept with a woman,'* I journaled, recalling what my doctor had said to me. *'But at 22, I haven't ever kissed a woman on the lips. And I consider celibacy?! ... pah!'*

*'And, have I ever really lived? Or, have I not always "answered" the world with prescribed doses of Catholicity?'*

*'I entered to be a Marist, not a teacher. The irony is, I may end up a teacher but no Marist.'*

*'I do not believe. Or, rather, I do not believe enough to base my life on it. I'll not be a fake. To continue would be an inadequate and inauthentic response to all that.'*

I journaled: *'I cannot pray; but I can write. And with words will I find my true self hidden.'*

I remembered seeing a film about a priest or brother having a vocational crisis. It had a scene shot from underwater. He is swimming naked. I journaled: *'We see this, and it is representative of his hidden, unexpressed sexual self. Like him, to stay in the seminary, I pretty much have to deny my sexuality, sexual desires and any sexual expression. Why anyone ever thought that could be a good thing, I do not understand!'*

I recalled reading Karen Armstrong's book *Through the Narrow Gate*, her story of leaving a convent. I journaled: *'I thought it was brilliant. I remember its climax: the scream – written in capitals. And then she realised it was she who was screaming.'*

But on 25 March, my spiritual director visited me at Avila. I asked him why he had suggested the retreat.

He replied: 'I thought it might be a prayerful chance for you to change your mind.'

## #45

Remembering how I chose to stay in religious life during my retreat of March 1984 is humbling. My spiritual director said: 'You have been under pressure. You had a difficult experience of obedience. You got your fingers burned in celibacy. You've been studying hard. And you haven't been praying.'

I was pleased he didn't want me to leave. I had always been open with him and he still believed in my vocation.

I said: 'I need you to be open to what I decide and to what's best for me.'

'I am,' he replied. 'But perhaps you should have a different director. You may see me as being too involved in your decision.'

'No. I'd prefer you.'

Maybe I worried another director might encourage me to leave.

I journaled: *'Yes. I would prefer him to direct this retreat. It is not right that the one man who believes in me more than anyone else, knows me better than anyone else, cares for me, tries to listen to me, that he should wash his hands of me simply because I no longer take all his thinking or his counsel piecemeal.'*

He didn't *'know me better than anyone else'*. I, alone, did. But I didn't realise that yet. I distrusted my personal perceptions, feelings and judgements. It was frightening to trust what I had called in my journal my *'inner workings'*.

My spiritual director said: 'I am against the idea of your leaving, although your heart is fairly set on it. There are all sorts of other things you could do, like taking a whole summer to work at something, or in a few years, to take longer off.'

I journaled: *'He's really dead against the idea of my leaving.'* It was flattering.

On 27 March, he said that the Superior wanted to give him something to give to me. I journaled: *'It'll be interesting to see what, if anything, JH gives me.'*

I went for a cycle and afterwards reflected that the two inner arguments calling me in different directions didn't speak to each other. *'Each has a strongly put, deeply felt, case. Each demands the total dedication of my will. Each obliterates the other. Neither is particularly rosy.'*

The 'stay' camp was winning. I sketched the outline of a play. *'All his life he'd listened to God's Word. He saw it as the fountain of life ... Much-loved seminary only at the prospect of leaving it; and still a hiding place at that ... Through the ages, Christ calls his own to himself. He chooses wisely.'*

*'You cannot leave Christ and be happy,'* I journaled, dialoguing with myself. *'Does Christ even figure in all this talk about leaving? When, during this retreat, did you know peace? At the thought of being in the Marists for life. Do you not see that the Marists have been for you a most gracious blessing from God? You run from this and you run from yourself and all you hold dear. You cannot settle for a lesser love than Christ's.'*

I had not forgiven the Superior for the mistake he had made about my subject choices at university. *'To go back to Milltown demands that I forgive the Superior,'* I journaled. *'It'll involve trusting him again and living my belief in reconciliation.'*

Disregarding my *'inner workings'* and with nothing more than a leap of faith, I journaled: *'It is God's will that I be a priest: so be it. Alleluia! Let us find our identity in Christ.'*

131

On 28 March, I journaled: *'I no longer believe I can or should or will leave. Shite! Am I in for life?'*

*'I've an almighty distraction: what the bloody Hell is JH going to give me? Will it make any difference to my decision whatever he sends me? If it is a letter, might I not again be leaning on the crutch of his approval rather than a self-reliance and freedom in my own choice? If anything arrives, I shall not open it!'*

*'I have already decided to stay. He does not know that. I can make my choice irrespective of what JH says. Of course, I'll always wonder what was in the bloody letter. But I'll have achieved a great freedom, a freedom I feel already!!! ... Phew! I'm in, and with God's continued mercy, it's for life.'*

He never wrote the letter, as I returned to Milltown on April Fool's Day 1984.

One of my confrères gave me a bear hug.

'Did you make any radical life decisions?' he asked.

'Yes.'

'Are you leaving?' he asked, worried.

'No. I'm staying!'

'Don't do that on me!' he beamed with joy.

I was glad to be back.

But on 3 April, I was awoken by a dream: *'There is a storm. My only memory of it is of not being able to move. Its ferocity is such that it is impossible to go out in it.'*

# Chapter 4

# Twists and turns

### #46

My relapse back into religious faith and my return to the Marist Fathers seminary on April Fool's Day 1984 heralded an intriguing period.

It began with relief, calm and serenity, at having made a decision.

'You look the picture of happiness,' a confrère said to me a week later. 'That retreat did you the world of good.'

The Superior told me he had never seen me so serene, and that the Provincial had remarked to him how much I'd matured.

But within a fortnight, my solitary difficulties with celibacy resumed.

'You were walking on water after your retreat,' said my confessor. 'Now you've been pulled back to earth.'

My mother attended the Easter Vigil on 21 April. I would have liked a speaking part during the liturgy given her presence – she had never heard me read at any event in Milltown. But I still lacked confidence speaking in public and always opted for a silent role.

133

'It was all above my head,' she said disparagingly after the mass to Father Denis Green, whom I think had presided.

*'I don't know how to describe what mood she was in,'* I journaled, *'but I've seen her in it before and don't like it.'* I wondered was she jealous, vengeful or bitter. *'She was nervy and ill-at-ease. And I was embarrassed for myself.'*

That Easter night, for the first time since my return to Milltown, thoughts of leaving returned. *'No. I'm not leaving,'* I journaled. *'But I put on that cap and shoes again and thought, why? I've now more or less been convinced that I'm called by God.'*

My adult self appreciates my use of *'or less'* there; and the unconvincing tone of my religious reboot, just weeks after I'd come close to leaving, and to honouring my uncharted *'inner workings'*.

Back at UCD on 26 April I sat beside Verena (not her real name). *'She is very nice,'* I journaled. *'She's lovely trusting eyes. And, I may be wrong, but I think she likes me. I'd bet 60/40 she'd go out with me if I asked her. Were I not a seminarian, I think she'd come out with me OK.'*

That same day, another attractive woman whom I knew invited me to join herself and a nun for a weekend in Kenmare. A person of impeccable integrity, she was visiting Mount St Mary's.

I decided to go, on the strength of her invitation, to a place I loved, for three days. I felt I needed to check that was OK with the Superior but he was away so I asked my spiritual director.

'Can you afford the time?' he asked, disapprovingly. 'Your exams are close.'

'I've been wrestling with the decision for twenty-four hours. I think the break would be good for me.'

'I think your fancy is dictating your decision,' he said. 'I'll leave you to decide but I expect you to decide responsibly.'

'Go, for God's sake, go!' said a confrère to me. 'He's using the language of freedom but not really leaving you free.'

I didn't go. I caved in, afraid of making the wrong decision; of risking my director's, or an imagined deity's, disapproval; of stepping away from the safety of obedience and, in my wildest dreams, losing my virginity in a weekend of unbridled pleasure – although I'm absolutely certain the idea of that was very far indeed from the mind of my friend!

I stayed and fumed, annoyed at my director and at myself, sleeping in late on Sunday morning; so not getting much study done.

It was a microcosm of what had happened when I was minded not to renew my vows: I decided to go: I talked to him: I allowed our interaction to undermine my decision: I stayed.

Religion demands the submission of the mind, heart, will and body to man-made rules and a man-made god. For example, Islam means submission to God. But submission is the opposite of personal adult maturity – thinking and deciding for oneself and accepting the consequences of one's decisions.

It took me a lifetime to grow out of submitting to religious people and their religious concepts, controls and laws – all of them man-made. God did not create man in the image of himself. Rather, man created God in the image of himself.

Indoctrinating infants and children into religious belief is the most insidious intellectual and emotional abuse of children. Mature adults learn to perceive, understand, judge, decide and act for themselves as autonomous, critical and responsible human beings. Having one's mind wired to religious dogmas and beliefs makes that task more difficult.

'I think I misjudged things about the weekend away,' my spiritual director subsequently said to me.

I told him that the consequences of the decision were fine when what I really wanted to tell him was that he used the language of freedom while not leaving me free.

But I'd a lot more growing up to do before I could speak truth to power. And even more work to do before I could own my personal power and make my own decisions for myself. Yet it was good of him to admit his mistake to me.

Next day, back at UCD, Verena was practically the first person I met. *'Shit, I think she's lovely,'* I journaled.

But I didn't tell her.

### #47

Do you know why I was sent here?' Father Bill Carney asked the Superior out loud in the refectory one day.

There was something brazen about his question. It was broadcast at full voice, without reticence, shame or fear, knowingly audible to many members of the community.

Father Carney was standing in front of me, just on the far side of the table at which I and others sat. He was facing the Superior, who also stood on the far side of the table, to my left.

'The Archbishop asked if we could let you stay here for a while and we agreed,' replied the Superior, looking at Father Carney searchingly.

'You really don't know?' persisted Bill, sounding incredulous.

'No,' said the Superior.

'Ah, it was the drink,' said Father Carney.

At the time, I regarded this exchange as extraordinary.

Father Bill Carney lived in Mount St Mary's during a substantial part of 1984 and for sure at times between April and September. He was not a Marist and I did not know why he was there.

I suspected the reason was more than 'the drink' – not least because it was the one offered by Father Carney at the tail end of that weird public interrogation of the Superior. If Carney knew the answer was alcoholism, why had he asked the question?

He presided at a penitential service in the seminary on 18 April 1984. My journal records: *'Bill Carney presided, excellently.'* I was impressed by him. He seemed to me to have a great pastoral empathy with people.

On 25 July, an entry reads: *'I like having Bill Carney around. Bill is human. He lives his faith. He's weak and he knows it.'* It's interesting that I sensed from him self-knowledge of his moral weakness, which I assumed concerned an alcohol addiction. I believed him to be a man of religious faith.

He was affable, encouraging and affirming of others. On 22 September, I journaled: *'Bill Carney said today I'd a lovely voice!'*

But there was a mystique about him. Why had a diocesan priest come to live with us when he wasn't a Marist?

I was stunned, decades later, to hear Father Bill Carney named as 'a serial sexual abuser of children, male and female' and 'one of the most serious serial abusers investigated by the Commission' in the 2009 Murphy

Report, the report of a Commission of Investigation by the Irish Government into sexual abuse in the Catholic Archdiocese of Dublin.

The Murphy Report states: 'He pleaded guilty to two counts of indecent assault in 1983. The Archdiocese of Dublin paid compensation to six of his victims.'

The next year, he lived with us – and worked with children in the local parish of Clonskeagh. His parish priest, Monsignor Browne, a lovely and astute man whom I knew, told the Archbishop that Father Bill Carney was 'reliable, punctual, always available for more work than he had been assigned'.

The Murphy Report confirms that the Marist Fathers had not been told why Father Carney had been sent to Mount St Mary's.

Religious congregations operate within a diocese with the permission of the bishop. I assume the Marists felt it was not their place to ask why he was being sent to them.

Likewise, Monsignor Browne was not told about Father Carney's history of child abuse. Indeed, the Monsignor commended the priest's celebration of mass, including class masses in local schools. 'Teachers,' according to the Murphy Report, 'felt this was a priest who could "really communicate with the children".'

Two years after staying with us, in 1986, he abused more children in Crumlin, Dublin.

When he was being transferred from Clogher Road parish in Dublin in 1989, parishioners complained that he was being moved because he was a 'wonderful priest', echoing my initial estimation of him from the reconciliation service he had led.

The Commission was aware of 'complaints or suspicions of child sexual abuse against him in respect of 32 named individuals' and said there was 'evidence that he abused many more children'.

Bill Carney was extradited from the UK in 2013 and died in Midlands Prison, Portlaoise, in 2015, aged 65, while on remand awaiting trial for historical abuses.

Although I had been fondled by a Christian brother as a young boy in primary school in the 1970s and was forced to strip naked by another Christian Brother, I had never spoken of those incidents until I was an adult.

In 1984, when Father Bill Carney lived in my community, the term 'paedophile priest' had not yet been coined. The international news scandal of paedophilia in the priesthood and its shameful cover-up by Church authorities had not yet broken and shaken the Church to its foundations.

When it did in the late 1980s, I wondered: who now could want to be a priest?

### #48

One month after taking my leap of faith and returning to the Marists, I'd a profound sense of dissatisfaction. The visitor who had invited me to join her and a nun for a weekend in Kenmare had left Mount St Mary's. Her departure triggered loneliness. Celibacy was as difficult as ever.

*'Father Denis Green today spent some time telling me how fine I am,'* I journaled – Denis was a great encourager – and he was thankful that I felt dissatisfied.

139

'If anyone is satisfied with themselves, they've opted out of the human race,' said Denis. 'We are characterised by a discontent, a longing for something. The wholly "happy" man is a fake.'

I was asked to lead a prayer meeting for confrères on 3 May 1984. I wrote on the community notice board: 'Perhaps we might share tonight of Our Experience of the Mystery of Our Coming to Birth in Christ.'

*'It made me tense,'* I journaled, when I overheard two confrères saying the notice was well worded. Having my written words applauded was like a singer discovering an audience liked his voice. I journaled: *'My writing helps things emerge. I think good with my pen.'*

After the prayer meeting, I journaled: *'Before speaking, I was nervous. But I told myself: this is a good thing. Just before opening my mouth, I reminded myself of the key: "mystery". Then, each of my thoughts was directed towards this.'* I was starting to lose my anxiety about public speaking.

I shared at the prayer meeting that, regardless of how well or how much I prayed, I *'sinned'.* Despite my repeated efforts to live celibacy in *'perfect continence',* I failed.

It was reality beckoning, undercutting my inherited religious and clerical presumption that sexual abstinence was morally superior to any sexual activity.

Confrères liked that prayer meeting. Coincidentally, each of those whom I recorded in my journal as having spoken at it eventually left religious life.

At spiritual direction on 6 May, I was gaining much needed distance from the counsel of my director. I journaled: *'His platitudes were met with my telltale nodding head. He noticed and stopped.'* He had admitted he had misjudged and mishandled my aborted weekend in Kenmare.

I wonder if he ever considered whether he may have misjudged and mishandled my attempt, that March, to leave religious life, saying it wouldn't be a 'free decision'. However, I allowed him to do it, by agreeing to do the retreat and by wanting and confirming him as my director for it. Had I been ready to leave, I would have done neither.

Next day I journaled: *'Father Jimmy Carr told me this morning he believes I have a vocation and has no difficulty seeing me saying mass. That put the day on a good footing.'*

But doubt was my constant companion. I journaled: *'There is no faith without doubt, no trust without fear, no hope without something like despair.'*

And on 9 May, my struggle with faith was again evident: *'What is "faith" if not a leap of confidence into the hands of the living God? What is trust if not the terror of not knowing but believing?'* Reprimanding myself for doubt, I journaled: *'What use is the man consecrated to God whose faith collapses under strain?'*

I grappled with the idea of human freedom and God's will. If I was called by God to be a Marist and left, would I be unhappy? Would to leave be perverting God's will by deafening my ear to His call?

A spirit of cynicism and backbiting held sway in Mount St Mary's that month. A priest in another Marist house was disparagingly referred to as a 'simple priest'; another priest was deemed 'repugnant', while another confrère was derided as having his head in the clouds.

I closed in on myself, wondering what was being said about me behind my back. Mass, for me, became a sham, the sacrament of our disunity. Tension was palpable and the harmonious spirit of novitiate was but a distant memory. Except for a few friends, the community had, for me, become emotionally barren.

# IN MY GUT, I DON'T BELIEVE

By mid-May, just over a month since choosing to stay, I had lost the battle of celibacy and felt powerless over my solitary pleasures. Prayer and spiritual reading made no difference. I felt humiliated, like an alcoholic unable to stop drinking.

I journaled: *'Is it that Christ wants me to have more understanding and mercy for my fellow sinners in the confessional? Or is it that sin is the most humiliating thing for me? Perhaps I've got to acknowledge more often – even daily – my yearning for conjugal sexual pleasure, apart at all from the intimacy and enrapture of intertwining my body around a woman. I long for this. There is no denying it!'*

Most hot-blooded 22-year-old men would agree. But most wouldn't be committed to celibacy, nor their minds and emotions warped by Catholic guilt about sex.

#49

By 15 June 1984, Morning Prayer had lost any meaning for me.' I journaled: *'It didn't matter if I got up, it didn't matter if I didn't.'* I saw *'cynicism'* in Milltown about *'faith'*, observing that it wasn't just me, but other members of the community too, who doubted.

*'My prayer is dead,'* I journaled on 21 June. *'I feel depressed. I'm lonely. I feel like I'm in Limbo. I've no particular inclination to have spiritual direction. Celibacy is as hard as at its hardest before. Desire is high. Pining. Want.'*

I was invited to accompany a busload of middle-aged and elderly women on a pilgrimage to the Marian shrine of Knock. Against my will, I was expected by the tour organiser to play the role of the devout seminarian, leading several rosaries on the bus.

142

When we stopped for lunch at a hotel, she expected me to sit at the top table. This was how priests could develop a sense of entitlement. It all felt wrong. The Gospel (Luke 14:10) has a story of Jesus telling his disciples not to take places of honour.

Unwilling to accept the role into which I was being cast, I declined the invitation to the top table, choosing instead to sit among the pilgrims. But the organiser insisted I move and I felt forced into the stereotype. I did not want to play this role. I wanted to be authentic.

I couldn't identify with the devotion of the pilgrims on the bus, or at the shrine, as they rattled off rosary after rosary. I tried discussing with the organiser the need for an informed, intelligent and critical faith. She was appalled by my suggestion that Catholics should think for themselves.

She retorted: 'Sure, then we'd be just like Protestants!'

When I discussed the pilgrimage with my spiritual director on 25 June, he reprimanded me: 'You should have accepted the position of honour. Those people have a deep spirituality that you would know nothing about.'

I was stung by his criticism, which I regarded as unfair. Their piety was passive and unthinking. They could as easily have been devout Muslims, Hindus or belonged to any sect, given their passive acceptance of the dogmas and devotions of the religion they happened to have been born into. Was that all religion was – perpetuating the religious bias of a given social or geo-political culture?

I had no wish to collude in propagating such tales. I journaled: *To play along with it is the perpetuation of a myth.'*

The morning of that spiritual direction, I dreamt I was a prisoner who makes repeated attempts to escape but each time I'm chased and I am put back in chains.

For me, the dream was about wanting to get beyond the myths of religion and religious life. I was the escaping prisoner but also the captor, bringing myself back, time and time again, by my infernal, internal struggle between doubt and faith, belief and unbelief.

*'Unbelief characterised today,'* I journaled on 26 June. *'Doubt. Absence of faith. Last night I lay awake thinking. Do I have a vocation? Will I leave in September? Will I renew for one year only?'*

Three months after my retreat, I journaled: *'I am again in the situation of instability, uncertainty, absence of confidence and doubt in my vocation or lack thereof. I am frightened and disturbed by this. I cannot smile. There is no life in my eyes. "Prayer" – public and private – is sublimated doubt.'*

That night I dreamt I'm being chased on my bicycle. I see a bridge. I cycle some of the way across. But the way is treacherous. The road is slanted. The bridge is of mossy, slippery rocks.

The philosopher Blaise Pascal (1623–1662) proposed that, when in doubt, to 'act as if' you believed and that this could cure unbelief. I think my entire faith life was based on that principle. 'If' Jesus was God, then that had to change everything. And there were lots of days when I managed to believe.

On 28 June I journaled: *'A good day. I believed in Christ and his love, mercy and call to me. The problem is never other's doubts of my vocation but mine.'*

A symposium of Marist Fathers, Brothers and Sisters on 4 July revitalised my belief in Marist spirituality, modelling oneself after the exemplar of Mary, the Virgin Mother of God. Hearing, two days later, that I passed my first Arts exams further improved my mood.

*'Today could be regarded as one of the happiest days of my life,'* I journaled on 7 July. *'As I lay prostrate just now in the chapel, my heart beat, reminding me of my fragility. I prayed. Mary is the key, dare I say, to my happiness, authenticity, spirituality and vocation.'*

## #50

My mother cajoled me into teaching her to drive. On 17 July 1984, she practised on Dollymount Strand and drove home. Despite a few hairy moments, we arrived at the top of Belton Park Avenue. Approaching our house, she was going too fast because she needed to turn left at a ninety-degree angle into the short car-length drive of our house.

'Brake,' I said.

This elicited no response.

'Brake,' I repeated.

She went faster.

'Brake!' I yelled.

She depressed the accelerator, turned ninety degrees at speed and crashed with a loud bang into the front of our house.

'Did we hit something?' asked my mother.

I couldn't believe my ears.

'Did we hit the pillar?' she specified.

The pillar was behind us, untouched. She seemed oblivious to the unusual proximity of the house, the mangled car bonnet right there before her eyes and a large crack quaking up the pebbledash.

That night, she confessed my father had tried to teach her to drive and he had given up.

'Why?' I asked.

'I crashed and he said I should never get behind the wheel of a car again.'

\*

The car crash was a metaphor for our relationship. On 3 August, I journaled: *Today I came clean with my mother.'*

She said I hadn't respected her for three years, citing my attitude to her during our ghastly pilgrimage to Lourdes two summers earlier.

*'Now, at last,'* I journaled, *'she knows I don't enjoy being in her house or company. She's quite philosophical about our relationship.'*

'Some of the best relationships die,' she said.

*'That struck me,'* I journaled. *'It seemed refreshingly containable.'*

I told her I distrusted her; a trust sundered by her failure to tell me that my missing brother David was gay, even during my search for him while our father lay dying. It could have helped me find him.

Perhaps it never occurred to her it might help. She didn't think it was fair that I should hold it against her.

'There are skeletons in every house,' she said.

As for her treatment of David, who disappeared from home aged 17, she said she had known nothing about homosexuality nor how to handle it. When I reminded her of the negative beliefs and attitudes that she had instilled into me about sex, warning me masturbation was a 'very serious sin', she couldn't remember saying it.

In a meeting with the Superior on 22 August, he said my gift of journaling was magnificent. He reminded me always to keep my diaries and never to throw them away.

Three nights later I was awoken by a dream. All I could remember from it was a repeated phrase, something like

146

'You, only you' or 'You and you alone'. I asked myself: what if I alone of my novitiate stayed in the Marists for life?

A week later, I discussed with my spiritual director the dire state of my relationship with my mother.

'Beware,' he cautioned, 'lest it become irreparable.'

My mother went to London to meet David around this time. *They spent a considerable part of the day together, fruitfully and pleasantly,* I journaled. *'And that's only their second encounter in nine and a half years. It is the first since the family reunion some two and a half years ago.'* Perhaps my conversation with her prompted the reconciliation with her stepson.

'What are your thoughts on renewing your vows?' asked my director.

'I think I'll renew for two years,' I said.

'Good. This will be your last temporary renewal before final profession.'

Final profession was when you committed yourself – and when the congregation committed to you – for life. It was the first time it had been mentioned to me personally. It suddenly seemed close.

'I'll be only twenty-four when these two years are up. That's young for a life decision.'

'Not really. Lots of people are married by your age, Joe.'

We did our annual retreat leading up to the renewal of vows. On 31 August, just days before we renewed our commitment, the Superior summoned the whole community together.

'I've very bad news for you,' he said.

I wondered was he going to announce that the congregation was folding. The students in the common room made up the bulk of Marist seminarians in Europe.

'Father Keith Murphy (not his real name) is leaving the priesthood and religious life.'

I was stunned. Father Murphy was a member of the formation staff in Milltown. He had been my spiritual director for much of 1982.

Next day, a much-respected confrère from my novitiate told me it was unlikely he would renew his vows. I felt desolate.

That night, I could not sleep. My confrère's wavering and Father Murphy's departure taught me, and I now realised it at an existential level, that absolutely anyone could leave – even the Superior or the Pope.

#### #51

Knowing that a priest who had been on the formation staff at Milltown was leaving the priesthood and religious life sent shockwaves around the community in September 1984. That he had been my spiritual director for much of 1982 made his departure even more personal for me.

I had the sense of a panicking Society of Mary. Father Denis Green hugged me, sensing my desolation. It was mutual support. This was his brother priest who was leaving. I journaled: *'I think I detected high emotion. I think I supported him.'*

I tried to dissuade the confrère from my novitiate, who had told me he was minded not to renew his vows, from leaving. I told him I'd faced a similar dilemma at my Easter retreat and that I had chosen what I called the 'higher values' of religious life.

'In those terms,' he replied, 'the higher values for me are those now appealing to me to leave.'

Another confrère from my novitiate who had been a good friend had left that summer. The Superior had described us during novitiate as 'kindred spirits'.

I coped with these losses by consoling myself with the Gospel words: 'He who loses his life for my sake will find it'. I felt responsibility for the faith, strengthened by my mother's recent meeting with my brother David. I journaled: *"Put out to deep water," says the Lord, "and cast out the nets for a catch." Remember, "nothing is impossible to God."'*

I tried to support my confrères. My two retreats that year, and the shock departure of confrères, added zeal to my decision to be a Marist. *'Christ, I am convinced, has a particular call to me to strengthen my brothers, to appreciate them (and not only when I hear they are going), to serve them, to accept them as they are, to upbuild them,'* I journaled.

'You need a veil to shield your brightness!' Denis said to me on 6 September, emboldened as I was by my reinvigorated faith and sense of responsibility towards my community.

I renewed my vows on 12 September 1984. But the very next day I felt again the loneliness of celibacy and the desire for an exclusive relationship. I journaled: *What is the basis for unity in religious life? Is vocation a matter of call or choice? I am most at peace when I choose to believe that I have a call. But is there assumed communion? To what extent did Marist priests become finally professed for similar reasons?'*

I wrote of the *'lamentable solitude of the human heart'*, while on a short holiday in Galway with three confrères. *'Each of us lonely, being human. How different it would be were we not celibates, if we were two boys and two girls, or married couples. The*

149

*Lord, though bountiful, is a hard master. Let me not neglect the yearning within my heart for intimacy. This is my cross. Can I bear it for life?'*

I headed off alone for a few hours to the seashore. It rained soft to the touch. I didn't get soaked and I was amazed to see the field beside me avoided the shower. Immersed in the splendour of life surrounding me, I journaled: *'I sang and sang to my heart's content. Nobody could hear me. Yes, I sang holy songs. Nothing else sprang from my heart but the Gloria.'*

Abstinence remained difficult after renewing my vows. Having confessed on 21 September to solitary pleasures, my confessor said I should thank God for my weaknesses *'because "otherwise you'd be unbearable". I was on a high after confession,'* I journaled.

The extent of my 22-year-old sexual naivety is embarrassing. On 29 September, I journaled: *'I slept with no clothes on last night. It was terrific.'* But then, when seminaries accepted boys as young as 17 and 18, what legitimate opportunities were there for sexual experimentation, exploration or maturation?

The only licit place where sex can manifest for celibates is in shocking, riotous night-time dreams, where the unguarded subconscious has licence to roam, unrestrained by religious constraints, morality or social mores. Unbridled in sleep, the dream-self of even a holy Pope might be a murderer, a rapist, a necrophiliac; or all three in the same dream.

On 2 October, a confrère and I got drenched on our way back from a pub. I undressed in my room. I journaled: *'It would have been stupid to change into other clothes, and stupid to stay as we were. I didn't hang about taking time undressing. I was into bed in a jiffy. I don't think he even saw my penis. He kissed me on the forehead as he left.'*

I had forgotten about that uneventful encounter but my journal reveals there was more to it than met the eye, as I shall next explore.

### #52

On 2 October 1984, less than three weeks after renewing my vows, that seemingly innocuous encounter took place in my bedroom. I'd had two pints with a confrère in a pub. We got soaked in the rain on the way back to Mount St Mary's. As I journaled: *'It would have been stupid to change into other clothes…I was into bed in a jiffy. I don't think he even saw my penis.'*

Let me dig deeper. Why, 35 years ago, did my confrère come into my bedroom when presumably he was saturated too. And why did I let him in?

Confrères and priests were often in each other's rooms. I'd say it was a daily occurrence. But my journal records: *'He said earlier he may be aroused by my privates. He communicated prior desire.'* I don't recall whether he said this in the pub or in my room. I journaled: *'His seeming willingness to fondle my penis. His request. His "guiltlessness".'*

My journal doesn't specify, nor can I recall, what, if anything, his request was. Perhaps he asked if he could touch me and I was struck by his ease, which contrasted with my sense of shame and sinfulness about sex.

I journaled: *'It is lovely to feel wanted and desired.'* And I wondered was it *'really so very serious were he to handle me?'*

Sexually abused as a young boy by a Christian Brother, I had, after the abuse, worried: *'Why me?'* His abuse had

151

undermined my boyhood confidence in my masculinity and my emerging sexual identity. I had felt confused and isolated and there had been nobody I could talk to.

Now I was a sexually inhibited young man, my head full of religion and the supposed virtues of celibacy. But I could not deny my normal human needs, my desire, craving and yearning for sexual release. Try as I did, I never managed to abstain for long from solitary pleasures.

I thought of a film I saw in which boys experimented with each other's privates. I had never done that. 'Curiosity,' I journaled. 'No babies,' I reasoned, 'no nooses to be hanged upon to accompany such mild homosexual activity.' I wondered had my confrère 'lent a hand' to other confrères. From one thing he said I gathered he hadn't. From something else he had said, I wondered if he may have.

He leant over me 'softly touching my shoulder and arm'. I became aroused. 'I asked him to get up. He mentioned going at least twice – I didn't discourage him. But he stayed. Neither did I really want him to leave.'

He kissed me on the forehead as he left.

'I do believe,' I journaled the following day, 'that if I said to him to come to my room tonight and lend a hand and explore that area – he had indicated he would like to and be willing to – I think he would come. I am "free" to do it, allow it to happen, even repay him a little.'

What was scary for me was: 'I feel that I have a contact. I don't think he'd ever raise the issue in spiritual direction. I'm quite willing to have a go.'

However, I noted two problems. 'One: I am almost absolutely certain that I would have to raise the matter in spiritual direction. Two: We are at the concrete choice again – to love celibately or to seek sexual gratification. Such activity diminishes the spiritual *life of the Church, the Marists, most specifically this community and, above all, my capacity for charity.'*

I journaled: *'Damn it, celibacy is hard! Why does the life I want so badly to live well have to exclude this kind of intimacy? With male or female, and preferably female. The beauty, warmth and closeness of my youthful body next to that of another young adult.'*

*'I've an intense desire to sin. I know somebody who is willing and able to fondle my penis. If I say "come", he will surely come. I feel it not to be so terribly serious. Mutual exploration. Mutual consent. Mutual silence, if necessary.'*

There was one subsequent sexual experience with that confrère. I don't remember when it occurred, presumably sometime after this. We were watching TV in a darkened room in Milltown. Sitting beside me, he placed his left hand on my right thigh. I did not object. A hand is a hand, and his worked up to my genitals. I became aroused. We both went to my room. But reason, conscience, guilt, shame, distrust or fear gained the ascendancy by the time we got there. I withdrew my consent to whatever had started in the TV room. He left my bedroom shortly after we'd arrived, nothing further having transpired between us.

### #53

That night of desire and vulnerability occurred less than three weeks after my renewal of vows on 12 September 1984. I felt there was someone in my community willing to lend a hand to ease the aching loneliness of celibacy and sensed how close I had come to availing of that release.

That night of temptation prompted me to review my journal, adding words in the margins testifying to my reawakened doubt. I saw no correlation between time spent in prayer, or its perceived quality, and my repeated failures shouldering the yoke of celibacy. I could pray earnestly for an hour and succumb to solitary pleasure minutes later.

Wherein lay truth – in a prayerful relationship with an unseen, silent, inscrutable god, who may not exist? Or in the natural, inner dynamism towards wholesome sexual release, a desire for companionship, and a personal need for a relationship with some visible, audible, corporeal human being?

My journal reflections of 2 October, after my openness to infidelity to my vows earlier that night, show the continued coexistence within me of belief and unbelief. It was exhausting exploring everything, quasi-simultaneously, through the perspectives of both faith and doubt. But I wouldn't have had it any other way. I couldn't understand, and I did not envy, those who did not doubt.

The day after my confrère's visit to my room, I went to confession. *'I didn't feel better after confession,'* I journaled. *'Yes, it was good to go to confession immediately. But I felt sick almost physically at what I had done.'*

As nothing had transpired with my confrère, and I didn't specify in my journal 'what I had done', I assume there was something unusual about my succumbing to solitary pleasure after my confrère had left. I know that on one occasion, during a lapse from 'perfect continence', I reached for a rosary beads; and thereafter felt guilty of sacrilege. I wonder might it have been that night.

The rosary, representing purity; the male organ symbolising the 'necessary sin of Adam'. Both irreconcilable. Belief and unbelief. Superego and id. Virgin Most Pure and 'original sin'.

All of the contradictions of Catholicism are there in the rosary beads and the penis: the joyful, sorrowful and glorious mysteries of the faith, with the Virgin Mother at its heart, and the life-giving pleasurable messy male organ of desire, intimacy and fecundity.

*

Father Larry Duffy, who had so inspired me to enter the Marists, had joined a new mission in the Philippines. I received a letter from him on 16 October, conveying his excitement at being involved in the project. Larry asked me to imagine the amount of work there was for only two priests and a few workers in a parish of 40,000 people, with elementary and high schools, a university, a hospital, clinics, and a convent. There were sixteen barrios, each with a chapel, and tribal Filipinos *'some of whom live away in the hills and have not been evangelised yet'*.

He said the place was *'crawling with sects'*. But I was increasingly aware that the Catholic Church was also a sect – just bigger than most. Larry wrote that he hoped a lot of us in Milltown were thinking of volunteering for the foreign missions. I felt that his letter was perhaps intended to encourage me to do that. But, though respecting him, I never saw myself following in Larry's footsteps again.

*

A few days later, one of my best friends in the Marists told me he was thinking of pulling out of religious life. Like me, he had come close to leaving before.

'Next time,' he said, 'I'll only tell people after I've decided and I'll be gone within the hour.'

It cut me to the heart that so close a friend might decide to leave without my awareness of his crisis and depart at any moment. Our collective band of brotherhood, forged

155

in novitiate, was increasingly illusory. Before the end of October, another scholastic had left.

'I hope you will remain a Marist,' the Superior, Father Hannan, said to me on 1 November, adding humbly that he was happy I was taking him off a pedestal.

On 20 November, my mother visited me for the most bizarre 'conversation' of my life. I journaled: *'She read her thoughts to me from a list. She held a notebook in her hand, reported to me all she had to tell me and, when finished, looked up as if to say, "Well, you're very quiet. Have you any news for me?"'*

## #54

By November 1984, I was becoming disaffected with spiritual direction. Contemplating changing my director, I countered in my journal: *'He knows more about me than anybody else.'* Clearly, I still had not learned that *I* knew myself better than anyone.

Outgrowing religion would involve me coming to recognise and respect my personal perceptions, understanding, judgements and decisions. I had to take back the power that I had given to others; a power that I should never have given away in the first place and that was always mine alone to keep. But I had yet to learn that lesson.

*'He was there for that Easter retreat – a milestone in my life,'* I journaled.

In fact, I had undermined my personal decision to leave earlier that year because of his contention that it would not have been a free decision.

156

Now in November, months after that crisis, I journaled: *'There aren't any heroes. There aren't any saints. I sin. And, presumably, he sins.'*

\*

Meanwhile, my religious faith was taking a pounding at UCD. I got on well with Dr Michael Richter, (1943–2011), who would, in 1987, become professor of medieval history at the University of Konstanz. In his UCD lectures, Richter argued that Bede's *Ecclesiastical History of the English People* was a work of Christian propaganda, rather than an objective history. He maintained that the pre-eminence of Rome in Christianity had been an historical accident.

Later, I would confide in Dr Richter about my vocational doubts and, unlike all the priests who counselled me to stay, he advised me with insight and wisdom to: 'Take your chance in the world!'

On 26 November, I got a high score in a history essay from my tutor Professor F.X. Martin (1922–2000), the famous medieval scholar and Augustinian friar who campaigned to save the Wood Quay archaeological site in Dublin. Encouraged by F.X. Martin saying I was getting 'even better', I journaled: *'One o'clock and I'm wide awake and I'm by no means blue. There is something exciting going on in me. Is it a reawakening of a long-lost self – studious, intelligent, confident, hard-working. Is it an abandoning of superstition, bondage, silliness?'*

Another learned priest–historian admitted to me that the greatest challenge to religious faith is the history of the Church.

Probably because of my interest in history, I was appointed house archivist at Mount St Mary's. In the archives, I found a delicious 1925 letter from the then Superior General on the dangers to the faith of the radio!

It was a fascinating find and I displayed it on the community notice board. But someone took it down almost immediately; its swift removal indicative of the weakness of religious faith when confronted with factual historical evidence.

*

*'Maybe changing directors,'* I journaled on 10 December as I approached my fifth Christmas in the Marists, *'is preparing me for a change in direction'.*

Looking back aged 57, I'm astonished at what I next wrote: *'I want to do something different. Nobody has yet tried to persuade me to leave. I'd love to.'*

There it was in black and white: *'I'd love to leave.'*

I continued: *'If only for the exhilaration of launching forth on my life, making my decisions, doing something unpredictable. Yet something as minor as putting up that bloody letter often backfires and turns out badly.'*

This suggests that some of what kept me in the Marists was fear. If posting an interesting historical letter on the notice board gets torn down summarily, making the biggest decision of my life might lead to catastrophe.

*'I'd like to have an affair,'* I continued. *'Kip up with some nice lady. Fuck it, I'm 22 and I've never kissed a lady.'*

Interesting choice of language by my 22-year-old self: 'lady', not 'woman' or 'girl'.

I wondered if I might leave after my BA, emigrate, get a job, sleep around, find a girlfriend, get married in my late 20s or early 30s. Live my own life, freed from celibacy, choose my own work, have a car, a house, holidays, luxuries.

But as soon as I introduced 'God' into my thinking, I presumed it was better to be a priest. I journaled: *'It's like*

158

*as if He is my Pull; and I'll not be fully His if I left and married. I'd be selfish. Would I? Ought I to have the freedom to leave? In what sense is it different to the freedom I have to sin? Could it be that God would be just as happy with me in the married state? Would He bless my choice as much as if I am someday ordained?'*

I wasn't praying and I wondered if I was trying *'to sink the ship of my vocation'.* I added: *'How much I would like to tell Verena that I think she's really nice.'*

<h3 style="text-align:center">#55</h3>

Disentangling myself from my unhealthy relationship with my mother was as traumatic a trek as transitioning from belief to unbelief.

On 4 December 1984, my 22-year-old self journaled: *'I was always very close to my mother.'* I wondered if my *'closeness'* to her had led to my *'high-affectivity needs. Don't I need a woman behind me to help me, encourage me, be with me? Women sympathise better than men. They are more appealing. The chemistry is better and more complementary. Who cares if I leave?'*

My mother offered to type the Marist Provincial newsletter. I dropped home in February 1985 to collect it. There had been a problem with her typewriter but she had kept typing. It was awful. Nobody could publish it.

On 3 March, I journaled: *'Exasperating experience yet again with my mother.'* I don't remember what happened on that occasion. I drove her to Howth on 14 March and journaled: *'Felt frustrated that we are so far apart.'* Two weeks later I phoned her. I heard a *'horrid lifeless voice'* at the other end of the phone.

'What's wrong?' I asked.

159

'Come home only if you can be pleasant to me,' she said. 'You have treated me with contempt for three and a half years. I couldn't have done anything to deserve that. Don't tell me you haven't noticed your attitude to me. I've read books about members of a family hating one another after somebody dies.

'You just use the place. Why do you come home at all? Duty? At first, I thought you were trying to toughen me up. Then, I decided, no, it's just contempt. I'd rather not have you. Thursday was the last blow.'

I had no idea what Thursday she was talking about. I hadn't seen her the previous day (a Thursday), and the Thursday before that I'd been away with confrères.

She continued: 'I thanked God at the end of the day for the trip to Howth and the weather, the scenery, but not for that clown.'

Now I realised she was talking about three Thursdays back. Considering all else she had said, her designating me a 'clown' was comic relief.

'I see it all as God's will,' she said. 'Now I know how your dad felt with his two sons. Nothing could justify your treating me with such calculated contempt. What is it?'

I would be condemned if I spoke and if I said nothing. So, I spoke: 'You never loved my father. I doubted your grief.'

To my astonishment, she replied: 'That is understandable. It is admirable.'

Then she changed tack: it wasn't admirable. She cried. I cried. There were long silences on the phone.

'There's no point talking to her,' my father had confided to me years earlier. 'You can't reason with her. Nobody can.'

'Your father said he was twice as happy with me as he was with Joan,' my mother now said to me on the phone. 'I loved Arthur. I miss him.' Her next words left me staggered by her self-deception: 'Everyone knows what a close marriage we had.'

After that phone call, I was consumed by guilt. 'Honour your father and your mother.' 'Do not turn from your own kin.' I felt humiliated that I could not love her and found her contemptible.

I had changed my spiritual director. My new director was Father Denis Green. On 1 April, we discussed the dire state of my relationship with my mother.

He suggested: 'It could be good to see her tomorrow, if only to say it would be better not to go home after Easter. It wouldn't be good to allow that telephone conversation to enter into a long silence.'

I agreed.

'Think about your parents' marriage,' he said. 'Your father's wife died. He was left with two little boys.'

I imagined my bereaved father. He had to work, and his sons were passed around among relatives. Paul told me they'd go to sleep not knowing in whose house they'd wake up.

'Not every marriage is for love,' suggested Denis.

Hearing someone else articulate this made it easier to accept.

'And there's her excessive praying. What's going on there?' asked Denis. 'It's pathetic the way she goes on. You are humiliated not only by her inconsistency, her fluctuations from excitement to sedateness, but because she's your mother.'

He was right. I was humbled by her attitudes, irrationality and behaviour; and that she was my mother, my progenitor; my source of life and faith.

'It's better that this has happened,' said Denis. 'It might not ever have happened if you hadn't left home. People can live adjacent to each other without being honest.'

## #56

I took to heart Denis Green's advice on April Fool's Day 1985 to make a short visit home to see my mother lest the awful phone call three days earlier entered into a long silence.

Next day, I cycled home. My mother insisted I talk. The conversation was getting nowhere. My perceptions, memories, feelings and thoughts were dismissed, as ever.

Relatives from three families – hers, my father's and my brothers' mother's – had spoken to me about the family tension I had known and absorbed from my earliest childhood. My mother knew people had been talking to me. She demanded names.

Our relationship in tatters, I named just one person – my father. I told her he had said to me: 'The things that woman did!'

She needed no other names. Given her dearth of self-knowledge, it was ironic that my mother often misquoted Robert Burns: *'Oh would to God the grace He'd gie us, To see ourselves as others see us.'*

Now, she had a glimpse of how her husband saw her.

That night, I journaled: *'I never thought I would, or could, say that to her.'* But it was a breakthrough. Having expressed it to her, it lost its grip over me. My mother shifted from denial to some recognition of reality. It led, temporarily, to an improvement in our relationship.

*

Constrained sexually by the vow of celibacy, I yearned, aged 23, for a soulmate, an emotionally intimate friendship.

Verena was gorgeous, tactile and affirming. I loved the touch of her hand, our occasional hugs and innocent kisses on the cheek, and the rare moments when we were alone together. I felt the attraction was mutual. Unshackled from celibacy, I imagined a happy future with her. But I didn't want to hurt her emotionally or to use her for sexual gratification.

'Are you happy?' she asked me, while walking the cliff path in Howth with other college friends after our summer exams. We held hands when the path became uneven. I loved it – the touch, comfort and emotional connection.

'It's the best place for me,' I replied, repeating the self-disparaging phrase I'd used in novitiate.

Later, I drove her home. Outside the car, we kissed. The touch of her hand was firm. We parted and I drove away, regretting that I wouldn't have an excuse to see her until the new term in October.

I had also become friends with Tom at UCD, a fellow seminarian from a different religious congregation. He was a great listener. We explored profound life questions together, weighing our possible 'call' to the priesthood against the attractions of women and sex, and making our own way in the world. We had fun, drank pints, loved literature, laughed and supped some of the joy of life together. He became my best friend at UCD and, together with Bríd, a girl from Donegal, we formed a strong bond of friendship, playfully referring to ourselves as 'the diabolic trinity'.

But I invested most time, thought and energy into another friendship in 1985. Kevin (not his real name) was intense. He was popular, good looking and intriguing. But as I got to know him better, I discovered he suffered a lot inwardly.

I sought, as best I could, to help him. I cried with him out of compassion for his suffering. It was a new and intense experience of emotional empathy for me. He was profoundly honest with me, revealing the most intimate things about himself.

For me, our friendship was encapsulated by lines from Thomas Gray's *Elegy Written in a Country Churchyard*:

*He gave to Misery all he had, a tear,*
*He gained from Heaven, ('twas all he wish'd) a friend.*

But that rare and cherished friendship did not endure. I had to learn the hard way that friendship requires reciprocity. I had to relinquish the role of helper and acknowledge my needs to receive in equal measure from my friend. At 23, with Kevin, I found that hard. The fault was mine; not his. But I learned, and that lesson has stood me in good stead ever since.

In June 1985, I joined four fellow Marist scholastics on a camping holiday near Dingle. I was more at home in my skin than ever before. I headed off alone one day, exploring the breathtaking landscape. Enjoying my solitude, I walked along a beach, then climbed a hill to a tower. An unexpected panorama awaited me, overlooking the bay. Exhilarated, I was attuned to the marvellous spectacle.

164

I had an exuberant awareness of my masculinity, my height, my youth, my beauty, my strength, virility and power. I felt like a stag running proud in the fields.

I knew I wanted more than celibate relationships. As a sexual being, I wanted to shake off my stoicism and never again underestimate the power of my sexuality.

## #57

*I have a need for an exclusive relationship,'* I journaled on 29 July 1985, aged 23. *'My desire to be a priest must not ignore my sexual needs. My need to kiss and be kissed. My need for touch.'*

Days later, on 5 August, in France for summer pastoral work, my head still filled with religion and the supposed virtues of celibacy, my subconscious broke further through. I journaled: *'In my desires, yearnings and longing, I crave for genital intimacy with a woman. In my dreamy-conscious self, the guardsmen of my ideal image suffered to allow surface an actual choice I made last night: to choose celibacy, probably, but virginity, probably not.'*

*

Gay Byrne on his RTE Radio One show in the autumn of 1985 put a 'hot tip' on a story I'd written to win a competition. It didn't. The task was to write a piece of romantic fiction, the first meeting of him and her, leaving the reader wanting to read more.

But hearing my words, read by a professional actor, Dan Riordan of the RTE repertory company, on Ireland's national public service broadcaster, bit me with the writing bug. It gave me an amazing buzz.

I submitted it under a pseudonym and didn't tell Gay that I was writing it from a seminary (I gave my mother's

165

address) or that the story was true. It was written from the perspective of an older man looking back at his 23-year-old self, set on becoming a priest, but whose questions about the veracity of religion, and whose hormones, cravings and desires, were leading him elsewhere.

Here's the script.

*It was only the third time I had as much as seen her, yet now promised to be the first, and it then seemed, final possibility of an encounter of hearts.*

*'I knew I would meet you before I left France,' I said.*

*She gave me a tiny icon, a symbol and proof of our extraordinary, immediate and seemingly mystical communion of hearts. For we were strangers, and yet we felt we had known one another since birth.*

*I was, at that time, five years in the seminary. She was 33, ten years my senior. She had been an enclosed Carmelite and had left after seven years. Her persona radiated a curious and exceedingly attractive mystique.*

*I suggested we pray together. It was night. We entered a dimly-lit oratory and knelt together, holding hands.*

*'Let us go to a more lonely place,' she said, for we were not alone.*

*Close by, stood the chapel. In the sanctuary we knelt together holding hands. Instinctively, spontaneously, beautifully and in a most natural, peaceful manner, she laid her head on my breast.*

*Christ! It was beautiful. I had embraced and been embraced by others before, both male and female. Each was a moment of intimacy, of fondness, of vulnerability, of friendship. But this was of an altogether different order and ignited an altogether different response.*

*She was especially womanly, and her head gently resting upon my breast, was, to me, as the harmony of the universe itself. We were male and female expressing, chastely, our divinely ordained depth of intimacy.*

166

*We heard somebody in the chapel. Annoyed, somewhat embarrassed, we withdrew to catacombs at the back of the chapel. We were now, certainly, alone.*

*Why was I here? Why had she led me here? I put my arm around her shoulder and discovered her bare arm. Trying still to pray, I became conscious of my breathing.*

*Who was this woman with whom I shared this heavenly embrace? I knew then only what she had told me; that throughout her life she felt the tragic loneliness of abandonment. And somehow, by some heavenly design, inconceivably and incomprehensibly and so suddenly, she found, in me, her peace.*

*'May I kiss you?' I asked, when not to have asked would have been to ignore my deepest spirit.*

*We kissed. And several times again, we kissed.*

*In the rain, she drove me home. Making to go, our lips met once more. Her tender lips remained pressed against mine. Oh, glory!*

*I withdrew. Our eyes met, and I beheld her agonised expression.*

*We kissed again, this time into timelessness itself.*

*We parted, both of us exuberant.*

*In the solitude of my room, I knew only that I could not and absolutely must not see her again before I left France.*

*It was two mornings later that I received her invitation to meet, that Saturday, in Paris.*

*

I did not lose my virginity that Saturday in Paris, and I'm sure the idea of intercourse was far from the mind of the wonderful woman I kissed. But the dissonance between my ideal and real self, the fissure between my commitment to celibacy and my willingness to make love, left me feeling shattered and crushed.

167

## #58

That Saturday in Paris, 24 August 1985, precipitated four months of inner turmoil, vocational anguish and religious doubt.

My desire and willingness to cast off celibacy, if only for one night, my lapses from perfect continence and my carnal longing *'laugh at my praying and my faith'*, I journaled on 1 September. *'I'm left broken, beaten, crushed.'*

Beginning my sixth year in religious life that month, I wondered if *'Christ, hanging on Calvary with absolutely nothing to show for his decisions in faith, might have felt he had miscalculated'*. Instead of growing in virtue, I yearned for women, sexual intimacy, affectivity and male–female chemistry.

'The real trial of your celibacy,' Father Denis Green said to me on 6 September during spiritual direction, 'is the loneliness occasioned by your personal warmth.'

I was learning, too, the hard way, that any friendship founded on my pastoral concern for someone in need was unlikely to grow into a soul friend relationship based on equality and interdependency.

Two scholastics, one from my novitiate, left on 10 September. I felt low, weary and empty. But the following day, one of my very best friends from novitiate left; the confrère who had warned me a year before: 'Next time, I'll only tell people after I've decided and I'll be gone within the hour.'

I rang him, trying to change his mind.

'I can't,' he said.

I cried for two hours, including during mass. I skipped supper and cycled to Dún Laoghaire, where he and I had often spent a Sunday afternoon, walking the pier and then

168

a pint in a pub; but this time without my pal, saddened to the core. I couldn't sleep that night.

'That one hurt,' said a confrère to me, a grief shared.

Though supported by the shared loss within our shocked community, I felt desolate, isolated and abandoned. I journaled on 16 September: *Is Marist life for me? Self-doubt and doubt of God so easily get the upper hand with me.*

He was the tenth of my novitiate of twenty to leave. There had been as many as thirty-eight seminarians, including two Englishmen, a Norwegian and a German, in Mount St Mary's in 1980. By 20 September 1985, the student body of Irish seminarians, despite new entrants, had reduced to 25, at least nineteen of whom would later leave the Society of Mary, several after ordination.

A week after my friend left, I listed reasons for me to leave, including the absence of affectivity; my need for sexual expression and intimacy; my doubts about the point and purpose of the priesthood; and my *'confusion, disaffection and alienation from so huge a body of Roman Catholic faith and expression.'*

The vow of poverty, it seemed to me, kept adults in a permanent state of financial and adolescent dependency. I found it doubly humiliating: if we needed to buy anything – like a shirt – we had to ask the Superior for permission, and then ask Father Bursar for the money.

I had only been given twenty pounds' spending money for a full month's pastoral work that summer in France. It had not been enough. I'd been given three gifts, of five, ten and fifty pounds. My former spiritual director had become the Superior. He let me keep the two smaller gifts, but resentment surged as I handed in the fifty quid.

It also kept some priests within religious life who wanted to leave or who no longer believed in God. As a priest pointed out to me, older priests rarely left, not only because they were institutionalised but because they often had no other financial options.

*'There's something up inside me,'* I journaled on 27 September. *'I know from my presence to the community, my disinterest in prayer, my arriving late to, and leaving early from, Eucharistic adoration.'*

I was moved by a poster of a beautiful young woman and child and I hung it up in my room.

I journaled: *'Am I on the way out? I must attend deeply to my felt life. I feel empty and inadequate. In community today, I felt exposed, like I'd lost my grip over my religious life and had fallen slap on the face like a slippery omelette.'*

On 30 September, I journaled: *'Why am I crying? Why did I just leave the chapel?'* Prayer seemed meaningless; my resolutions to practice perfect continence ineffective. I journaled: *'How I would love somebody to come into the room. But nobody will come in.'*

I wondered on 26 October if the woman I had kissed in France might visit Ireland. *'Wouldn't I be tempted were she to suggest we spend some time together, albeit without long-term commitments? Why not? Isn't it a possibility? And isn't it desired? Couldn't she perhaps come to Ireland for a week or so, stay in a cottage – for two?'*

She would have been horrified by my fantasy, given her deep religious faith. But that fissure between my ideal self and my willingness, even once, to lie with another, was leading me into dangerous territory.

## #59

In the midst of the apathy, indifference and depression of the last quarter of 1985, I journaled on 29 October that religion had *'disrupted my life plans. Damnit, I'm 23 and very, very different to when I joined.'*

Father Denis Green said to me: 'You are one of those for whom vocation is so caught up in your psychology that you might not be able to leave here and be a Christian.'

On 1 November, I met with the Superior. I cried in his presence, speaking of my work, friendships, yearning for a married relationship, doubts about the faith, indifference and apathy.

He advised me to see Denis more often and to keep writing my journal, adding: 'You are talented with words.'

The piece of romantic 'fiction' I'd written for the Gay Byrne show was rebroadcast on RTE Radio One's 'Playback' programme. Hearing my work performed was a beacon of hope in those bleak months.

Days later, I received a letter from the French woman, whose kisses and invitation to Paris had ignited my desire to lose my virginity with her. Already, the gap had extended and deepened between my ideal and real self.

She thanked God for *'this kiss of the Holy Spirit that we received'*, and prayed *'for you, and with you, resting on your breast'* that I would become a holy priest.

There ended my notions of a romantic cottage!

*'I still doubt a lot,'* I journaled on 5 November. *'Reading the story of an American priest who is reported to be healing the sick, I was completely cynical and disbelieved every word of it.'*

171

I felt guilty attending a careers seminar and spending a lot of time with an attractive girl at UCD. Eucharistic adoration on 7 November was *'an enormous bore for me'*.

Depression persisted. I was frustrated by a phone call from a neighbour from home who wanted to become a priest. I skipped Morning Prayer, felt *'pissed off'* at mass and *'beaten and disheartened by masturbation'*.

Denis Green invited me out for a walk. He told me to *'cool it'* with a confrère I was fond of, saying it wouldn't be a friendship of equals and it would be an escape for both of us.

Two days later, the confrère visited my room.

'Are you just tired?' he asked.

'Yes, just tired,' I lied.

I found Denis's request that I back off our friendship difficult.

*'Do I want to live like this for the rest of my life?'* I journaled on 10 November. *'The alternative – to write – is becoming more real. Maybe religious life is one big escape for me? Maybe it always was. Something behind which I could hide my sensitivity, vulnerability, fears of not being accepted.'*

Perhaps my vocation as a writer was, and is, to dare to share my human vulnerability with the reader. To show it's OK to be human, and to encourage others to accept themselves as they are.

My religious faith was in freefall. Mother Teresa, seen even then as a living saint, I'd heard was a control freak. Her congregation had a house beside a Marist presbytery in Dublin and a senior priest had told me that the nuns couldn't even make small decisions in the house without the express permission of their founder on the other side of the world.

The Church under Pope John Paul II had gone right wing, with conservative organisations like Opus Dei and the Legionaries of Christ in the ascendancy. Some Marist priests who had once inspired me no longer did so. Charismatic renewal, which had played a significant part in my teenage life, I now regarded with scepticism. The Society of Mary seemed to be dying. Confrères – students and priests – were leaving.

*'Tonight's conference on prayer I found insufferable,'* I journaled on 11 November. *'Deep-seated questions refuse to go away. Confronted again with stark reality: an empty room, a single bed, doubts, prayerlessness, new possibilities, new meaning. Can I leave here and be happy?'*

*'Is glas iad na cnoc i bhfad uainn (Faraway hills are green),'* said a priest in Irish, when I shared with him my angst.

Beware anyone spouting platitudes! My life as a responsible adult began when I left the Marists. But I had not yet walked through the glass wall of my self-imprisonment.

Haunted by the story of the rich young man who declined Christ's call and went away sad, I journaled: *'It is more than an academic question of the existence of God. It is my happiness that is at stake. To leave here is to leave part of me. What part of me is dying?'*

On 12 November, I journaled: *'I just feel very inauthentic here – I profess things that I do not do.'* Much of the day I spent thinking *'when'* I might leave – not if.

173

## #60

My decision, when it came, on 15 December 1985, in the middle of the night, a sleepless night, was definitive.

As a boy of 23, I deemed it, *'the loneliest decision of my life'*.

After months of heightened anguish and discussions with the Superior, my spiritual director, confessor, confrères, and friends at UCD, attuned to myself, I weighed the evidence and I made my solitary choice, surging up from my gut.

\*

I tried to imagine God loving me into being in my mother's womb, loving me for who I was, not for what I did. I had learned that true love is one's presence with another person, rather than doing things for them.

I needed to appreciate myself for who I was, not for what I did. As love can't be 'won', why was I in a seminary? If life wasn't about helping the needy, if those who did that might be motivated out of their selfish need to be needed, it changed everything.

There were no brownie points for sacrifice. The paradigm I'd grown up with of self-sacrificial love needed radical revision. And anyway, from my knowledge of myself and others in the priesthood and religious life, at that moment I couldn't think of anyone who was a priest or religious for other than delusional or selfish motives.

I'd seen enough of religious life to opine in my journal: *'Scratch beneath the thin veneer of community life and you will find the alienation of each individual within it.'*

At college, I warmed to Verena anytime I was near her. I wanted to kiss her when she touched me, hugged me or came up close to me. Whenever we parted after a few minutes together, loneliness pained me.

It was around this time that my history lecturer Dr Michael Richter at UCD urged me to take my chance in the world. Here was a caring, intelligent, authoritative adult suggesting an altogether different responsible choice than the one presented to me in the seminary as the best one.

'Commit to yourself. It is you who is important,' he exhorted. 'Make yourself your priority.'

I dreamt of leaving the Marists. When I woke up, I could see myself going. Next night, I'd another dream in which, I journaled: *'I'm running down a lane heading home.'*

I mused: *'God is not a vindictive god. He won't insist that I become a priest to be happy. He won't make me miserable outside if I choose to leave. It's an idea put into my head as a child.'*

Later that day, there was a festive Christmas atmosphere in Grafton Street. Sipping coffee, I waited for my mother and sister in the packed Powerscourt Townhouse Centre. A pianist began to play and the music soothed me, lifting my mood. Then the full-voiced choir of the Glasnevin Musical Society blasted out Joy to the World! My angst had dissipated by the time they arrived. I even managed to tolerate my mother's obsessive talking.

I asked her to enquire about getting a grant from Guinness's for a master's degree. If she interpreted this request as she might, she didn't show it.

During a reconciliation service that night I went to confession out of habit. I didn't feel contrite for my 'sins' and I couldn't have cared less if I hadn't received absolution. The sacrament had become an empty ritual.

I sat in the chapel and I imagined telling my confrères. I owed it to them. Then I thought I might write something in their honour. Maybe this is it. I loved the place. It had been my home. I loved these men; well, most of them. I wondered how I would go – would I be driven home in a house car or would my sister collect me.

I no longer needed to be a priest. I had to realise that I was loved and lovable. It was a breakthrough.

I journaled: *'I don't have to be here to be happy. It's a choice, not a necessity.'*

That night, I could not sleep. My mother was enquiring about a grant for a master's degree. My university fees were paid. I had a medical card. Hopefully, the Marists would give me some money. I needed to get down to study. My life's future shape would depend on it.

The tears came like a river, bucketing down my face, unknotting my stomach, as I passed through that threshold, knowing I had to leave. I could do no other. Still the tears came. I was heaving now; terrified, and relieved, at the death of my dream for the priesthood, and stepping into the unknown.

I had decided; and I needed to tell someone. As my director, Father Denis Green was away, I knocked on the Superior's door in the middle of the night. But his bedroom was on the far side of his office. He was asleep and he could not hear me.

## *Chapter 5*

# Loss of self

### #61

My decision to leave the Marists was made in the early hours of the morning of 15 December 1985.

I told Father Denis Green, when he returned to Milltown, and I cried.

'You would have made a fine priest,' he said. 'And if that's what God wants, that's how you'll end up eventually. Is there anything I can do for you?'

He understood how, since my return from France that August, the question had been plaguing my mind incessantly. I felt respected by his accepting my choice.

'You must be free and you must love,' he said. 'Perhaps you have to go elsewhere to clear up something sought, something missed, something not quite ready or resolved.'

*'It was quite easy in the end,'* I journaled. *'I prayed: Lord, walk with me.'*

Denis suggested we go out for a drink. But first, he left his room to tell the Superior.

That night I journaled: *'Last night – golly did I cry. And tonight, in Denis's company and in his absence, I cried. Up to this, I needed to stay. Now, I need to leave: to perceive myself, and life, other than from the perspective of Milltown and the Marists.'*

\*

Denis was gone a long time. When he returned, he had totally changed his tune.

'You had a bad day on Saturday,' he said. 'Is there an outside influence? Why not wait another month and see if things look different then?'

At first, I felt flattered. Then, insulted. What he had listened to, understood and appreciated, was now reduced to a bad day.

*'I sat. I listened. It was actually embarrassing,'* I journaled. *'So radically different from Denis's actual, earlier, response – a response that gave me dignity, self-respect and freedom.'*

This had happened to me before, on 14 March 1984, when my then spiritual director – the Superior whom Denis had just consulted – had said it wouldn't be a 'free' decision if I left. I had allowed his opinion to undermine my decision.

*'When the straw breaks the camel's back,'* I journaled, *'the Superior seems to me to rearrange the bundle rather than admitting a spinal break. My spine is broken. As for Denis, how could he be a credible director after such a backdown on his part!'*

'Don't tell anybody yet,' said Denis.

I was sad to be going. *'But it's a courageous, necessary step to be faithful to myself,'* I journaled. *'This is the only opportunity in my life to experience the kind of freedom I need and to experience myself just as self. It is my choice, an act involving my whole self. I must accept the consequences, good and bad. Maybe I will return. Maybe not. My future is unknown. Lord, walk with me.'*

178

I yearned just to be me – without vows or a mission or pastoral identity. I wanted *just to relate as me*.

It wasn't easy to leave. Mount St Mary's was my home. I journaled: *'These are the men with whom I have shared my life for over five years and who have shared their lives with me.'* Close to UCD, it was convenient to stay. I had financial security. I lived with pleasant, interesting and gifted people. I liked my Marist identity, mission and status. There was psychological security in belonging to the Society of Mary and the Church.

But I needed, at least, a break. Not yet ordained and without final vows, I saw this as my opportunity to experience life outside religious life. *'When I leave, I will be well and truly gone,'* I journaled. I wanted *'to stand alone. To be free. To trust in God's abiding love, mercy and guidance. This decision demands faithfulness to myself, courage, and trust in God.'*

When I met the Superior on 18 December, he poured me a whiskey.

'It's possible you might be making the right decision,' he said. 'But I'd love you to become a Marist priest and my bias is very much in favour of you staying. You have tailspins. Your lows are very low. I don't know whether it's developmental or chronic.'

I was offended at his use of medical language, as if vocational doubt was a diagnosable condition.

I said I might come back – I wasn't turning my back on the priesthood forever.

'You might not be accepted back if you reapply,' he said.

I countered: 'Well surely that would confirm I was right to leave!'

'If you leave, I think you should move into a flat rather than going home to your mother.'

179

As I didn't have a penny, I didn't know how he expected me to do that. I wondered if he was thinking that the Marists might fund accommodation for six months while I finished my degree, but he didn't say and I didn't ask.

'I'd like you to stay one more month,' said the Superior, 'and if you still want to go, do so then.'

## #62

At the meeting with the Superior on 18 December 1985, I agreed to delay my departure from the Marists until the end of January.

I couldn't sleep at all that night. Father Denis Green had asked me not to tell anyone I was leaving but I told some confrères and best friends in confidence.

I got drunk, and *'publicly'* told three confrères I wasn't getting on well with in Milltown how I felt about them. After 35 years, I can no longer remember the details, but I was amused to find the following nugget in my journal: *'Did I have to use the word "obnoxious"?'*

On 20 December, I met my uncle Tom in Clerys restaurant. He cried when I told him I was leaving the Marists. He wiped his eyes with his handkerchief and offered me £1,000. He said it would be enough for me to rent accommodation and feed myself for the six months until I finished my degree.

'I would fight to make sure you do not go back home,' he said. 'David could never forgive her for the way she treated him. She was the incarnation of the cruel stepmother. And she's getting worse with age.'

Then came his *coup de grâce*: 'She's the last unstrung bitch!'

180

I'd always thought he was my mother's closest sibling so I was disarmed by, and appreciated, his unexpected candour.

'And stop calling me "Uncle Tom". Call me Tom.'

By his generosity, two major obstacles to leaving had been removed: I wouldn't need to live with my mother and I'd be able to support myself until I graduated. I journaled: *'God is good. I am frightened about leaving. Tom said I had courage and am brave.'*

\*

I met the Provincial too that day and told him I was leaving.

'I'm disappointed, naturally, Joe – not in you but for the Marists, but your freedom is essential.'

'I feel a bit guilty,' I said, 'that the Marists have paid my university fees.'

'Nonsense,' said the Provincial.

He asked if I would go into teaching. While I never wanted to be a priest–teacher, I would have to earn my living as a layman. At a time when teaching jobs were hard to get, I suspected I'd be a strong contender, if I wished, to teach in a Marist school.

'Now don't go making any big life decisions for at least two or three years,' he advised. 'If there is anything I can do for you, let me know. I'm disappointed for us,' he repeated. 'I'll remember you in my prayers.'

\*

Later, in my room, I felt lonely, scared and tired. I wasn't sure if I could wait until the end of January. Next day, 21 December, at Evening Prayer, I was nervous.

The Superior prayed aloud: 'Lord, help all Marists to remain faithful to their vocation.'

I couldn't help but feel that this was directed at me.

Later that evening, Denis invited me to his room. He played dirty.

'I'm dissatisfied with your decision,' he said. 'The Society of Mary is a work of God. I feel you caught me unawares that day you told me you'd decided to leave. The Superior was right to ask you to stay until the end of January. You manipulated me. You hastily arranged that spiritual direction after I'd been away for the weekend.'

Speechless, I couldn't fathom how he couldn't understand my need to talk to him. I journaled: *My head would have burst if I had not been able to tell him.*

'It may be very difficult for you to be allowed back,' he said. 'You would be leaving against our advice. You wouldn't listen to us.'

He said my final vows could be four years away and I didn't need to be certain yet.

'Do you really want to leave the fellowship of the Marists for the loneliness of some dingy flat? Celibacy would be more difficult after having a fling with a girl or two.'

I was angry and thought of getting up and walking out of his room. The following day, I journaled: *I consider that Denis psychologically raped me last night.*

I loved Denis and, in 2012 when I was making my RTE documentary, I asked him about his intervention; but he couldn't remember it.

On Christmas Eve, 1985, I journaled: *I've grown accustomed to this place. It's very easy for me, therefore, to swim back into the melody and disregard my real decision in the dark of the night that this dream is outmoded and of my childhood. I did not and do not feel free to stay. After what Denis said, neither do I feel free to go.'*

At home for a week from 26 December, I was glad to be away from Milltown. I didn't want to leave with the sour taste in my mouth of that conversation with Denis. But my credibility to myself was on the line.

## #63

*L*ast night I slept with Samantha,' I journaled on 28 December 1985. (Not her real name.) I had spent that afternoon in Howth with my friend Father Tony Ward, who was visiting Dublin.

*'He said he thinks it's the wrong decision to leave,'* I journaled. He said to wait for at least six months. He had 'resigned' from the General House four times. He was fond of me. The Society of Mary was committed to me until September, when my temporary vows would expire. He said Denis had mentioned to him I was a bit unsettled.

Later, I drove to Samantha's. She had invited me. I hoped I might lose my virginity that night.

*'She suggested I sleep with her rather than on the couch,'* I journaled.

'We won't do anything,' she said.

'No?' I intoned, disappointed. 'Not even touch?'

'Nothing.'

I stripped; my first time naked with a woman.

I cajoled and coaxed to no avail. She realised her power as a woman, knowing I would do nothing without her consent. I couldn't believe it – for years I had yearned to make love to a woman and now that I was naked in bed with one, she wouldn't let me touch her!

*'For most of the night she was very disciplined,'* I journaled. I was so frustrated, I masturbated. She knew.

183

*'By morning, she yielded. We didn't have intercourse, nor oral sex, nor did either of us handle each other's genitalia. We kissed, cuddled, I touched her breasts, bottom; she my tummy; and I led her hand down to feel my pubic hair.'*

She said that had we started earlier it would have been harder not to go further. But hope did not die: *'She invited me back.'*

Ironically, establishing what I hoped could become a full sexual relationship with Samantha removed one reason for leaving. Perhaps I could catch up on what I was missing in life while remaining a Marist for now.

*

On 30 December, a good friend, who had joined and left a convent, called to see me. We had what I regarded in my journal as a *'most significant conversation about vocation, happiness, God's will and self-will, and my proposed leaving'.*

I told her I was not a very good Marist. Given I had imagined at times that she and I could have a future together, I was surprised when she said that to leave involved less courage than to stay.

I also met another girl I knew. She suggested I wasn't missing out on all that much by being in the Marists. None of the girls in her rented accommodation was going with anybody.

'It's yourself that counts,' she said. 'A relationship is only possible when you are at peace with yourself.'

*

On New Year's Eve, I journaled: *'To stay involves daily effort, suffering, sin, dissatisfaction, crises, some difficult relationships in community, daily toil. To leave implies a supposed freedom which is not so; material and sexual gratification which fails to satisfy; intellectual freewheeling which is untrue; and irresolute will.*

184

*'We are only given one vocation in life. A gap exists between my will, and what I must admit I deep down believe to be God's will for me.*

*'One answer is to cease to believe in my vocation. The other is to work humbly with my questions, doubts, disbeliefs, sins; trying to conform my will to God's. My life is at breakdown. I must reconstruct it.'*

A benefit of the crisis was, I journaled: *'I am now learning to reveal my needs to others.'*

My week at home was a disaster. *'Things were never worse with mother,'* I journaled on 3 January. Escaping early to Milltown, I found Tony Ward had handwritten Robert Frost's *The Road Not Taken* for me.

My Uncle Jack, a stranger to subtlety, had posted me John Greenleaf Whittier's poem *Don't Quit*.

But I knew that on that crucial night in mid-December, I journaled: *'I simply did not believe in my vocation. I hadn't got one. That was the whole self-realisation. The temptation to just slip back into daily living is very present. But at what cost?'*

My confessor joined the fray. He said: 'It's the wrong decision to leave. I believe you have a vocation! The very least you should do is to put it out of your head until you have finished your BA this summer.'

By 7 January, I deemed my self-realisation of mid-December a mistake.

'I think it's the wrong decision to leave,' I told Denis.

'Thank God!' he replied, 'For the sake of the Society of Mary and for your sake.'

But the reversal of my decision came at a catastrophic cost. Unable to sleep that night, I journaled: *'I doubt my own mind and thoughts, my "insights", my "decisions". I distrust any "arguments" that I begin to formulate.'*

## #64

*The Lord, to use Denis's word, is "destroying" me,'* I journaled on 18 February 1986. Whatever of 'the Lord', I was doing an effective job of self-destruction. Under significant pressure from others, I had denied my self-realisation and decision of mid-December 1985 that I needed to leave the Marists and, on 7 January 1986, I had reversed my choice.

My decision to leave had emerged from deep within me in the dark of the night that mid-December, when the tears had flowed like a river, bucketing down my face, after more than five years of deliberation. I had known I had to leave.

But religion, and its attendant, fear, warps rational thought. I wasn't strong enough yet to trust my gut, my reasoning nor myself. My resolve dissolved before the counterarguments of others, the Superior's request to delay my departure, my spiritual director's extraordinary volte-face and 'psychological rape', and my many fears: of making a mistake; of the unknown; of trusting myself; of bad consequences of my decision. And I was confronted with the explicit threat by the Superior and my spiritual director of not being allowed back if I wanted to do so as I hadn't listened to their advice.

I buckled under all that. I set aside my personal perceptions, feelings, yearnings, desires, insights, tears, understanding, judgements and my major life decision to leave, even though it had come from my gut. I distrusted my personal self-realisation. I doubted myself.

186

On 3 March, I journaled that three or four weeks earlier, the Superior said he had been *'quite prepared to let me leave, that Denis was of the same mind and that I was brave to stay.'*

How unfair, I thought. Had it not been for both of them I would have left before Christmas.

*

My awful relationship with my mother plummeted to new depths in 1986.

On St Patrick's Day, I journaled: *'On the vocation front, I have never felt more at home here. More and more my sense of my having found my home is dawning upon me. I am beginning to accept myself as I am — and that includes accepting without self-condemnation the hatred I feel for my mother.'*

I wrote her a short letter on 19 March, acknowledging that we were *'not getting on so well together. At the moment I feel incapable of bettering this sad situation. I suppose you do too, since you have not contacted me since Christmas. As both of us need space I think it best not to go home at Easter. You know where I am. I hope you will contact me if you need anything or want me for any other reason.'*

She sent me a horrible letter on 21 March which I reread repeatedly; her words acidic. After a week or so, I ripped it up.

On Easter Sunday, 30 March, I journaled that our relationship caused me *'grief, guilt and shame. The cakes have stopped coming. The phone calls have ceased since Christmas. Post is forwarded anonymously. I am angry with her. Others go home tomorrow. I do not go to my mother's house.'*

My journal continued: *'There is guilt, shame, confusion and tears when a married couple separates. But when a mother and son cease relating, the mother is seen as the aggrieved party, and this woman capitalises on it splendidly. She has had practice with two*

187

*stepsons already. I feel angry with God: Christ never had to contend with a mother like mine. Jesus was not maimed by his mother.'*

My mother had been my first educator. At 23, my life's work seemed to be to unlearn what she had taught me. It was like having to learn to walk again.

In a journal entry, I imagined I was talking to my mother: *'I joined the Marists partly to get away from you. You stifled me. You dominated me. You have maimed me. My healing began when I got away from you. You're a liar. I do not trust you. My Novice Master described you as "an incredible woman". Your brother described you as "the last unstrung bitch" and the archetypal wicked stepmother to my brothers; whom you always referred to as "those two brats". Home was a ball of tension – always.'*

I felt guilty and ashamed feeling as I did, given the commandment: 'Thou shalt honour thy father and thy mother.' I journaled that I was angry, *'at her persistent inability to acknowledge anything wrong in herself. It's all my fault, is her attitude to me.'*

On 16 April, I updated the Superior on the dire state of my relationship with my mother. At the same meeting, four months after my decision to leave, I told him: *'I am thinking in terms of final profession in September 1987.'*

## #65

The grievous state of my relationship with my mother disturbed my sleep and manifested in dreams. My stomach was a ball of tension.

On 9 May 1986, during spiritual direction, Father Denis Green said: 'The reason your stomach is tense is that's the part of you that was attached to your mother. You're cutting the umbilical cord.'

188

I cried. Denis was, I journaled, *'unorthodox and marvellous'.* Asking my permission, he reached across and placed his hand on my tummy.

My father had touched my stomach once, when I was in bed with a sore belly as a young boy. I recall the heat of my father's hand; the moment of tenderness, intimacy and trust; the pain going away; and my astonishment at my father's seeming healing power.

As a boy, I needed my mother's approval. I had witnessed how cruelly she treated my brothers. I was terrified of getting the wrong side of her, of being banished like Paul or vanishing for a decade like David. She had traduced them, repeatedly, to me, to relatives and to others. I believed I needed to be 'good' to survive: to protect myself from her wrath.

Now 24, I was finally facing and feeling my mother's disapproval. She refused to accept any responsibility – her lifelong habit – for the state of our relationship. I had chosen not to see her since I returned to Milltown early after the post-Christmas break at home. But I thought of her every day. Every difficult decision not to contact her, with its associated anger, guilt, fear and shame, was, for me, a new moment of liberation and personal growth.

'You've kicked your mother on the shins!' said Denis with verve, approvingly. 'You are dependent upon her. That is why this is causing you such pain. This will be the making of you.'

It seemed my relationship with my mother was irretrievable. I wondered if she would be at my conferring, my final profession or my ordination.

On 20 May, my journal records a dream in which the breakdown of our relationship becomes public: *'Then comes the break. I go public. We begin to argue. I see a neighbour and I ask him: Is this just? and Am I right? He says I am right. I ask two more neighbours: Speak to me. Tell me. Am I right? They say they know her well and yes I am right.'*

*'She's dead now,'* continues the dream. These and other neighbours from home gather to *'assist me to pass the threshold of believing my own eyes and ears and feelings and thoughts'.*

The dream validated what I'd seen, heard, felt and reasoned. In waking life, my mother had always undermined my perceptions, emotions, insights, understandings and judgements, leaving me doubting my own eyes and ears. I felt good after that dream. I wasn't crazy.

The dream finished with me talking with my Uncle Billy, an elder brother of my mother's, realising: *'It's extraordinary the effect she had on my life.'* He asks about my vocation. *'And I said yes, that I was sure the she'd had a huge influence there too. And I've yet to think through, to fully research and explore, that one.'*

While I never knew how she felt about me studying for the priesthood, and she had, after my father's death, tried to get me to leave to take care of her, my mother's excessive religiosity, her negativity towards sex, and the total submission of her mind and will to the teaching authority of the See of Peter, profoundly affected me; imbibing, from infancy, her distorted view of reality.

On 5 June, I journaled: *'As I entered the sacristy to serve mass, five priests were already there and vested. I was almost embarrassed as I sensed my communion with them. It was a good moment; of trust in myself; in my faith; in my calling to the Marist priesthood.'*

*'I loved facilitating the bereavement support group tonight,'* I journaled the same day. *'I am convinced it is God's work. My pastoral work humbles me. And tonight, as I listened and helped*

*others to listen, I longed to be a priest to celebrate the Eucharist with this group.'*

A journal entry for 22 June reads: *'I am grateful to God for being a Marist today. He has given me so many opportunities, has blessed me so much. My community, its people, prayer, support, education, expertise, its care. Its acceptance of me as I am. Growth through suffering into freedom. Breaking past patterns. Becoming myself.'*

That day too I journaled that I had said goodbye to Samantha that night. I had never returned to her bed. I had avoided her, following my decision not to leave the Marists. She shed some tears, said she didn't think badly of me and that she cared for me a lot. It was a good ending.

### #66

My mother phoned me 27 June 1986 saying, *'She loved me, she missed me.'* It was her first phone call since her toxic letter of 21 March and a note in April stating her earlier letter *'still stands'*.

On 6 July, my uncle Tom visited me.

'Forget about her,' he said. 'She's either a bitch or a mental case. She's had her way for so long and got away with it. You'll be better off the less you have to do with her. You're not responsible for her attitudes. She's brought it all on herself.'

But next day, my pastoral director, a woman, said, 'Flesh of my flesh,' quoting Genesis. 'You'll have to meet her sometime.'

Journaling on 9 July, I articulated *'a truth of 24 years' standing: I am afraid of her. I have seen what she can do to people. And, soon, I realised I was actually trembling.'*

191

In the early hours of 15 July, I journaled: *'My mind is racing all over the place, preventing sleep. The idea of having a wife, actually loving another, properly, and receiving love, is on my mind.'*

Realising the dysfunctionality of my relationship with my mother, allowed me glimpse the possibility of a healthy relationship with a life partner. Moreover, in the bereavement support group, I admired a married couple, Paul and Marie Toomey, who, for me, modelled a healthy marriage.

On 18 July, I had a dramatic dream. *'My mother and two other women are setting out together. I, and two other guys, watch the three ascend steps adjacent to a massive concrete wall, like a skyscraper.*

*'The women climb up, chattering. I'm glad I'm not with them. I sense my mother's hurt and despondency. They turn sharply along the sheer face of the concrete mass, ascending the far side.*

*'Myself and my friends ascend too. Now, both parties go up the third side. It is just as steep. We have gone up a considerable distance.*

*'Water starts to flow down, gushing beside us. It's dangerous: the water is powerful, strong, relentless, frightening and terrible. To survive, each has to hug tight to the wall.*

*'My mother is swept mercilessly down past me by the surging mass of water. Seeing her, I abandon my position of relative safety. I climb down quickly, running precariously along the top of a hand rail.*

*'My mother looks up and sees me running to save her. She reaches out her hand from the mass of water and says: My son will save me.*

*'Our hands meet. The mass, the weight, the sheer terror of the water is alarming. I grip on to her with my outstretched arm. The Sea is still pulling. Am I strong enough? Will she be swept away? At least I try. Seeing her, I love her, and try to save her. She sees my love and she shows her love and this is consolation indeed if, as indeed I think, she dies.'*

On the morning of 20 July, I met up with my brother Paul, his wife and two young children. In the afternoon, we were joined by my sister. Later, for the first time since Christmas, *'I met up with my mother.'*

But any hope of reconciliation was soon dashed. She prattled on, dismissing any possibility of her having hurt me, stuck doggedly to the contents of her odious March letter and insisted I owed her an apology.

That night, I journaled: *'The woman is demented. She has me half-demented. In the Marists, I am accepted for who I am – including my irreconcilable estrangement from my mother. Here, at least for the moment, and, I hope, for life, I can learn to be me.'*

At a meeting of the bereavement group, I talked about my mother. A woman in the group said she perfectly understood me, since she had hated her father.

On 8 August, I dreamt that *'my mother's deep disturbance was becoming the issue of my family'.* I awoke, dozed and slipped back into a dream in which *'somebody explains the earlier dream to me: "You've got to love yourself."'*

My BA final exams started in late August. On 28 August, I met my Uncle Jack, my mother's eldest brother.

'Go your own way,' he counselled. 'You are responsible only for you. Your mother was always as she is now, difficult and domineering. She never matured or developed. Don't take her too seriously. Her self-righteousness lacks the acts to justify it. There was always something missing, something lacking. You are not responsible for her unhappiness.'

That night, I dreamt, *'my mother rings me. I listen to her as best I can. I tell her that I love her. I then ask her to consider seeing a doctor, listen during the long subsequent silence, and eventually I tell her that I have to go now.'*

#67

On 13 August 1986, I envied four confrères who were preparing for final profession, the ceremony when a Marist committed himself to the congregation for life.

I worried that if I applied to take my final vows the following year, in September 1987, that my vocational crisis of December 1985 would be held against me. Instead, I should have been concerned about how I had allowed other people's opinions and interventions to change my decision to leave.

'It doesn't matter what the Provincial, or anyone else, thinks. What matters is what you want,' said Paul Toomey. 'It was good that you were honest and open about that crisis.'

Paul was right. But he had intended it as encouragement for me to proceed towards final profession. I should have been applying its wisdom to re-examining my decision to ditch my self-realisation of December 1985 that I needed to leave.

Paul and his wife Marie I now regarded as my adopted parents. Together, we had set up the bereavement support group, following the death of their son, Mark.

Two days later, I wrote to the Provincial applying to renew my temporary vows of celibacy, poverty and obedience for one year.

On 5 September, during days of recollection in preparation for renewing our vows, a priest led us through a guided fantasy. My imagery was of myself as a stone statue, crouched and doubled over. *I did not like the statue. It*

194

*had a gaping great wound: a whole limb was missing and the tissue where an arm had been was distorted, the mangled flesh captured by the sculptor. I was ashamed.'*

Within the fantasy, I was glad I was alone. *'I want nobody to see this. Nobody must be let in.'*

It says a lot about how I saw myself and why I chose celibacy.

*'A contrasting characteristic was its young face,'* I journaled. *'I was looking up. There was hope in my eyes. The youthful, hopeful eyes; the gaping, irredeemable wound: opposing images.'*

As the priest proceeded with the guided imagery, I thought – this is a fantasy. Just as I had conceived a solid statue, crouched with a gaping wound, now I chose to let the hope in its eyes take over. The statue came alive as a human being, unfurled its beauty, stood tall, swayed gracefully – and danced.

Identifying in my imagination with the statue, *'I stood beautifully. I was naked. I cared not. My legs were beautiful. My movement glorious. Gaping wound and all, I danced as I am. And people came and marvelled at the graciousness of every movement, at the individuality of me. See, they cried, his gaping wound and yet his dance. Happy and free to be his complete self.'*

We were asked to write the obituary that we would love to have in our wildest dreams. In mine, I died a Marist priest, *'a man very much alive and alert, happy to be himself. He basked lovingly in self-acceptance. In love with God, others were touched by him and strengthened to carry their sufferings.'*

I saw addressing the conflict in the North as the greatest pastoral need in Ireland. My 'obituary' imagined that my life as a priest had helped bring about reconciliation, *'where once Catholic and Protestant hated and feared one another, they now live*

195

*in peace. He was not a busy man. His ministry and achievements were in the realm of who he was, not what he did.'*

I reviewed my *'faith autobiography'*, from the capture of my imagination as a child to be a priest, to the *'deep, deep peace in the decision to stay'* in the Marists that January, following my verdict to leave a month earlier.

*'Here is the place where I can become free, can become me,'* I journaled. *'Here is where I am learning – albeit often painfully – about love. Experiencing love and being taught by God to love myself.'*

But despite this inner religious revival, I journaled the same day – the eve of the renewal of my vows: *'Now – loneliness, absence of a sexual partner.'*

I renewed my profession on 8 September 1986, my vows concluding, as at my first profession, with those words considered most intimate to Marists: *'Strengthen, O God, the work of your hand. Mary, most loving mother, I am yours; by your power and intercession secure my everlasting welfare. Amen.'*

There followed a time of hope, growth and gratitude, and *'my increasing capacity and willingness to share my needs'.*

On 4 October, my BA results were out and I was happy. With religious fervour, I journaled: *'If we take sorrow from the Lord, we must also take joy! Today, I have taken joy. God bestows good fortune upon the earth.'*

A month later, on 5 November, I told the Superior I would like to be finally professed. I added: *'But I don't think that I know myself well enough.'*

### #68

On 20 October 1986, Father Denis Green accompanied me home for a brief visit to break the ice with my mother. She clung to me but it

196

was not a good hug. Denis, to my relief, released me from her grip and we departed.

My mother attended the conferring of my BA. Afterwards, my best friend at UCD, Tom, and I, and our two families, went for a meal together. He protected me from my mother, so she could not spoil my big night.

Two weeks after finishing my BA finals at UCD, I returned to the Milltown Institute to start a degree in theology.

I journaled on 11 November: *What is my fear? Having to stand up before people and be me.'* Next day, I stood before a packed hall of students of the Milltown Institute and was elected Vice-President of the Students' Union.

On the weekend of 21 to 23 November, two other Marist scholastics and I attended a workshop for members of religious orders, male and female, close to taking final vows. Dozens attended, unimaginable numbers today. I learned that less certainty was needed before proceeding to final profession than I had assumed would be required.

It was a period of happiness for me. On 28 November, I journaled: *'Sometimes I just want to smile a massive smile from the depths of my being. I'm beginning to be more natural, more myself.'*

I did an eight-day silent retreat at Manresa House, near Dollymount, from New Year's Day to 10 January 1987. I told my retreat director about the vocational crisis twelve months earlier and my painful extraction from my mother.

'Your self has now been established,' he said, encouragingly.

Later that day, 3 January, a heavy mood descended. Sex was on my mind. *'Maybe I do not want to surrender my sexuality to God,'* I journaled. *'Is there a kind of grieving going on for what can never be if I remain a Marist? Celibacy, and the extra sacrifice of virginity. Do I want this life?'*

In the meditation assigned to me by my spiritual director, I wasn't convinced that 'God' was talking to me. Feeling low, I went for a cycle along Dollymount Strand in the dark. I wasn't in the least bit 'holy'. Instead, I later journaled, there were the *'secret thoughts of my mind and what I do and would do behind closed doors and my mixed motivations'.*

But after more encouraging subsequent meditations, I journaled on 7 January: *'I think I have decided to apply for final profession this year. If I cannot bear the risk of being refused, I should hardly be able to bear the weight of being accepted. By September, I shall have been seven full years in the Society of Mary.'*

However, while deciding *'what my heart wants'*, I journaled: *'But my body knows a different drummer. During the night I felt it perhaps literally cry out for sex, for physical union, for a woman. And, upon waking, upon recovering from a disturbing dream, I wanted a son.'*

In the nightmare, *'a hideous little bastard has grabbed me by my genitals and castrated me'*. I awoke frightened, so real had been the dream. The *'hideous little bastard'*, I presume, represents the part of myself that was willing to proceed towards lifelong celibacy to the detriment of my sexual self and of the genetic imperative to procreate.

On 9 January, I journaled: *'My ideal self does not exist: only I do. Icon and handkerchief: and the agony born of the conflict of God's will and my will.'*

In early February, the Superior suggested I try to force a decision. He said: 'To live in a state of uncertainty for too long is not good.'

But caught between surges of faith and doubt, I journaled: *'I still find myself coming down firmly on the fence.'*

Also uncertain was what I would do the following year. The choices were to go straight into second year theology, do teacher training or take a pastoral year in the North of Ireland, where I wanted to work as a priest, trying to reconcile a divided community.

I had never wanted to be a teacher, yet I feared I was being pushed towards teaching. I could never fathom how the sacrifice of celibacy made sense when one's priestly work was teaching.

But if I could carve out for myself a ministry of reconciliation in the North, I felt I could proceed towards the priesthood with greater resolve, confident that my pastoral vision would be respected and accommodated within the Marists.

I put a lot of time and effort into researching the possibility of a pastoral year in Belfast. Finally, I put in a formal request to the formation staff for permission to do so.

I would learn anew, on Ash Wednesday, that the vow of obedience was as painful and traumatic as celibacy.

## #69

Ash Wednesday, 4 March 1987, saw my dream of a pastoral mission of reconciliation between the divided communities in Belfast go up in flames.

I could see meaning in being a priest if it was for the sake of work that I believed in. The conflict in the North seemed to me the greatest need in Ireland. I had explored the possibility of doing a pastoral year in the ecumenical Columbanus Community in Belfast.

199

Almost 25 years of age, I had been studying all my life. I had only a fortnight off between finishing my BA and starting my degree in theology. I needed a break from academia. Moreover, I was in my seventh year living in Mount St. Mary's.

Some confrères had spent a year or more in England or Germany. Two peers were heading to Senegal and Brazil that autumn. My request for a year in Belfast was modest in comparison.

I was enraged when I learned that my request had been turned down. I journaled: *Do what you're told and say your prayers. Think about your future, discern it, and after we've fooled you, we'll still tell you what to do and mould you according to the mould.*

*'How can I seriously again engage, without cynicism, in these endless discussions about our vision for the future of the Society of Mary, new apostolates, reading the signs of the times, when my reading of those signs for a Marist mission is dismissed?'*

My disappointment, disillusionment and depression manifested in lust, laziness and indiscipline. Celibacy and obedience were biting hard.

*

Final profession – committing to the Marist Fathers for life – was approaching.

*'It all comes down to an act of faith,'* I noted at a talk by the Superior on 14 April for scholastics nearing final profession. *'I will never have certainty. It's about taking a step in the dark.'*

He wanted us to decide by mid-May, four weeks away.

'Perhaps you are beginning to believe in your vocation,' the Superior said to me, walking in the grounds of Mount

200

St Mary's, linking my arm to consolidate his point. 'You're the one who needs to be convinced.'

Some days later, he said to the elderly Father Eugene McVicar, that I'd been a Marist a year longer than another finally professed confrère.

'You should be ordained by now!' said Father McVicar.

When the Superior gave me my monthly allowance, he said that if I were finally professed, I would get more. He handed me a sheet with the dates for final profession, its preparatory events, trips and pre-profession retreat.

My spiritual director, Denis Green, said: 'The only way to know what it's like to be finally professed is to take final vows!'

A finally professed confrère said: 'From all your journal-keeping over the years, you're ahead of many people in self-knowledge. You can apply and still work things through later.'

Overcoming my fear of rejection, I decided to apply.

'Congratulations, brother,' said Denis, 'I am happy with your decision.'

Later, walking in the grounds, he added: 'Remember the responsibility you're taking on with celibacy. It is a public commitment. We cannot overestimate the need for caution in the sexual sphere. Priests – fine men – have had to leave their provinces because of sexual misdemeanours that might appear of the slightest kind.'

When I told the Superior, he said: 'I am very happy with your decision. You have explored these issues thoroughly over the years. I don't expect the formation staff to have difficulty with it.'

'Will the recent issue about Belfast come against me?'

'I don't see why. You worked through it. It was not a vocational issue.'

'What about my telling the Provincial the Christmas before last that I'd decided to leave?'

'I don't expect that will be an issue for him,' he replied. 'Throughout the time I have known you, openness has always been your forte. Keep it up. It is the finest quality.'

That Thursday, I met the Provincial.

'Do you think it's too soon after the vocational crisis of Christmas 1985?' I asked.

'No,' he replied.

'I expect you know I didn't handle the refusal of a pastoral year in Belfast very well?'

'We can all go down cul-de-sacs,' he replied. 'It's perhaps necessary to go down them. Soon you get a nose for them. As in a long maths problem, we get to identify patterns more easily and avoid them the next time.'

*I am known by these men,* I journaled. *They know me very well. If they wanted to refuse me, they have plenty of material with which to do so. If they accept me, it will be accepting me as I am.*

Shortly after a Provincial Council meeting on 30 May, 1987, the Superior congratulated me that I had been called to final profession.

## *Chapter 6*

# Tail wags God

### #70

The months following the Provincial Council's acceptance of my application to take final profession were typified by anger, depression and suffocation.

My relationship with my mother was as bad as ever. Invited together for a meal with a mutual friend on 2 June 1987, all was well until I mentioned my brothers Paul and David. *'Then you could cut the air with a knife,'* I journaled. *'I feel a fake. I feel angry with my mother and with myself at being affected still by her; angry and self-doubtful. She makes me into a twisted scapegoat for her pretence and guilt.'*

Perhaps I felt a fake too because I had allowed the opinions of the Superior, my spiritual director and others to undermine my decision to leave in December 1985. *'I feel crushed, helpless, weak,'* I journaled on 5 July.

We wrote our wills on the eve of our final profession, 12 September 1987, leaving everything to the Marists. In an optional section, I bequeathed *'my personal diaries, journals and letters, for their destruction, to the Society of Mary'.* For the record, I have rescinded that will.

My retreat before final vows was restless. We received our profession crosses during the ceremony, the Provincial placing one around each neck. The image of a hangman comes to me now. In a photograph taken from a pew as I exited the chapel, bedecked in white hooded alb, profession cross upon the chest, strung from the neck by Marian blue cord, my face is a study of dejection and defeat.

A month later, on 13 October, I wrote to my friend Father Tony Ward in Rome: *'God get me out of this house!'*

Aged 25, I still had to ask permission to telephone outside Dublin, to be out after midnight, or to use a car. But what pushed me to breaking point was when the Superior directed all seminarians to submit to him a minute-by-minute account of how we spent our time.

In my letter, I told Tony of my ongoing difficulties with celibacy, *'my recurring doubt that I've actually been called by God to be a Marist, and a heavy dose of self-rejection'.*

On 22 October, I asked the Superior to transfer me from Mount St Mary's by the following summer.

Angry, depressed, run-down by a persistent cough, and skipping Morning Prayer and a theology lecture, I journaled on 3 November: *'Everything I do at the moment is a chore. My heart is heavy. Yesterday was a disaster. Two classes, my first teaching day. Twenty-two completely uncontrollable pupils. Wrecked after it.'*

My new pastoral work was to take two classes of religious education every Monday at Chanel College. I'd never wanted to teach and here I was being sent teaching.

My UCD friend Tom was doing his novitiate in the North and we could only communicate by letter. On 5 November, I wrote to him: *'Denis says there's no cheap grace. I feel vaguely inconsolable. Perhaps it's post-profession depression.'* After final vows, I asked *'all the same questions as at any stage before. The same feelings are there too. The Greener is a consolation. He'll just come up and give me a big hug. I love it.'*

Nine remained of my novitiate of twenty. One was living in a small community. A second, who loved teaching, worked five afternoons a week in a school. A third had lived in Germany and London and would soon be ordained. Two more were in Africa and Brazil. A sixth was ordained and had dwelt in London and Scotland. A seventh had resided in London and was soon to be ordained. An eight had also stayed elsewhere.

My proposal to do a pastoral year in Belfast had been turned down so I was in my eighth consecutive year at Mount St Mary's.

On 10 November, I journaled, *'one of the formation staff came to my room. He touched a nerve. I let loose my anger, my deep anger, at being here this year. I cried. I cried a lot, in his presence.'*

'You should tell the Superior how you feel,' he said. 'This will be the making of you.'

Next day, I broke down before my confessor too.

'I find it difficult living here. Why am I here? I'm unhappy,' I said.

'Often in religious life you will not know why you are where you are or why you are doing what you're doing,' he replied. 'Christ learned to obey through suffering.'

When I visited the doctor that same day, worn down by my chest infection, he said he saw before him a man *'embittered, sunken'*. He likened my situation to that of an adolescent ready to leave home but forced to comply with the house's regulations.

Except I wasn't an adolescent. I was 25.

On 13 November, I shared with the Superior my aversion to living in Mount St Mary's and said I understood why another confrère had recently left the Society during his eight year there.

By 25 November, I journaled: *'I'm sick to the teeth of Milltown. I hate it.'*

## #71

Realising my difficulties controlling pupils' unruly behaviour during my two lessons a week of religious education at Chanel College, an experienced priest–teacher suggested I try reading them a story.

'That'll settle them,' he suggested.

I chose Irish writer Oscar Wilde's short story *The Devoted Friend*, hoping to explore the theme of love and self-sacrifice.

At the start of the lesson, I began to read the tale aloud when, to my horror, I spotted an alternative meaning to the words at the end of the opening line, which I expected would not be lost on this class of prepubescent boys: 'One morning the old Water-rat put his head out of his hole.'

How could Oscar have missed this? None of my class did. As anticipated, those ambiguous words elicited in the minds of these Dublin boys a vision of contorted cranial dexterity by the rodent, its head emerging from its anal cavity.

The room erupted in Pandemonium. Laughter resounded. Palms pounded desks. Missiles hit the ceiling. And that was just the start of the lesson. Bedlam reigned

206

until the Headmaster swung open the door, rebuked the class, ignored me and left again as if I hadn't been there.

*

Pedagogical disasters aside, my appeal to be transferred from Milltown seemed to be getting nowhere.

I was a member of the Marists for longer than at least five of the recently ordained – people who hadn't done a 'secular' degree – yet I was still subjected to restrictive seminary rules, despite being finally professed. Being based in the seminary, I was even given a lower allowance than finally professed confrères in other communities. It was unfair.

A member of the formation staff had told me I needed to tell the Superior how strongly I felt. But when I did so at a meeting on 27 November, the Superior replied that no decision could be made in light of the 'vehemence' of my request. It was my third time trying to address the issue with him in five weeks.

*'Tom, I've just been crying,'* I wrote to my friend from UCD, later that day. *'Heads they win, tails I lose. And that's what made me cry. A sense of utter frustration, of banging my head off a stone wall, of their wanting me to be other than I am. Cool and objective, whereas I am fiery and passionate; distant and detached, whereas I am vehement and determined. The buggers have beaten me and I'm full of anger, depression and self-pity.'*

During a Provincial visitation of Mount St Mary's, I spoke to the Provincial. Asked what apostolate I would like to do, I said working for reconciliation in the North, or counselling or parish work and, a very poor fourth, teaching. He more or less told me that I would be going into teaching. He asked me what timescale I had in mind for ordination to the priesthood. We agreed it would probably be in about three years.

He understood my sense of injustice about still being in Milltown. 'Not only does it seem unfair keeping someone eight or nine years here,' he said. 'It's not good for them.'

One student is OK in another house, he said, but when it's two it becomes a semi-formation house. He said I was unfortunate that others got out there before me. However, I would definitely be out of Milltown by the time I finished theology and possibly after second-year theology.

I had spiritual direction with Denis on 9 December.

'I'm ashamed of you,' he said. 'There was no need to use all that emotion with the Superior. Jesus left his disciples in the dark. He was badly treated. You must learn to live with uncertainty.'

Another priest told me he resented me inflicting my depression and heaviness of heart on him; while another priest said he was 'going off' me.

I journaled on 10 December: *'I just want to sit in a corner, be alone, and clasp my temple in the palms of my hands. How to accept and be done with this frightening, controlling depression? It's a reactive depression. I wonder how close it is to a nervous breakdown? Why can't I shake it off? Why is it going on so long? How can I finish with it?'*

Two confrères were ordained deacons on 12 December, one of whom entered after me. When I got to my room that night, I saw a piece of folded red-coloured paper inserted into the nameplate on my door. I recognised the handwriting as the Superior's. It read: *'Joe, lest I do not get the chance to see you on your own tomorrow I would like to tell you that the Provincial Council has agreed in principle to your residing outside of Milltown next year.'*

## #72

Hearing, on 12 December 1987, that I would be living outside Mount St Mary's within months was a profound relief. I grew in confidence that my needs could be met within the Marists. I journaled: *'Slowly, I became happy.'*

I met with the Superior on 18 December. He said this was new ground – for somebody to leave Milltown while studying theology; adding that it was the right decision.

By 13 January 1988, I journaled: *'This has been a very special and happy time for me. My last Christmas in Milltown. Knowing that I'm leaving it, I can now appreciate it and enjoy it. That's good, healthy and natural.'*

Loneliness surfaced on 22 January. Tom, my best friend from UCD, was still in novitiate, so I couldn't see him. Another best friend, the Marist confrère I'd gone to school with, was in Senegal. Yet another great buddy had left the Marists and I found his departure so painful that I had let that friendship come to an abrupt stop. And neither of my two more intense friendships in the Marists had ended well. As for Verena, I did not keep in touch with her after graduating.

I worried that I couldn't keep a friend. I journaled: *'Make them I do. Keep them, I don't. I can hardly put myself forward for the diaconate if I cannot keep a friend.'*

Apart from Denis, my spiritual director, there was only one other member of the Milltown community that I used to share with. Now, I felt he was avoiding me. I journaled: *'I'm fond of him. I like him. I've cried in his presence a long time back.'* I had shared with him about my relationship with my

209

mother. *I've shared my pain with him. In that sense, we have been emotionally intimate.'*

On 24 January, I chatted with him and told him I was impoverished by our not keeping in touch. That same day, the Provincial asked me if I would join a Northern Ireland committee to investigate the possibilities of the Marist Fathers becoming involved in the North. And that evening I had an enjoyable time with my cousin Mary. It was a good and significant day.

On 2 February, I told Denis I was thinking of being ordained a deacon that December. He was very positive and said there was no need for another big analysis. In fact, he asked: 'Why not September?'

I told the Superior on 22 February that I was thinking of the diaconate for December. His response was positive and heartening.

'Time is a factor in canon law,' he said, 'but given your year's novitiate, your BA and that you'll be in your ninth year and your final year of theology, it should be possible.'

Some days later, my uncle Tom died – the man who had cried when I told him in December 1985 that I was leaving the Marists and who had offered to fund my rent and subsistence until I finished my BA.

*I headed over to the hospital the morning he died, with communion,'* I wrote to my friend Tom on 1 March. *I hoped to administer Viaticum which I can do as an acolyte but I was "cheated" of that too as he was dead by the time I got there.'*

Viaticum is giving the Eucharist to a dying person as food for the journey into death.

I hadn't heard for months from the girl I'd known before I entered the Marists. I had last seen her at my final profession on 12 September. I thought she was involved in a relationship so I judged it best to leave things alone. But she attended my uncle's funeral. I journaled: *'I treasure her friendship. It is a friendship characterised by real and deep intimacy and mutual knowing, constancy, freedom. I thank God for our love.'*

On 22 March, I wrote to Tom: *'Life is still good with me.'* I told him of my sustained efforts to abstain from solitary pleasures, which I called *'an escape from reality'*. In triumph, I added: *'I've had my first wet dream in ages!'*

Letters to others that March, show that I was settled, contented and happy. I was gaining further confidence speaking in public; even singing solo the *Exultet* – the lengthy sung proclamation during the Easter Vigil – on 2 April 1988.

I was learning that life wasn't all about serving other people's needs. I could sing and be myself. There was no need for self-deprecation.

At a time of Anglo-Irish tension and atrocities on both sides in the North, I hoped that the Marists might yet begin a new ministry of reconciliation. I was living a balanced lifestyle, cycling, studying theology, and even improving control over my unruly classroom pupils. I had a renewed belief in my priestly vocation.

### #73

I met the Provincial on 25 April 1988. He told me I would be moving that summer to Catholic University School (CUS) – a Marist Fathers' community and school near St Stephen's Green in central Dublin.

He said diaconate could be in eight months, December 1988, and I could be ordained a priest in summer 1989, nine years after entering. I would complete third-year theology at Milltown Park while living in CUS. He wanted to move on a new mission in the North but wanted to take the Province with him.

I was encouraged by our conversation. On 6 May, I journaled that I had told a confrère: *"I'll be ordained priest summer '89." I wasn't so rash even to say that to myself yet! But deep down the decision has been made.'*

Next day, I journaled: *'This is a time of deep consolation and contentment. I am more myself now than I think I've ever been.'*

On 11 May, my friend Tom wrote telling me he had decided to leave his congregation. I felt numb – sad for me and happy for him. I hoped our friendship would survive his departure from religious life.

That night, I dreamt of *'an advancing tornado and I'm looking for somewhere to hide'*.

The Superior told me on 20 May that I could expect to be doing the Higher Diploma in Education after finishing my degree in theology. I journaled: *'It was like as if I hadn't spoken of the All Hallows pastoral diploma at all to him. He also said I can expect to be teaching for the first four or five years of my priestly life.'*

'I would prefer parish work to teaching,' I said.

'But there are already enough priests working in our parishes,' he replied.

Feeling uneasy, it seemed I had no control over what work I would do. When I had joined the Marists, I thought I could decide later about my apostolates. Now I realised it wouldn't be my call. The prospect of teaching filled me with emptiness.

The Superior said that he didn't expect me to be a deacon for longer than a year. If diaconate was in

December 1988, I would be ordained a priest by the following December at the latest.

My 'adopted' parents Paul and Marie offered help with the 'eats' for my first mass. Paul said he'd like to be a part of it and that I could be upfront with him about my needs.

I had my last day teaching at Chanel College on 23 May. I had just two weeks of second year theology to go, with essays, presentations and oral exams to pack in.

On a long cycle later that month, I visited my brother Paul in Castleblaney. Discussing my approaching ordination, I told him I felt like someone before a parachute jump. Am I ready? Am I able? Do I jump next summer?

'Jump!' said Paul, adding: 'I'll pray for you.'

On 31 May, I dreamt: *I've moved house. A huge window which I thought was locked is open. The window without a latch opens. I look through it.'*

To my mind, that dream reveals a retrieved inner openness to leaving religious life and the path to the priesthood.

By 4 June, I had *'a sense of being truly unsure, very insecure in myself, confused by my own perceptions'*. I felt like a *'soldier losing his nerve. Panic sets in at the thought of jumping.'*

It is said that 99 per cent of men masturbate and the other one per cent are liars. But the Church calls it 'an intrinsically and gravely disordered action' (Catechism 2352).

As a man and student priest struggling to abstain from masturbation, I journaled on 10 June: *'Sex is so powerful! It's an escape from loneliness. I can imagine my being hugged and loved. My masculinity. Its fullest self. I often sleep better after it. My*

213

*imagination, combined with my body, mind, memory, desire, my relationships, my tiredness, all combine in the urge towards orgasm.'*

I began a retreat at All Hallows in Dublin on 17 July 1988. My spiritual director was a woman. She said: 'The only person who sees masturbation as an obstacle to ordination is you. Is it an excuse for remaining indecisive?'

She asked me where I found pleasure in life, if I really wanted to be ordained, what was my motivation and did I want to teach.

'As a Marist priest you will surely be teaching,' she said. 'You really must decide. Decide one way or the other. Don't be vacillating between this way and that. It saps energy.'

That night I journaled: *'If I want to be a priest, then summer 1989 is the right time. I have answered the 'when?' But my question has shifted focus back to whether or not I want to be ordained.'*

## #74

Women were challenging, encouraging and affirming me as a person. At a party in Milltown Park to celebrate the end of the 1987–1988 academic year, a vivacious African nun wearing multicoloured ethnic dress danced with me.

'I see you like dancing,' she smiled, teaching me to let my body go a bit more.

'Not usually, but I'm enjoying this,' I replied.

She was herself. She was free. When I went to leave, she walked me to the door of the college, explaining that that was normal in her culture.

In June 1988, I was master of ceremonies for the ordination to the priesthood of three confrères, two from my novitiate. I planned the liturgy meticulously. My pastoral director, a lay woman, knew how much I had put into it.

Wisely, she asked me to choose one thing to do imperfectly. So, I decided not to polish my shoes. Her advice was an insightful and practical antidote to perfectionism; and one that has stood me in good stead ever since. I relaxed, remembering that perfectionism is a vice, that nothing is ever perfect; and the ceremony went really well.

As mentioned, my spiritual director during my retreat at All Hallows in July 1988 was also a woman. My discussions with her had brought a new feminine perspective and unparalleled clarity to eight years of vocational churning.

And, at that same All Hallows retreat, most participants were women; an extraordinary and welcome counterpoint to my eight years living in an all-male community.

The retreat aimed to help us to become more authentic and more ourselves; to find our personal meaning in life. For me, that involved abandoning false humility and coming to a greater awareness of my needs. In a note after one session, I journaled: *The more I know and appreciate myself, the more I can love another. I must be in relationship with myself.*

I found the retreat freeing; and I savoured the company of these dynamic, supportive, life-enhancing women. We started each day seated in a circle, briefly sharing the first image that came to mind. On 21 July, mine was of 'a lovable dog who needs to be brushed'.

I was brushed to death all day! I loved it.

In one session that day, we were taught the basics of reflexology. We paired up, giving each other foot massages.

It was great fun, human, healthy, tactile, sensual and intimate.

There were two girls there I particularly hit it off with. One was exquisitely beautiful – she had a vibrant, shiny mane of jet-black hair, immaculate Indian tanned skin and deep, sea green eyes to drown in. She was sexy, sultry and a nun! And the other girl, who became a good friend, was a smiling Afro-Caribbean, from Trinidad.

We three clicked. They invited me out with others for a walk one evening. The girls danced on Griffith Avenue, singing that summer's hit single 'Mercedes Boy'. I half-hoped, with its suggestive lyrics, that they might be singing it to me.

We bought Chinese food in a takeaway, and ate it with our fingers, sitting in the dark on the lawn of All Hallows college, without a key to get back in. Our carefree chatter, singing and laughter eventually prompted somebody to open a door for us.

That night I journaled: *'A freeing day. Perhaps I am now free of the need to be ordained next year.'*

After the retreat, on 25 July, I journaled: *'I'm aware of a new-found freedom. I am Joseph before I am either priest or husband/father. I don't need to be a priest. I could accept it if I were refused.'*

I had yet to consider the still greater freedom of choosing not to apply.

Supported by these positive feminine influences, it was a time of growth, affirmation and consolation. I sensed I had made a quantum leap during the retreat. I was reviewing my stoical attitude associating pleasure with sin. Choosing pleasure and what I wanted could be good, further discrediting my old paradigm extolling self-denial and sacrifice.

I journaled I was *'coming into relationship with myself. Heaps of people have told me how well I'm looking.'*

Back in Milltown, surrounded only by men, I journaled on 5 August that I felt *'lonely, unsupported, frustrated, angry, directionless and discouraged. I'm not sure whether I want to be a priest.'* I met an ex-Capuchin seminarian, who looked well and happy, showing me that there was happiness beyond religious life.

Unable to sleep, early on the morning of 6 August I journaled: *'On one level, I have decided to apply for diaconate for this December and for the priesthood for next summer.*

*'On another level, I'm not sure what I want. Grasped by the idea of Joseph being lovable, young and beautiful, and my desires for female affection, intimacy and sexual relations, I am willing not to be a priest. The idea of not becoming a priest is no longer merely theoretical but existential.'*

## #75

On 6 August 1988, I had great hopes for a meeting between the Provincial and a bishop in Northern Ireland. I hoped that the meeting might lead to a new Marist Fathers mission of reconciliation in the North, which I was passionate about.

I journaled: *'It seemed to bear immediately on my life. The awful prospect of the HDip followed by five-to-15 years teaching faded. The attractive idea of doing an MA in Peace Studies or Ecumenism seemed real and immediate; or even being in the North as a priest in 12 months.'*

The Provincial sent letters to four Northern bishops regarding the possibility of a new Marist Fathers ministry in the North. I journaled: *'Had I had my pastoral year there, I could hardly have hoped for such a move.'* However, as I worked on the Northern Ireland Mission Statement, surprisingly, I found *'it was a bit of a pain doing it'*.

Another boon was that my UCD friend Tom, who had left his religious congregation, would be doing his teaching practice at CUS, the Marist school and community in Dublin where I would shortly be residing.

I moved into CUS, 89 Lower Leeson Street, in early September. A Georgian building, it had fine plasterwork on some ceilings. My room was massive, with an enormous bay window from floor to ceiling, overlooking the school playground. It was divided by a partition. The first part had a simple desk and chair, a cheap armchair and bookshelves, while the partitioned section had a single bed, sink and wardrobe.

In the attic, directly above my bed, was the tank for the entire house. It filled up at night when I was trying to sleep. I think there were about eighty steps to descend from my room to the community kitchen and dining room.

On 19 September, I journaled: *'I am happy here and now. I love my new room – so symbolic of my moving on: more space, more light, more freedom, more at home. I am coming more into relationship with who I am.'*

The CUS community was in many respects the opposite of the seminary. There, so much had been regulated and controlled. But at CUS, community activities were minimal and everyone had great latitude, which I liked. My time was my own and I quickly came to think of it as my flat in Leeson Street.

The community was full of characters. One priest was much taken by limericks, a fascination I share. He especially liked, as do I, the bawdy ones: they are the best. He also told risqué jokes. I recall his quip about a conductor rebuking a female cellist: 'Madam, the instrument between your legs was meant for the pleasure of many and all you can do is scratch it.'

The headteacher of Chanel who had burst into my classroom of unruly pupils had since been transferred to CUS too. We got on well. We used to play pool in the community room. He taught me how to hold the cue properly and jeered me mercilessly when I hit a bad shot.

The Superior was an affable man, caring and easy to talk to. He used to pat his paunch while chatting. A highlight of his year was when the international rugby season began and he and most of us in the community watched the games with passion and enthusiasm. He teased me for never rushing to answer the telephone. 'Hurry, Joseph, it might be for you!'

Feeling that what I most wanted was to be a priest, and encouraged by others to do so, I had submitted my application to be ordained deacon that December. I felt at peace with my decision; although, having done so, as ever, my fear of rejection came to the fore.

I began the third year of theology on 3 October. I was dismayed, on 6 October, to hear that the Jesuits were no longer ordaining men to the priesthood at the end of their third year of theology, and that the Passionists had also adopted that policy, seemingly due to a stricter interpretation of canon law at the Vatican.

Diocesan priests tended to be ordained within six or seven years. If the Marists adopted the new policy, my path to the priesthood could take ten, rather than nine, years.

When I mentioned this to Denis Green, he dismissed my concern saying: 'Since when have you been influenced by canon law!'

## #76

Trepidation had descended upon me from 6 October 1988, having heard of the two religious orders who had stopped ordaining deacons during third-year theology. That they were no longer ordaining priests soon after theology also perturbed me in the increasingly rule-observant Rome.

The Marists had not yet changed their policy. I had already applied for diaconate, the presumed date being December, just two months away.

The Provincial had told me he considered nine years was sufficient preparation for the priesthood and had encouraged me to consider priestly ordination for June 1989.

My spiritual director had dismissed my concerns about canon law. Encouraging me to apply for diaconate for December 1988 and for priesthood in June 1989, Denis had said: 'You are you: unique, different, called, chosen. It's what's right for you that's important, not when others are called.'

Before my application, another priest, watching me dithering, had said: 'Go up to your room now and apply for the diaconate!'

The Jesuit President of the Milltown Institute had also said to me: 'Sure you'll be ordained priest next June, won't you?'

I would be ordained deacon in December 1988 or June 1989. It was only six months either way. So why did the earlier date matter to me?

On 7 October 1988, I journaled: *'I spent this summer dwelling on the decision of "when". It felt so right. I felt so good. My "when" was my core question. Then the "whether" was unexpectedly reopened. Both are very tied up.'*

My personal, religious faith and its veracity mattered to me. I was staking my life on it. I wondered how could God call a confrère to the diaconate during third-year theology 12 months ago but no longer be doing so in deference to canon law? Was the tail wagging the god?

I journaled on 8 October it mattered because: *'I chose, or believed myself to be chosen, for this December. I firmly and deeply believed it was and is right for me.'*

*'The depths of a man can only be known by himself, not by any other man,'* I mused in my journal, a reference to the first letter to the Corinthians (1 Cor 2: 11).

Did God, if He existed, have any part in it? Or was the Church just a human association like a golf club, imposing man-made rules, under the guise of divine authority, on gullible fools?

The issue for me was the convergence of my sense of an inner call with the external call of the Church. If those two 'calls' could not meet, then perhaps religious faith was fatuous.

On 11 October, the Superior told me that the formation staff would prefer me to defer. They were glad that I had

Leabharlann Baile Formaid
Ballyfermot Library
01-2228422

applied. There was no question of not being ordained; only when.

I responded telling him of the Provincial's suggestion for me to go for priesthood next June; and of my spiritual director being of the same mind; and that the decision had been the *'work of my year'.*

He was sympathetic to my view. I journaled: *'I felt a resurgence of hope for diaconate in December, priesthood in June.'*

I pondered: *'If I am accepted for diaconate in December, what is it that this means to me?'*

I would see it as an *'existential recognition of God's unique call to me'.* I would have felt the *'trust of others — the Order — in God's particular workings within me.'*

It would have been: *'A recognition and respect of my interior life with its movements of consolation and desolation. A confidence in myself and in my discernment, in union with the Church, of God's will for me. A belief in self as a place where God speaks and can be trusted, and that significant others trust the real me.'*

On 19 October, the Superior rang me to say that my application was on the agenda for that Saturday's Provincial Council meeting. He said the Provincial would be in touch with me after the meeting. He had asked the Provincial not to put it on the public agenda and he suggested I could probably read between the lines. I couldn't.

I journaled: *'Next Saturday I shall be called to the diaconate. The date of the diaconate will probably be June. Why do I feel so disappointed at this prospect? Why, to me, is it like a refusal, a rejection, of my deep self?'*

I dreamt that night that my room was a corridor. I was trying to settle down and make it my private space but people kept intruding.

222

My journal of Saturday 22 October records: *'Today at 1pm, the Superior rang me to say that I have been called to the diaconate, for December. Thanks be to God.'*

I felt numb. Suppressing an urge to announce it at table, I journaled: *'I need to tell me first!'*

### #77

After my call to the diaconate on 22 October 1988, I had a lot to juggle. I needed to organise my diaconate; attend theology lectures; do oral exams on the Eucharist, marriage and the liturgy; write essays on the priesthood and Saint Paul; have a retreat; continue my pastoral work with disadvantaged kids; write a report on the Northern Ireland study group; attend various committees; have the daily round of masses, prayer and the Divine Office; do spiritual direction and meet with the Superior.

I had a discussion with an Assistant General from Rome about my hopes for a new Marist mission in Northern Ireland.

'Go for whatever you can get,' he advised on 27 October, saying I was not too young, aged 26, to strive for it now. He said I could be up North next year in my first year of priesthood.

That night, I dreamt I was in a boat. *The boat is some kind of taxi service for an island. It stops at various places. If you want out, you get out here. But if you get out, the boat goes off and leaves you.'*

Perhaps 'island' represents my identity, how I would define myself, my 'I-land'. And with ordination so close, staying on or getting off the boat would define me.

I had often dreamt of waiting for a boat at a terminal. *'Now I'm* in *the boat,'* I journaled. *'It's circling the island, stopping here and there. Am I sure I want to stay in this boat before it takes to the high and open seas? If you go out, there's no coming back. If you get out, the boat leaves without you.'*

I wondered: *'Do I want to get out?'* I felt *'Caught – not really free to get out.'*

On 2 November, the Superior said my diaconate would be 17 December and he presumed I would be ordained a priest in summer 1989. The Provincial congratulated me on being called to diaconate.

I got measured for my diaconate suit. My Uncle Jack paid for it. My mother bought me a new alb.

A good friend stood me up for a date on 4 November. *'She means a lot to me,'* I journaled. *'Yet I can't figure her out.'*

I spoke separately to Denis and my pal Tom on 8 November about her non-appearance. Later that night I journaled: *'I was very depressed today. Sunken. Angry. Embittered. Heavy. Why?'*

I wondered if it was that my friend had stood me up; or that I had too much work on; or that the Provincial *'hadn't had word yet about the indult'.*

I needed an indult, or licence, from Rome authorising my diaconate during third-year theology. The Superior had assured me it was only a matter of form.

*'The whether/when question seems open again,'* I journaled.

I was back in good form next day. My friend had been in touch and I would see her the following night. We met and I was glad to renew our friendship.

The weekend of 12 November, I spent with the Superior and the 'already-but-not-yet' – finally professed and deacons who were not yet priests.

*'I felt dissected,'* I journaled. *'My innards microscoped. I felt very vulnerable. Towards the end, I could barely speak. I was afraid I was close to crying.'*

The Superior and another confrère suggested I reconsider the timing of diaconate given my other commitments.

I journaled: *'I am anxious in myself these days. I don't think I'm free. I am pressurised. Perhaps I need to see a counsellor to sort myself out. The whole decision has been a very rocky ride. I feel I should be more at peace. I'm afraid it might be the wrong decision. I've been called. I've even got a date: 17 December. Now, I'm losing my nerve. I don't feel supported in the decision. I'm anxious, unsure, distressed.'*

Next day, on 13 November, left alone in a car while the Superior went into a house, I had a calm moment of profound inner freedom. I imagined a new direction. I could choose a different life.

Four weeks to diaconate, I was open to an abrupt about-turn. I was inwardly free to explore leaving; even, this time, to act on it.

When the Superior returned to the car, I said: 'I am open to postponing diaconate.'

'I'm struck by how free you are,' he replied.

On 16 November, he wrote me a note saying the Provincial had just received a phone call from the General House saying they could not apply for an indult.

The Superior apologised for 'the messing and the wasted energy' and for giving the impression that it would not be a problem – things had changed since earlier precedents.

He wrote: 'It seems that the question has, after all, been taken out of our hands.'

# IN MY GUT, I DON'T BELIEVE

## *Chapter 7*

# Taking charge of my life

### #78

At first, my response to the postponement of my diaconate on 16 November 1988, due to a stricter interpretation of canon law at the Vatican, was calm. My understanding trumped anger.

I was encouraged that the Province had believed in me enough to call me to diaconate for that December. I knew it wasn't personal. Policies in Rome had changed. In fact, I had been more aware of these changes than the Superior, the Provincial and my spiritual director.

Moreover, given I had been inwardly free to postpone it myself, and was open to doing so, at the start relief exceeded disappointment. I was free to concentrate on my final year of theology, without the distraction of diaconate.

There was some embarrassment. I had told people I would be ordained deacon on 17 December, and my mother had broadcast it to a multitude. It was pointless offering her a canonical exegesis for the delay.

But the most significant development was my idea, on 12 November, that I might *need to see a counsellor to sort myself out*; followed by that moment the next day when, alone in a car, I had an existential awareness of my inner freedom; imagining a new direction; knowing I could choose a different path. Though so close to ordination, I could still leave.

On 21 November, I recollected that radical freedom in the car when I had considered *'a new scenario for my life'*. A cousin, close to marriage, had cancelled it and entered a seminary. *'His was a brave and admirable decision,'* I journaled.

*'There was I,'* I continued, *'four weeks before my diaconate, and I really considered a similar about-turn. To "postpone" diaconate. To go to counselling – to come to know myself better. Probably to leave. Possibly to marry.'*

I'm struck by the boldness of *'Probably to leave'*, written a month before my then still scheduled ordination to the diaconate. And the inverted commas around *'postpone'* were in my journal, suggesting I wanted cancellation more than postponement.

*'Probably to leave. Possibly to marry'* reminds me of a journal entry of more than three years earlier, 5 August 1985. Some three weeks before kissing that beautiful French woman and heading off to Paris hoping to lose my virginity, in my dreamy-semi-conscious waking self *'the guardsmen of my ideal image suffered to allow surface an actual choice I made'* that night: *'to choose celibacy, probably, but virginity, probably not.'*

By November 1988, that had become: to leave, probably; celibacy probably not.

228

But the human psyche is complex and my mind was a mire of confusion: I was being pulled, or propelling myself, in opposing directions. In my ninth year in religious life, I still wasn't sure what I wanted, so I could never know if I got there, even if I had arrived. I hoped counselling would guide me through the jungle of my mind.

After some days, anger surged; bringing in its wake, depression. I wondered on 21 November: *Is it anger at myself for being here? Better to know now than in 10- or 20- or 30-years' time. Do I really want this life? I feel trapped, disheartened, discouraged, upset, disorientated.*

In counselling, I wanted to explore *'my lack of faith in myself. When it comes to relationships, I don't believe in my psychological capacity to live a happy and full married life.'*

On 24 November, I journaled: *'I'm not happy. What would I do if I chose not to be ordained?'* I answered with one word: *'Writing.'*

Two days later, I journaled: *'I'm not looking forward to Mother's birthday party tomorrow. There'll be people there who know of our falling out. I'll feel watched, judged; and some of them will be expecting my diaconate in December. I'm frustrated, angry, tense, isolated, lonely, self-doubting.'*

As things stood, I would be ordained deacon in about six months, and a priest six months to a year after that. *'I'm almost there – at the end of a long 9 to 10 years. But,'* I added, *'do I want to get into teaching? No. Do I want to do this with my life? I resent that I entered religious life so young. Why didn't I sow wild oats?'*

On 27 November, I journaled: *'Mother's party went very well. A kind of exorcism for me. A public gesture of reconciliation.'*

I wanted to see a counsellor to *'double-check'* if diaconate and priesthood was *'right for me'*. I knew I might *'postpone diaconate indefinitely in an effort, through counselling, to get myself more together.'* I had a sense that *'exterior time'* was *'converging on interior time.'* I determined to *'enter fully into counselling';* to *'seek freedom within and the right decision without.'*

On 29 November, unsettled, unhappy and unsure, I wondered if I was annoyed for having wanted ordination so much; or for having wanted it at all.

## #79

I met the Superior on 14 December 1988, telling him I wanted to do counselling to get to know myself better and to explore my motivations. He gave me permission, offered me the phone number of a counsellor and said it could begin after Christmas.

That same day, I remembered the night exactly three years earlier when I had *'cried and cried and cried having just told Denis of my decision to leave. I was actually doing it.'* But I had allowed the interventions of my spiritual director, the Superior and others to deflect me from that decision which had emanated from the core of my being.

Now, as I prepared for counselling, I asked myself: *'When I sound confident about my vocation, am I being honest? Why do I find it so impossible to make and keep a decision?'*

My bias favoured authority. I journaled: *'Why would I like other people to make my decisions for me? Why am I so confused and muddled up?'* In confession, I admitted my doubt and disbelief in Christ, in my vocation, and in the 'Kingdom of God'.

On 7 January 1989, I journaled: *'During my holidays, I became very sad one night in bed. I remembered the day I met my uncle Tom in Clerys restaurant. I told him I had decided to leave the*

*Marists. He cried, briefly; advised me against going home; and offered me £1,000 to get by until the end of my BA.'*

I was sad that he wouldn't be at my ordination. But I was sad too that I had buried my decision to leave, having consented to the request of the Superior to stay for several weeks; and that I had been swayed by my director, who completely changed his tune from his initial respect for my decision, following his discussion with the Superior.

I journaled: *'I read today that Irish graduates who try at all can find jobs in London. Go over? Find a job.'* I wondered if I might invite a friend to join me there later. I was fond of her. *'Could marry her if she was willing. But don't know if I love her.'*

My journal continued: *'I joined at 18 years of age. I seemed, then, to really believe in God. I wanted, needed, to get away from home. Nothing, not even the death of my father, would take me back. In some senses, I feel trapped. My courses will soon be finishing. It will be embarrassing if I don't get ordained deacon in June. I hate obedience. I dislike celibacy – who'd want it? I don't even try poverty.'*

I had phoned the number the Superior gave me, made an appointment and, on 19 January, I cycled to a house in south Dublin. I waited for a short while in a pokey area of the basement until I was called into the consulting room. A man and a woman were inside, both counsellors.

I had two sheets of paper with me. One was a mind map showing the issues I wanted to explore: motivation; diaconate, priesthood; my Marist future – teaching, the North; anger; friendships; mother; sexuality; feelings, wants and needs; and a named female friend.

The second sheet went into more detail on each topic, such as exploring my motivation for wanting to work for reconciliation in the North of Ireland.

The man said: 'You don't need that paper.'

231

In my notes after the meeting, the key word was 'unsure'. I was unsure of my vocation, intelligence, motivation, sexuality and relationships.

'You have to take authority for your life,' he said. 'You have to try to cut through the stories. You identified with your mother. You never identified with your father. You have a good intellectual grasp of your problems but this must filter to your emotions.'

Afterwards, I journaled that *'when'* the Superior *'asks if he may have permission to speak with the counsellors, I shall refrain from granting the necessary permission. I shall say no.'*

I remembered, on 21 January, my mother telling me that she had been expecting a girl. It had never occurred to her that I could be male. I knew that I lacked confidence in my ability to sustain a lifelong relationship. I viewed myself *'as so screwed up I wouldn't want to inflict myself on any children – as my mother did on me.'*

On 23 January, I rang the phone number again and spoke to the female counsellor, whose name I still didn't catch. I confirmed that I would do the counselling.

I journaled: *'They believe it best for me to have a woman counsellor. So, Ms D it's to be. I accepted both the gender and person.'*

To this day, I never learned her name.

'Are you willing to work very hard?' she asked.

'I am.'

'So, we begin this day week, 2.30pm.'

## #80

*I begin counselling today,'* I journaled at 4.30am on 30 January 1989, following a light sleep.

232

After our first session, I wrote: *'I feel threatened by her sexuality and by mine.'* In a flight of fantasy, I half hoped *'that part of the counselling might involve a sex practical – either viewing her semi- or fully nude or attempting intercourse.'*

*'Attempting'* was an interesting choice of words but, aged 26, I had never made love to anyone.

*'I felt attracted by her femininity – her eyes, her dress, her breasts, her sympathetic and needy presence.'*

I'm sure she would have challenged 'needy'. I was glad she was a woman. *'I am male,'* I journaled. I'm sorry to admit that I felt *'superior'* to her. I felt *'safer'* with her than had I been assigned to her male colleague, whom I imagined might have been *'tougher, less sympathetic'*.

She was a *'foreigner, an outsider, perhaps unmarried'*. I deemed her to be *'getting on'* – but I couldn't, even now, guess her age. Perhaps only in her 30s, I found her attractive, alluring and mysterious. I felt resentful for being *'the primary person-in-need'*.

My journal records nothing more of the contents of the first counselling session. However, a hint may be gleaned from a dream that night, in which, *I'm sitting, harmlessly, at table when, all of a sudden, I turn to the six or so people there and I tell them whether I like them or hate them'*.

When I get to one member of the community, *'I tell him I hate him. I shout it out. I yell and scream and holler.'*

I entitled the dream 'The Scream', and described its theme: *'Being how I feel. Letting it surface.'*

The following day, I almost enacted it in waking life, when a respected confrère in CUS announced at a community meeting his reluctant decision to lock the pantry. *'I reacted strongly against this,'* I journaled, perplexed that the community's food store would be sealed, which seemed to me to contradict the shared belief that this was our home.

Also, following that first counselling session, I showed confident leadership in a public speech at the Milltown Institute, voicing my opposition to a proposal to pull our college out of the Union of Students in Ireland.

I suspect the first hour's therapy also discussed my concern about maintaining long-term relationships, because I reflected on 31 January that it was I who had terminated some friendships, and so it was within my control to choose otherwise in future.

On 1 February, I dreamt: *'We are on some kind of a trail near the Dark Sea. But we did not bring a compass.'*

Perhaps the Dark Sea represents my subconscious, or sex and sexuality, and my awareness that I was journeying very close to it. With no compass, I couldn't be sure where I was; or where I was going.

*'There are four of us,'* continued the dream. Each, I suspect, representing an aspect of myself. *'We are very close to the water's edge and there is somewhat soft soil underfoot,'* suggesting that, through counselling, I was dipping my toes into my subconscious and my sexuality.

*'It is a deserted place,'* – a place empty of people. *'We stop by the side of the water – at a bus shelter!'* So perhaps many people come to this place after all, awaiting public transport. Remaining uncertain *'whether we're on the west or the eastern side of a very long lake,'* the dream concludes: *'Across the water is a foreign country.'*

On 3 February, I had my first session with a new spiritual director, a nun. After so many years of being guided and directed by men, I now had a woman counsellor and a

234

female director. The nun suggested I take a Gospel passage, use my imagination and see where the meditation took me.

Taking the cue from my recent dream, I read the Gospel story of Peter and the disciples fishing all night on the lake but catching nothing. Jesus appears and tells them to cast their nets on the other side. The disciples obey him and they catch so many fish that the boat almost capsizes.

As I imagined the scene, what was going on in me was sheer disbelief that it had ever happened as the evangelist recorded it. *'It didn't happen. It is a story,'* I journaled. And I wondered if unbelief had led three young men, whom I knew, to leave the priesthood recently, soon after ordination.

Perhaps exploring an alternative choice for myself, on 6 February I had a lovely evening on Dollymount Strand with the girl I thought I might have a future with.

Three days later, I told my counsellor: 'I hate my mother.'

'Do you find these feelings unacceptable?' she asked. 'If so, you find yourself unacceptable. Do you need to seek confirmation outside yourself for feeling and thinking as you do?'

### #81

On 9 February 1989, after my second counselling session with Ms D., I journaled: *What a waste of energy if I cannot be me in the here and now, if I need to go away and think and come back prepared. Just come as I am to the sessions, without being prepared.'*

Two days later, I journaled: *'I'm happy. Content. Counselling has considerably improved my confidence in friendships.'*

I spoke to my pal Tom about *'my unsureness about religious life and priesthood'*. I had *'demythologised Larry Duffy'*, the good priest who had so inspired me. Theology taught me to reinterpret the gospels too, free of their mythical elements.

Nine years of religious life had shorn consecrated life of the sacred. Liturgy had become empty ritual. Scrutinise their personal theologies and any shared meaning between Marists was minimal, I felt. As if to accentuate my loss of meaning, that Saturday, no members of the community turned up for Eucharistic adoration.

On 16 February, I journaled that I dreamt I had *'turned right rather than left at decision time'*. My dream suggested I *'might have made the wrong decision'*, and had taken *'a longer route – but I still arrive on the far side of the lake where I wanted to get to, though late.'*

This dream resumed that of 1 February, taking the plot further: now I have arrived on the far side of the lake. It reflects on my choice, in January 1986, to stay in the Marists, despite my profound personal decision a month earlier to leave. I made what I thought was the 'right' decision by staying – I had not 'left' the Marists. But, arriving on the far side of the lake, this dream anticipates what my waking consciousness had yet to comprehend.

Later that day, 16 February, I met Ms D for my third counselling session. She challenged me on my repeated use of the phrase 'I suppose'.

'Supposing, supposing, three men were frozen, two died, how many were left?'

I couldn't remember the answer to the child's riddle.

'None,' she said. 'You were only supposing. Stop saying, "I suppose I feel this or that." Or I feel "sort of X, Y or Z". Say how you feel. Own it.'

She also challenged me on my tendency to waste time telling her what other people thought. 'Discard the web of other people's perceptions and judgements,' she said.

What mattered was *my* perception, feeling, understanding and judgement.

'Limit yourself to that,' she said. 'I only want to hear what you perceive, think, feel, remember, judge. You should stop suspending your judgement. Don't go beyond your own experience, either in thinking or communicating.'

It was a pivotal lesson for me and my personal invitation to Cartesian doubt. René Descartes (1596–1650) proposed that we question, doubt and be sceptical about everything. It is the basis of the scientific method. Only by doubt, questioning and examining the facts, can we come to know the truth. Descartes famously said: '*Cogito ergo sum* – I think, therefore I am.'

Nobody can think their way into a 'revealed' religion. By limiting myself to my thoughts, feelings, insights, understanding and judgements, I would have to set aside other people's opinions, focusing solely on mine instead. At last, I had a compass to find my way through the jungle of my mind.

It was *'a powerful message, borne out by the rest of the day,'* I journaled. *'I feel very happy, very content. Hopeful, as I felt this morning. And confident and at peace.'*

*'I had the opportunity to try out my confidence in my perceptions tonight,'* I journaled. That night, a confrère and I were to go to a novitiate reunion. He was sure it was in one pub. I thought it was in a different one. Rather than doubting my judgement, I took authority for it and I was right.

At the reunion, I envied three friends who had left the Marists. *Why am I here? Pride? Too stubborn to leave? Unsure of*

237

*my capacity to live my life with a woman? Comfortable? Relieved of the bother of having to earn money? Insufficiently in touch with who I am and so this is the easy option? Or some residual belief in Jesus?'*

That night, I summed up the lessons learned so far in counselling. Feeling *'unsure'* about many things, I needed to, *'Be me in the here and now';* and to *'Bother only with my perceptions, feelings, understandings and judgements.'*

On 20 February, I *'enjoyed myself very much'* with two confrères in community. *'Was myself. Outgoing. Taking initiative and participating in the fun.'*

At spiritual direction the next day, my new director asked me: 'If the proposed North of Ireland mission doesn't come off and if you end up teaching, would you leave the Marists?'

'Yes,' I replied, surprising myself with my clarity.

### #82

*A difficult session. I felt embarrassed, awkward, uncomfortable,'* I journaled after my fourth counselling session on 23 February 1989.

*'I've only met Ms D five times, including the initial consultation with her colleague, yet I was asking her to tell me if I am intelligent or not.'*

She threw the question back at me.

'I don't know,' I responded.

'That's a good starting point,' she said.

I went blank and lost my thread answering some question. The answer concerned a memory of my mother's selfish reaction to the only bad school report she had ever received about me, when I was in fifth year in secondary school.

I had 'found God' in the charismatic renewal and stopped studying for the Leaving Certificate. I did so partly because I feared I couldn't repeat my high performance at my Intermediate Certificate and partly due to my fear that if I did so I might abandon my desire to be a priest, lured away from 'God' by ambition, success and money.

My journal records my mother's delight that in second year UCD I came first in my class, a feat not repeated in third year. But my good result at my Intermediate Certificate and in second year UCD failed to excite me.

Towards the end of the session, Ms D asked me about my sexuality. I didn't expect it, especially coming so late in the hour.

Having spent almost nine years with a vow of celibacy in an all-male community, I hadn't had much opportunity to explore my sexuality. Attracted to men and women, I clammed up, my mind went blank, my muscles tightened, my emotions shut down, time stood still, and I was dying for the session to end.

'What am I meant to say?' I asked.

'What are you afraid of?' she asked.

I couldn't answer her, as I didn't know.

'How do you feel about me?' she asked, unexpectedly.

I found her attractive, sexy, alluring, enticing, engaging, playful and mysterious. I had enjoyed fantasies of having sex with her. But I didn't tell her that. My mind blanked. I was lost for words.

'When your brain shuts down, what are you left with?' she asked.

I was vividly aware of my loins, as if the entire focus of the room was on my genitalia. Embarrassed by my ineptitude in communicating with her, I was close to tears. Instead, I laughed.

'So, when you want to cry, you laugh,' she said.

I couldn't wait for the session to end, but it dragged on, excruciatingly. It was like spending an hour in a boxing ring, with her landing all the punches.

'You withdrew during this session,' she said. 'Your voice went low. You avoided questions. You did the same last time.'

I later journaled: *'Time did, eventually, save me. Or did it? Did not time run out but the problem remains?'*

Two days later, on 25 February, a priest in CUS said that I, and two other members of the community, treated the house like a hostel.

'You wouldn't care if the place was shut down in the morning,' he said, adding that priest–teachers in the Province were treated like second-class citizens.'

'On the contrary,' I protested, angry and close to tears, 'not wanting to teach makes me a second-class citizen in the Marists.'

That night, I met my mother. My sister was thinking of moving to France and my mother was planning to sell the family home. She said the modest terraced house was too big for her. It seemed crazy to sell her home in order to rent an apartment, but I said nothing knowing I'd be blamed if things didn't work out.

My journal records my antagonism towards her and the *'impossibility, as ever, of talking to her'.* She *'wanted to know – felt she had the right to know and came close to demanding – when I would be ordained.'*

I remembered her brother Tom calling her *'the last unstrung bitch'*; and I concurred, adding: *'If I cannot accept these feelings about her, I cannot accept myself.'*

Reflecting on my life context, I added: *'From rush to be ordained, to whether to leave to Hell out of the whole sham.'*

On 26 February, Denis rang me to say that the Derry Council of Priests had turned us down. My immediate reaction was to postpone diaconate, stay as finally professed, wait until completing my Higher Diploma in Education and *'then maybe leave'*.

My second reaction was to reflect on recent refusals. The Superior General not applying for an indult for diaconate because of changed Vatican procedures and now the Derry priests preventing the Marist Fathers moving to their diocese.

My third reaction was of disillusionment, disenchantment and disbelief. I journaled: *'The whole fucking thing is a sham. I'm a sham, the Church, religion – you fucking name it.'*

#83

During my fifth counselling session, on 2 March 1989, I asked Ms D if she felt I should leave the Marists.

'Thanks!' she replied, with mock delight. 'You've made my day! The power you've given me over you!'

I was confused. Wasn't she the expert on human psychology, the professional with specialised knowledge? Did she not have a view on whether I should stay or leave?

'Thanks, but no thanks,' she continued. 'That is your power alone to decide. Take it back!'

I was perplexed.

'How long do I know you?' she challenged.

'Five or six weeks.'

'And how long have *you* known you?'

'Almost twenty-seven years.'

'You do that to others too. You think your Superior or spiritual director know you better than you know yourself.'

We explored my decision to leave the Marists on 15 December 1985. In the lonely dark of the night, an ocean of tears welling up from my gut, I had decided to leave.

But the Superior asked me to wait several weeks and my spiritual director told me he was unhappy with my decision, that the Society of Mary was a work of God. He had characterised my choice as leaving a community of brothers for the loneliness of some dingy flat to have a fling with a girl. Both told me that if I left and regretted it, I might not be readmitted as I had ignored their advice.

My decision shifted from my choice to leave, to *'we decided it wiser to wait a while'* and then to: *'I appreciated the wisdom of waiting – this was my life I was dealing with.'*

Ms D. said: 'So, your pattern is you go to the dean. You're confident. You're sure. Then somebody else says something and your judgement caves through.'

I was learning what her colleague had said at our initial consultation, that I needed to take authority for my life: I alone should judge, decide and act.

On 4 March, I listed reasons to stay in religious life. I had taken final vows, for life, in public. It suited me – reflecting on the meaning of life. Being part of an international community *'staves off loneliness'*. There were confrères I was fond of and who were fond of me. And Marists espoused shared values.

I could make a *'useful priest'*. Financially dependent upon the congregation, the lifestyle was comfortable, secure, middleclass. Remaining offered me security of identity; and lifelong healthcare and religious surety.

*'But I must move the debate to a new level,'* I journaled. *'I must re-examine my crisis times and consequent decisions to stay.'*

I went home on Mother's Day, 5 March. *'I didn't' want to be there,'* I journaled. I felt *'angry, depressed, resentful, spiteful, bitter'.*

Back at CUS, a priest said: 'You should go home every Sunday and not pretend to be studying.'

'Fuck him,' I thought. He knew nothing about my mother nor our tormented relationship.

I rang my friend Tom, told him how awful I felt and discussed my shaky vocation.

'I don't think I want to do it anymore,' I said, 'be a religious or a priest.'

Next day, I felt very low. *'This is my worst patch since November 1987 when I wanted out of Milltown,'* I journaled. *'I don't seem to be able to lift myself out of it. I'm depressed, angry, furious. When I came home from Milltown Park, I dragged myself up the stairs. I went to bed at 2.30pm. Woke at 4pm. Slept again until 6.40pm. Got up at 8pm. Ate. Watched TV. Told [named priest] he had no right to tell me I ought to go home. He accepted that. Desolation is the best word for today.'*

I had a good chat with Brendan, a friend from another congregation, *'about how I am'*. I was grateful for him and my friend Tom. I journaled on 7 March: *'I talk to them like blood brothers. They know me well. I spoke to them both today about leaving. I was very depressed when Tom rang my room. He came up, accepted me as I am.'*

243

My journal continues: *'I spoke as someone who* will *be leaving the Marists. From "will I be accepted?" to "do I want this?" Being willing to follow my deep feelings, wants, desires. Not suspending them while I wait for "the" objective view — that is to remain a boy. If I could find a woman like Marie Toomey and if I could have a marriage like that of Paul and Marie, I would leave.'*

With Brendan, I called to his friend Treasa. I held in my arms, and connected well with, her nine-month-old baby.

'Are you the eldest in your family?' asked Treasa.

'No, the youngest,' I said.

I delighted in the child. I wanted to be a dad.

### #84

On 8 March 1989, I spoke to Father Denis Green about my hoped-for new Marist apostolate of reconciliation in the North of Ireland. He had more bad news for me.

*'Not only has the Council of Priests in Derry said no,'* I journaled, *'but the Marist Council of the Province was against the idea. The real likelihood of the Marists going North is next to nil.'*

I indicated to Denis my vocational turmoil. He heard my confession and spoke both of my 'pig-headedness' and his affection for me.

I shared with a confrère in CUS that I was receiving counselling and religious life was on the agenda. I told him: 'I'm feeling shit.'

I journaled: *'I'm frightened of leaving, of my future, of what I will do, of what I will miss, of the possibilities I will be leaving behind.'*

So much remained unexplained to me. I got it wrong in applying for diaconate and, before that, for final profession and, still earlier, in deciding to remain, reversing my choice to leave in December 1985. How could I be confident in my decision making, now or in the future?

One of the women who worked in the kitchen in Mount St Mary's said to me on 8 March that it would be a 'waste' if I became a priest.

*'I smiled. She guesses,'* I journaled.

Of one thing I was sure, committing to my journal: *'I do not want to be a Marist priest–teacher.'*

I drafted my curriculum vitae on 9 March. Nine years of studying for the priesthood didn't qualify me for anything – a year's novitiate, two years' philosophy, a BA in English and History, and a degree in theology, which I would complete that June.

I cried and physically shook later that day during my sixth counselling session with Ms D. We discussed my seeming decision to leave, although now that I was speaking to her I was unsure whether or not I had decided.

'I am frightened giving up the Marist dream,' I told her, 'my meaning, my role, my purpose. Just being me, devoid of my Marist identity, earning my own living, abandoning the security of Marist life.'

*'I physically shake now – as I write this,'* I later journaled, *'just as I did during the session.'*

'How do you feel about me?' asked Ms D.

'I was looking forward to coming,' I said.

She asked me about my sexual fantasies.

I hesitated.

'You need to speak out your feelings and partial thoughts before they get passed to the head. I appreciate counselling is difficult but you should not waste time. Avail of this opportunity of testing out your thoughts and fantasies with me in my professional role.'

'I fantasised that you stripped and we had intercourse.'

'Tell me about the fantasy.'

We explored the imagery, in which I had *allowed her to take the initiative and so took less responsibility and rationalised my compliance on the grounds of professional counselling*.

On 10 March, I reflected upon my setbacks within the Marists. Wanting to study psychology to become a priest–counsellor but not being allowed to. Having to start a new degree just two weeks after finishing my BA final exams. Not being granted a pastoral year or study-free year. Having to fight to live outside Milltown. My proposal for a Northern Irish mission turned down. Never wanting to be a priest–teacher yet destined for the classroom.

I walked through the grounds of the Milltown Institute feeling depressed, thinking about leaving. I wondered if wanting out of Mount St Mary's so soon after final vows was a reaction to my taking final profession, and that what I truly wanted was to be out of the Marists, not just the House of Studies.

My inner battle still raged between what I felt I *'ought'* to do, and what I *'wanted'*. I wondered if the dichotomy between what I *'want'* and the *'right'* thing might converge. I journaled: *Doing what I "want" may, for me, at this time, be the "right" thing. Again, tonight, I would say I'm leaving.'*

My pal Tom and I went to O'Donoghue's pub in Merrion Row for a pint. I journaled: *'I felt frightened and depressed, self-conscious and uncomfortable going to the pub tonight. I was thinking of just being Joseph Armstrong, without the Marist identity. I was frightened. Then, in the pub, after a while, my night was made. Three different girls spoke to me and I was happy and responsive and assured.'*

246

I was sexually attracted to one of them, my mood lifted and I was thrilled when she gave me her number. I was like any other guy out on the town.

My brief encounter with that girl gave me hope and confidence. That night, I journaled: *'I can make it. I'll do okay.'*


#### #85

On 11 March 1989, I drafted a letter to the Provincial seeking dispensation from my final vows.

I had made final profession *'with the intention of becoming a priest, with the hope of working in the North as a Marist'*. Now, it looked *'almost certain that I'm destined for the classroom'* and I felt *'no vocation to be a priest–teacher'* and I had *'said that throughout my formation. Even Marist parishes, which would interest me, are full up.'*

While becoming a priest had *'been my dream, my love, my hope'*, counselling caused me *'to pause'*. I felt *'unsure'*; and it *'would be wrong to proceed with Orders feeling unsure'*.

My draft continued that I needed *'time and space and freedom to find myself'* before I could be ordained. I was grateful to the Marists for *'my excellent formation – spiritual, academic, theological, human, social. I love the Marist dream and I am frightened at the thought of leaving.'*

I regretted *'any pain caused to the Church or Society of Mary by my seeking dispensation from final vows. I did not enter into final vows lightly and cherished, as my most prized symbol, my profession cross for life.'*

I had been inspired by the Marist vision and dream and it was *'with considerable personal cost that I now seek dispensation'*.

This was not the draft of a non-believer. It stated that I loved the scriptures and the Church and that I longed to play my part in its *worship and mission*. It concluded asking the Provincial's prayers *'that I may keep faith in Jesus and the Catholic Church'* and that I may *'walk humbly'*.

Two mornings later, I had a *'deep sense of panic at the thought of leaving'*.

Meanwhile, I was in the middle of theology exams. Feeling rotten later that day, I did a poor oral exam on the Church. Examiner Dr Chris O Donnell said: 'Not to worry. You did a good essay.'

I had three more exams on 14 March. Either preparing for an exam or in a subsequent private meeting with him, I had a pivotal, self-empowering discussion with Dr Jim Healy, a Jesuit priest and moral theologian, about the Catholic doctrine of conscience.

I told him I was unsure about proceeding with the priesthood but given that I had taken final vows, I wanted to check with him if I understood the Church's teaching on conscience. He gave me an article entitled 'Forming my conscience' by Jesuit Conn O'Donovan in the April 1972 edition of the periodical *Doctrine and Life*.

That article and my conversation with Jim Healy blew my mind. It left me feeling that conscience was the least understood, and most rarely taught, of all Catholic doctrines. It is revolutionary.

Sitting in his office, I checked with Dr Healy if I understood the article and doctrine correctly.

'It's the Church's teaching that I must always follow my conscience,' I said.

'Yes,' said Jim.

'And conscience isn't a little voice in my head nor is it doing what the Church teaches.'

'Correct,' he said.

'Conscience is, instead, my personal honest judgement?'

'Yes, that is Catholic teaching. You must be honest, aware of the human capacity to fool ourselves. And it must be a considered thought-through judgement – not a feeling or an impulse. And you alone are the one who must make your personal honest judgement, not anybody else, not your Superior nor your spiritual director nor even the Pope.'

'And I must always follow my personal honest judgement – my conscience – even if it breaks a church or civil law or my final vows,' I said.

'Yes,' he confirmed.

'And so if, after due diligence, asking all the questions, and aware of our propensity to fool ourselves, I form the honest judgement that I was wrong to take final vows, then not only may I leave religious life but I must – in order always to follow my conscience?'

'Yes. In fact, if, having formed that judgement, you stayed, you would be acting in bad conscience,' he confirmed. 'Aquinas taught us you must always follow your conscience even if it involves disobeying the Pope.'

This was revolutionary – and the antithesis of what was generally understood as Catholics always having to obey the Pope or following Church teaching. If it's my honest judgement that I should leave religious life, get a divorce or have an abortion, Catholic teaching says that you must leave, divorce or terminate a pregnancy.

It was liberating discovering this, the best kept secret in the Catholic Church.

The word 'exclaustration' appears for the first time in my journal on 15 March. Meaning 'outside the cloister', it is formal leave of absence for a finally professed religious, usually for a year or two. It would be a less definitive break than leaving outright, allowing the possibility of return.

Next day, during my seventh counselling session, we talked about sex.

## #86

It is difficult for a seminarian to explore his sexuality and become a mature, self-aware adult, especially if he entered the seminary as a sexually inexperienced teenager; as is the case with so many priests.

Committing to a life of celibacy as a teenager, with celibacy presented as an ideal and compulsory for the priesthood, can lead to loneliness, isolation, confusion, failure, anger, guilt and shame.

Living in an all-male community with teenagers, young men and priests, is not the optimum environment for normal human sexual development and maturation.

Committing to celibacy, the seminarian is not meant to take sexual initiatives with others. But the normal inner dynamism of the human spirit is to find a sexual partner and soulmate. This normal human need is stymied by celibacy.

It is all the more senseless as it is based on what the Church admits is a man-made law.

Celibacy hangs over you as a barrier to human intercourse, let alone sexual intercourse; hindering personal growth and inhibiting relationships. Priests used to be seen

250

as asexual, lacking sexual feelings, desires and not attracted to anyone.

The widespread, misplaced perception of priestly asexuality accounts for some of the shock to the Catholic psyche occasioned by public scandals when it became known that clergy fathered children in secret, had homosexual relationships, or sexually abused children.

If you're going to tell a lie, tell a big lie; and lies don't come much bigger than priestly celibacy. Priests are as sexual as anybody else. They can be as sexually confused, as sexually frustrated, as sexually potent, as sexually active, as sexually deviant, as sexually faithful or unfaithful as anybody else.

Priests have sexual fantasies just like any other human being. They become aroused, have nocturnal emissions, masturbate, enjoy sexual liaisons, have crushes, fall in love or in lust, like anyone else. Their subconscious can run riot with graphic sexual dreams when they sleep, just like anyone else.

It is little wonder that celibacy motivated by man-made mythologies of religious nonsense so often ends in tears.

In my seventh counselling session with Ms D on 16 March 1989, we explored sex.

'My most recent fantasy is of sex with you, here, standing up.'

'Who initiates it?' she asked.

'You do,' I said.

Another fantasy involved sex with her on the floor of my bedroom in CUS. She said I sought to legitimise my fantasies, by which I think she meant I didn't need to justify them. Better simply to accept them.

I must have asked her something about the significance of fantasies. She replied: 'There are a thousand ways of interpreting fantasy. It is what comes to your mind that matters. Your interpretation is the right thing for you.'

I told Ms D of my experience with Samantha more than three years earlier, in December 1985, a couple of weeks after I had decided to leave the Marists. Samantha had invited me over and I had hoped I might finally lose my virginity.

While I got naked with her and we slept together, she wouldn't let me make love to her. That night of frustration gave way in the morning to kissing and cuddling.

Ms D said I failed to take the initiative with her, leaving Samantha to invite me to her bed and for her to take responsibility for how far we would go. I didn't agree. I didn't want to presume that we would sleep together and I was willing to take responsibility for going all the way.

Ms D challenged me on why I had chosen to sleep with Samantha, when I preferred Verena. I hadn't taken the initiative with Verena, beyond an occasional kiss, hug or holding her hand.

I had lacked self-confidence. I told Ms D about my visit to the pub the previous Friday, 10 March. How, on my way there, I had felt frightened at the prospect of living without my Marist identity and just being me. Then, in the pub, chatting to three girls and one of them, to whom I was attracted, giving me her number and how I had left the pub feeling, 'I can make it. I'll do okay.'

By chance, on my way from counselling, I met a former Marist, who had been in my novitiate. We chatted over coffee, after which I journaled: *He may well surmise I'm on the way out. I left him thinking to myself, Yes, I'm leaving.*

Later I read the Irish Province Marist Newsletter, published that day. I journaled: *'I felt sad reading it, like as if I've already left.'*

During mass on Sunday 19 March, *'I didn't have a burning desire to be a priest – or, indeed, even to be at mass at all. I would have been happy not to go.'*

At my next counselling session, I confronted my deepest fears.

#### #87

'What a mess I'm in,' I said to Ms D at the start of my eighth counselling session on 20 March 1989. I laughed.

'So, you laugh,' she observed, as before.

'I have reinterpreted my November 1987 depression not so much as a wish to get out of Milltown but to get out of the Marists,' I said.

'And now, is that your interpretation?'

'I don't know!' I cried, despondent by the loop in my brain.

I journaled: *'I spoke of my fears, which coincided with my fear of leaving religious life, equated, perhaps, with my reasons for staying. I see myself more as a "psychological entity" than a person. My fear of leaving, my fear of myself, is that I am psychologically unstable, that I would be difficult for a woman to love or live with, that I could actually harm children born to my wife, that I could warp them as much as I am warped.'*

That negative self-image explains why, in 1985, when Verena, the girl I was fond of at UCD, had asked me 'Are you happy?' I replied that the priesthood was 'the best place for me'.

253

I felt close to despair. Only three or four months earlier, *'I would have been ordained deacon and wanted to be but was stopped by external factors beyond my control. Now, it seems likely that I may leave the Marists and the idea of priesthood forever.'*

My journal continues: *'I spoke to Ms D of my hopes for religious life caving in – that was when I cried. And I spoke of my new recognition of my need for a sexual relationship and my need for affectivity – not the superficial relationships in religious life.'*

I left the counselling session again feeling I would be leaving the Marists.

When I told my pal Tom the catalogue of fears I had expressed to my counsellor, about psychological instability, being unliveable with, unlovable, harmful to kids, warped and warping…he laughed.

'That's not the man I know!' said Tom. 'You've kept me sane at times!'

It was a welcome perspective from my best friend.

*

Next day, my spiritual director asked: 'What's your most treasured possession?'

'My profession cross was,' I replied.

'Was?' she reflected back.

My eyes filled, realising I had used the past tense.

I journaled: *'My assumption through years of spiritual direction, trials, doubts and questioning was that the right thing was to stay. I was to deny my likes, wants, needs, preferences.'*

I told her I felt guilty at the prospect of leaving: 'It feels like I'm doing the dirty on confrères, relatives, – even on the kids I do pastoral work with in Inchicore. Like I'm betraying them.'

'Nobody who cares for you would want you to be unhappy,' she responded.

254

I appreciated her fresh approach and detachment. Not a Marist, she had nothing to gain by me staying in the Society of Mary.

As a writer, I was not able to express myself uncensored as a Marist. My creativity and dynamism were stunted and rejected. Or I would have had to write under a pseudonym, as when my romantic 'fiction' piece was broadcast on RTE radio. I would have had to toe the party line or be silenced like so many priests and theologians.

I felt cheated and betrayed by the Marists. Anything I had ever wanted, except for my eventual move out of Milltown, had been denied. One of the reasons I had joined them was the variety of apostolates they did but, in reality, there was only one facing me: teaching, which I had never wanted to do.

I met the Superior on 22 March. He told me that the date for ordination to the diaconate was 20 May, less than two months away and earlier than the expected month of June. We discussed the possibility of postponing it until that December but I told him I would keep the May date *'as it focused the issue for me'*.

I journaled: *'I am still officially going ahead with diaconate this May.'* However, I added: *'I am unsure if it is the way for me to be happy, to be me',* showing a new healthier focus on my happiness and on my personal identity.

*'It is inconceivable that I could go ahead with diaconate at this time in light of my doubts and questions,'* I journaled. *'There is no rush.'* Moreover, I expected still to be doing counselling in May. Also, diaconate would be immediately before my final exams in theology. I concluded: *'I will definitely postpone diaconate.'*

But I needed space and I did not want the Superior getting involved in my decision making again, as he had done so often before, so I chose not to tell him.

## #88

Having decided to postpone my ordination to the diaconate, I went later that day to Howth with Father Denis Green and two other confrères. I was good company and there were many laughs. It was the best I had enjoyed myself for ages.

I felt free. I told jokes and bantered spontaneously, without self-censorship. The 'right' thing to do was to be me. I wanted to express my desires. I wanted an intimate relationship. And I realised that I didn't 'owe it' to anyone to be ordained.

I told Denis of my decision. He told me I should tell the Superior. I told him I wasn't ready yet.

'You should ring him tomorrow to tell him,' he said.

So, on Holy Thursday, 23 March 1989, I rang the Superior and told him. Later, I had a lovely night with my pal Tom, my sister and other friends, and told them all.

At dawn on Good Friday morning, I journaled: *'Right now, I cannot see myself staying in the Marists.'* Trying to pray, I reckoned I was just thinking and daydreaming. Depression resurfaced. I journaled: *'Somehow I'm protected from life in the Marists. I watch as a passive observer of people's struggles. Aloof. Secure. Superior.'*

In the community room, I observed older priests watching a television soap, dramatising the concerns of ordinary people – jobs, money, relationships. Those things were now more real for me but I reckoned the priests didn't get it. Insulated and institutionalised, the older ones couldn't survive outside religious life. I didn't find their lives inspiring. They had opted out of life.

Half in, half out of religious life, I journaled: *'I feel like I'm in Limbo.'*

On Holy Saturday night in CUS, I was *'delighted with my singing of the Exultet'*. Vested in an alb, I distributed communion to my mother and sister. I journaled: *'Wanted to. I thought: I've got to do this once anyway.'*

I liked my leadership role in the Christian community. I journaled: *'Am good at it. Will, or would, contribute much, by being me, as a priest.'*

I drove a confrère to Howth before dawn on Easter Sunday where some 200 people gathered for an interdenominational service on the clifftop. After a steak breakfast in Jury's Coffee Dock, I slept for four hours and awoke attracted to the security of religious life. I could 'hear' a CUS priest and my Uncle Jack thinking it 'madness' to leave.

On Easter Monday evening, I had a walk and a drink with my sister. She was getting ready to leave home to move to France. I journaled: *'Good to be with her and talk candidly to one another about ourselves and the Ma. I'm going to miss her when she goes to France.'*

My mother asked me next day if there was any chance of me taking a sabbatical. I went silent and did not reply. I journaled: *'I felt as if she was reading my mind. I haven't told her yet I've postponed diaconate.'*

Five days after telling the Superior of my decision, I went to the cinema to see Rain Man, *'with'*, I journaled, *'wait for it ... John Hannan. Spoke about my mother, my counselling, and postponing diaconate.'*

My former Superior and Novice Master, I imagine Father Hannan had been asked to meet me to figure out what was going on in my head – we had never gone to a movie together before.

That night, I told a good friend and confrère about counselling. I journaled: *'Marvellous chat: open, vulnerable, trusting, friendly. I took the initiative and gave him a big hug and a kiss on the cheek on parting. I was happy. He was happy.*

*'Is it just that I've never had the courage to leave? If I leave, and if I leave Ireland, it will be hard leaving many friends in Dublin.'*

I spent a few days in Curracloe with confrères. During a long walk together along the beach, I told another confrère, as I later journaled, about *'the Ma, counselling, postponing diaconate, possibilities of leaving, and my disillusionment with my life in the Marists.*

*'I wanted to hold his hand coming back from the pub – the human comfort of it. But it's so awkward and so easily misinterpreted. In the pub, a girl noticed me. I noticed her. Wouldn't mind. Would've been willing. But inhibited by local pub. Everybody watching us as strangers. She'd a pretty face and nice sexy legs.'*

Back in CUS, in the early hours of 3 April, I could not sleep. The tank above my bed was *'driving me bananas'.* I had twenty-one theses to study before my Bachelor of Divinity final exams in about eight weeks. I wrote that night to my friend and confrère Tony, and also to my Uncle Jack, telling them both I had deferred diaconate. But I still hadn't told my mother.

## #89

Counselling had heightened my awareness of sexual urges, wishes and fantasies. Brought up to think of Jesus as asexual, if, as the Church teaches, he was truly human, then he was sexual too.

I reread my final profession ceremony and final vows, and I perused a leaflet on crises as opportunities for growth. Having read both, I sensed I might remain a Marist.

I visited my friend and 'adopted mother' Marie Toomey on 4 April 1989.

She said: 'I'm not sure if you want to be a priest – you must be sure.'

I was astounded she got my two keywords – 'want' and 'sure' – together in one sentence.

'Take all the time it takes to be sure,' she continued. 'I love you whatever you do. It's not wasted time.'

I felt tortured by my incessant questioning and remembered Dr Jim Healy saying to me that I tended to see all 360 degrees of an angle at once.

Now, all my old questions – Am I called? Do I have a vocation? Is it right for me to become a priest? – had changed to: 'Do I want to be a priest?'

Unable to sleep in the early hours of 5 April, I wondered in my journal about *writing for The Irish Times a piece on why the IRA campaign does not satisfy the requirements of a Just War.*

I had other ideas for articles too but I journaled: *Being a religious, I am less free to speak my mind, to criticise bishops, to take political positions. I would be interested in journalism. In writing a play, autobiography, perhaps a novel.*

Still sleepless, I journaled: *'Reading Pope Pius IX's shite about Mary being on the steps of the throne of God and crushing Satan's head, I was reawakened to my thoughts about leaving the Catholic Church. Imagine, living as a journalist in Belfast, free to go to the Shankill without feeling a target for being a Catholic. Imagine: being able to speak my mind to Catholics, to Protestants. I have to continue now to think for myself. To perceive, to come to an understanding and judgements and be sure of where I stand, taking authority for who I am.'*

I reread the leaflet on crises as opportunities, this time from the perspective of leaving.

On 5 April, I turned towards Leeson Street from Upper Pembroke Street and, as I walked along the pavement, I saw two smug young priests perambulate towards me, dressed from head to toe in clerical gear. Walking in the opposite direction, I passed them by, hearing their self-satisfied voices and heels clicking behind me. I journaled: *'I felt I'd already left; that I had gone through all that and come out the other end.'*

Disillusionment is a good thing – outgrowing an illusion. It was better to cast off the delusion of God, the priesthood and my ideal self, and accept reality as it is; and me as I am.

I had my ninth counselling session with Ms D on 6 April. She told me to stop complaining. 'You can do that elsewhere. What do you want? Get in touch with your feelings, wants, desires. Feel them. Explore those in counselling.'

We spoke of a girl I was fond of.

'I might end up marrying her,' I said. 'Or I might end up as a Marist.'

'End up!' she snapped at me. 'You don't "end up" doing anything. You choose!'

I told her of my decision to postpone diaconate, and that I had told the Provincial I had doubts about my vocation.

'He has doubts too,' she said.

I felt she had broken some rule here and wondered had she spoken to him. I presumed she meant he had doubts about my vocation. But I was learning to check out my understanding in conversations. In fact, she meant that she presumed he too had doubts about *his* vocation.

Then she played a game with me: 'I don't believe you have a vocation!'

Again, I felt she was breaking a rule. Wasn't this meant to be non-directive counselling?

Promptly, she propounded: 'I believe you have a vocation!'

And then: 'I don't believe you have a vocation!'

And again: 'I believe you have a vocation!'

Her point was clear, reinforcing her key message to me, then, as always, that I alone needed to decide for me; and to disregard other people's opinions.

On 8 April, the Provincial showed me a letter from a bishop turning down the request by the Marist Fathers to start a new apostolate in the North. He asked me to consider moving from CUS to Chanel College from that summer, as the age profile in Chanel was old and they could do with a young man. I would also be company for two other confrères my own age.

However, Chanel was very close to Donnycarney, where my mother lived, and I feared getting sucked back into her lifelong web of dominance, dysfunctionality and manipulation.

## #90

On the night of 8 April 1989, a confrère drove me back from Milltown to CUS. I filled him in on my postponement of diaconate and decisions I still needed to make.

Afterwards, alone in my room, I felt the pain of celibacy, of longing and self-denial. Denis Green had warned me that, given my personal warmth, I would find my need for affectivity as difficult as sexual abstinence.

Now I felt both needs in equal measure. I journaled: *'Last night I went to bed thinking I would stay a Marist. Tonight, I think not.'*

'I'm in bits,' I said to a good friend and confrère the next day.

'Don't leave,' he replied.

I think I may have asked for my tenth counselling session with Ms D to be brought forward, as I met her on 10 April, just four days after our previous meeting.

I journaled: *'I felt "crowded" by so many decisions. I decided, during the session, to ask the Provincial to let me continue to live in CUS next year.'* Chanel College was too *'close to mother'.* There was *'enough hassle and unsettlement in my life'* without having to move house and community. *'I like CUS; having just settled down.'* I wasn't even a year there yet.

Moreover, I was peeved that the Superior of Milltown said CUS was unsatisfactory because of my *'unaccountability'* in *'informing people where I am'.*

In my mid-twenties, in Milltown, my natural and healthy drive for adult autonomy had reacted against the formation staff's insistence that all students submit a timetable accounting for how they spent every moment of every day.

It was one of the triggers that forced me to fight to get out of Milltown.

Now, aged almost 27, it seemed to me that the Superior wanted me again to account for wherever I might choose to go. I felt it was a gratuitous and overbearing control on my human right to liberty. If this was 'obedience', I found nothing godly or freeing about it. On the contrary, it felt oppressive and suffocating.

Deciding to ask the Provincial if I could remain at CUS involved me taking the risk of making a decision, sticking my neck out, and living with the consequences of the decision. That is what is involved in adult decision making. But the vow of obedience skews rational thinking, or at least it did for me.

In my religious thinking, I feared God might 'punish' me for acting on the basis of my desire to remain at CUS and for proposing to the Provincial my reasons for avoiding Chanel College.

'Or you might have to accept responsibility for your decisions and you can't blame anyone else,' Ms D suggested.

'It won't be my decision,' I countered. 'The Provincial will decide.'

'But expressing your views could prove decisive,' she responded.

We also discussed my sexual yearning. She asked why I wouldn't invite someone I was fond of to my room.

Shocked by her question, I replied: 'I wouldn't want to be kicked out of the Marists and it would not be true to my vows.'

'Again, the issue of reputation,' she suggested, 'how others might see it.'

Surprised by her words, I responded: 'I am more aware of my desires and wants. But is this incompatible with religious life?'

'You remain a man. And you won't always get what you want,' she said. 'Get in touch with your desires and wants as the man you are. It is at the level of your actions that you must accept the consequences for what you do.'

Later that afternoon, I visited the Superior and told him of my decision to ask the Provincial to keep me in CUS.

'Given your reasons,' he replied, 'it doesn't leave the Provincial free.'

In that moment the destructive dynamic of my time loop with the Superior was re-enacted: I decided, he undermined, repeated.

He reiterated that CUS was undesirable given the way its community was set up, that I was non-accountable, too free, and had too few controls and checks.

I also discussed with the Superior the possibility of my attending an orthodontist. I wanted to get a job during the summer to pay for it. But he said that if I did that the Marists would still be paying, since everything I earned belonged to them.

That evening, I journaled: *'I feel unsure about my decision this morning to ask the Provincial to let me stay in CUS. I wonder if the Superior's approach to me is bad for me. Rather than affirming my decisions, he undermines the stances I take and makes me feel unsure, and to withdraw the stance I take – like my choice to leave three years ago?'*

Back then, it needed that question mark. Hindsight is 20/20 vision.

## #91

Unsure of everything, I had spiritual direction on 11 April 1989.

Having spoken to the Superior, I was unsure of my decision, made during counselling the previous day, to ask the Provincial not to transfer me to Chanel College.

I was not praying; having come to the belief that I was just talking to myself in prayer.

As for celibacy, to quote fellow procrastinator Hamlet, it was more honoured in the breach than in the observance. Indeed, the Church's puritanical prohibition on masturbation is more honourably ignored than followed. But I just felt guilty.

Unsure, not praying, masturbating. 'Not a pretty picture,' I said to my spiritual director, and I cried.

She urged me to pray before the icon of Jesus in my room. She reminded me that I had made decisions – to enter the Marists, to apply for final profession and diaconate, and to postpone diaconate.

In my distress, she offered solace: 'You were accepted into the Marists, and for final profession and for diaconate – that says something.'

*

Later that day, I visited home. Hardly in the door, my mother tried to manipulate me. In front of a cousin, making it more difficult for me to say no, she asked me to borrow a Marist community car to drive her to Wicklow for a day, so she could socialise with relatives.

It was unreasonable. I couldn't justify taking a community car for a day for that reason. I journaled: *'She went up and down to Wicklow innumerable times by bus. She presumed that I could take a community car for her personal visit to Wicklow.'* Appalled at the prospect of *'my utter boredom'* on such a visit, I was exasperated by her pretence to my cousin *'that we get on well, whereas I despise the air she breathes'.* Finally, I was afraid it would *'set a precedent in light of my possible move to Chanel'.*

Back in CUS that night, I journaled: *'I feel like a lump of raw meat. I sat before the icon of Jesus, not knowing my future, unsure of decisions – those just made and those that must surely come.'*

I journaled an important insight: *'The feeling of being unsure was mine.'*

While studying philosophy, I liked the ideas of René Descartes, who said: *'If you would be a real seeker after truth, it is necessary that at least once in your life you doubt, as far as possible, all things.'*

He also said: *'Dubito, ergo cogito, ergo sum'* – I doubt, therefore I think, therefore I am.

And he said: *'Doubt is the origin of wisdom.'*

Cartesian doubt had arisen in my third counselling session with Ms D on 16 February. She had told me to discard the web of other people's opinions and judgements. My work was to get in touch with my personal wants, desires, perceptions and judgements.

Now, I was aware, at my core, of an authentic feeling of unsureness, of doubt, about everything. It was deeper than an intellectual doubt, deeper still than a feeling, mood or even attitude. It was at the baseline of my gut, an absolute certainty of feeling unsure about everything that I had ever thought was true, anything I had ever identified with, any value I had held, the whole panoply of faith and any worldview I had ever lived by or believed in.

This was an authentic, self-originating feeling from my gut. I could be sure of it. It was me.

On 12 April, I felt indifferent about a move to Chanel. I journaled: *'Right now, I don't mind. I dread the thought of living so close to my mother and her dragnet of misery.'* I would need to *'learn to say "no" to her. Indeed, I will have to.'* Moving house would be unsettling but, *'I'm young and not too entrenched in CUS'*. I would miss the city centre location, my big room and the freedom of CUS.

After an attempt at prayer, I journaled: *'I feel like a wet slop-wipe sponge, flung onto a damp sink.'*

My two images – a lump of raw meat and a wet sponge – lacked *'an autonomous centre'*. They were *'of use to humans'*, but dependent upon other people's choices *'to eat, throw out, wipe, squeeze or use'*.

Gut feelings continued to surface. I had my eleventh counselling session with Ms D on 13 April. I cried after saying, first inaudibly and then with full voice: 'I feel bad.'

'Why did you talk to the Superior about Chanel?' she asked. 'For 27 years you have checked out your decisions with others. You did that three years ago and again in the last three days. Isn't it time you tried something new?'

I said: 'But leaving the Marists is a major decision with lifelong consequences!'

She retorted: 'Staying in the Marists is a major decision with lifelong consequences!'

### #92

On 14 April 1989, I told the Provincial that I was willing to move to Chanel College.

267

I told him I could see the point of a younger Marist being sent there given the older age profile of Chanel. I disclosed just one reservation – living so close to my mother – telling him of the incident just three days earlier when she had tried to manipulate me to book out a Marist community car so she could socialise in Wicklow.

I acknowledged that if I didn't go to Chanel, she was indirectly determining where I could be sent within the Marists. I recognised the 'right' thing may be to go to Chanel and I concluded that I wanted him to feel free to send me there.

He thanked me for saying so, observing that, ironically, it left him freer to keep me in CUS. He knew there were cases where the norm of the dutiful son was not the correct solution. He would decide and tell me soon.

Two days later I journaled: *'I will be in Chanel next year,'* the Provincial having wasted no time in deciding. *'I think there is a greater chance of me remaining a Marist by going to Chanel. I think if I stayed in CUS I might leave.'*

In CUS that Sunday, I journaled: *'I was utterly and totally bored by the confirmations today. I kept reacting to what the bishop said,'* such as being obedient to parents. He's no psychologist, I thought, imagining a boy feeling guilty, if his mother was anything like mine.

Later, I bumped into a former seminarian from another congregation who had studied with me at Milltown Park. I journaled: *'Felt I would be leaving in talking to him. He reckoned I was "betwixt and between". I said Yes, I thought I was.'*

He told me he only got £200 from his congregation to tide him over after seven and a half years as a member. It made stark the financial realities of leaving.

On 17 April, I surveyed my options. They ranged from leaving outright; taking leave of absence; postponing leaving indefinitely; postponing ordination indefinitely; remaining a non-ordained Marist; or being ordained a priest.

I was in foul form on 18 April. Having slept badly, I masturbated; and later felt cross with a hairdresser. I journaled: *'Half price me arse! £5 for a dry cut. And left hairs down my back, vest and shirt.'*

I was angry with the Superior for *'disregarding what I had said to him the previous Monday about Chanel'*. Clearly, I had not yet processed my most recent conversation with Ms D, when she had challenged me for checking out my decision with him.

Moreover, I had failed to appreciate the importance of my conversation with the Provincial four days earlier, in which I had personally given him *carte blanche* to send me to Chanel.

Aggrieved that the Superior had not yet told me if I would be allowed to get a paid job during the summer, I was also vexed with myself for not studying, despite my final Bachelor of Divinity exams being just weeks away.

I journaled: *'I'm tottering on the brink of...I hate myself. I'm bored with studies, disillusioned with life, religious life, Catholicism. I'm pissed off. Depressed. Fucked up. Angry. Pissed about. Shoved to Chanel despite what I said last Monday to the Superior.'*

But I was beginning to unpack what I was learning in counselling. I journaled: *'I shift my position from "I'm asking you not to send me there," to "I'm willing to go. It might be right. I've one reservation, about my mother. But feel free to send me there."'*

I concluded: *'I said the fucking "right" thing, suspended my judgement, as usual.'*

I tried to pray and my image was of a three-dimensional mask, almost completely torn down the middle, from head down.

Things picked up later that night. I loved being with my sister for a meal and I was joined later by my pal Tom, and my school friend and confrère John.

I journaled: *'I got pissed. But I was happy to be with these three important people in my life.'* I admired and envied my sister that she had made her decision to leave her job and she would soon be moving to France.

*'I came back to CUS with Tom,'* I journaled. *'I was in a bad way. I cried walking home at one stage. I vomited in CUS – in the kitchen.'*

I marvelled watching my friend clean it up for me, grateful for our friendship.

Words had occurred to me earlier in solitude. I hadn't expressed them yet.

'Tom,' I said.

'What is it, old son?'

'Tom.'

'I'm listening, go on.'

'Tom,' I said, and out of the depths of me I uttered my authentic inner truth: *'I am most desperately unhappy.'*

#### #93

On 20 April 1989, I met Ms D for my twelfth counselling session. There was another gathering of the 'already-but-not-yet' scheduled for the following weekend – finally professed Marists and deacons who were not yet priests. From my gut, I did not want to go.

Ms D challenged me on changing my mind about asking not to be sent to Chanel College.

'Maybe the right thing was to stay in CUS,' she proposed. 'Your fear of having to accept the consequences of your decision makes it "safer" to go to Chanel.'

Later, the Superior rang me, informing me that I would be doing pastoral work in Inchicore that summer. I would not be permitted to do summer work to pay for an orthodontist. If I wanted to take it further, I was to see the Provincial.

'I said nothing to him about next weekend,' I journaled, and realised that I was shivering. 'It is cold; but not that cold!'

I remembered an idea from the philosopher B.J. Lonergan, that it is only at the level of decision that we emerge as persons.

I journaled: 'Might my complaining be a key to what I really want? I know I could be a priest.' But I wondered if my fear of the unknown kept me in the Marists.

I spent 21 April doing psychological tests and interviews for a pastoral course in All Hallows. I was honest in the tests, active in group work and my true self at the interviews. I journaled: 'I told the course director I was unsure about my Marist future. I was detached, relatively relaxed, as I wasn't burning with zeal to be accepted. I felt tired, unhappy and depressed after it all.'

Next day, after cycling to Roundwood, the Sally Gap and Glencree with a confrère, I faced my dilemma about the 'already-but-not-yet' weekend. I felt sick at the thought of not going, and whatever the consequences might be. I journaled: 'Is it possible to make decisions and remain in religious life?'

I skipped Sunday mass on 23 April. I didn't feel guilty. I reflected that, where I found joy in life, was in writing, like the buzz I got entering the Gay Byrne Show competition; and creating a story and watching it acted out by others on my All Hallows retreat the previous summer.

In a dream on 24 April, I was, *'a James Bond figure. I get into doors that have sentries. I escape from places that are thought foolproof. I've flown away before, but they'd prevented that one. Still, I get away. I dive back to where I'm meant to be. How do I do it? I have a mask made that fooled them.'*

I felt refreshed and exhilarated upon waking. I called the dream 'James Joseph Bond'. Its theme: I can do it. Its question: Why was I locked up? But I was anxious later that day, preoccupied by the coming weekend. I felt terror, fear, determination, anger and, as ever, uncertainty.

I had my thirteenth counselling session with Ms D on 27 April.

'Despite an upset stomach, sleeplessness and shivering at the thought of it,' I told her, 'I didn't consult anybody about my honest judgement and decision not to go on the weekend.'

'Why are you telling me?' she asked.

I told her my request to get a summer job had been turned down.

'You chose religious life,' she said. 'Nobody forced you to join, to take vows, to make final profession. So why complain? The way you handled the Chanel change was not mature. You spoke your mind to the Superior but said something very different to the Provincial. And then you feel angry about it. What happens when your honest judgement clashes with someone else's?'

On Friday 28 April, the Superior phoned me. He was returning earlier phone messages I had left him.

'It is my honest judgement that it would be better for me not to go on this weekend,' I said.

There was silence.

Then, he said: 'I respect your judgement. Obviously, you are free. Clearly, you were trying to contact me all day. Speak to the other guys about it.'

'For what purpose?' I asked.

'Just to let them know why one of our party won't be attending,' he said.

'Fine. Thanks,' I said. It felt good that he respected my judgement and left me free to decide and act accordingly.

As requested, I spoke to the two confrères in CUS who would be on the weekend. Both respected my decision. One said: 'You wouldn't find it helpful.' It wasn't a condemnation but an articulation of how it was.

I journaled: *Take a bow! At least for tonight, it is possible to be true to myself within religious life, and religious life does not, tonight, steamroll my true self.*

## #94

I went out with my sister for a drink on the night of Friday 28 April 1989, happy to have acted on my decision not to attend the weekend for senior Marist students. We met a friend of mine from UCD, a lovely, fine-looking fellow. He joined us upon my invitation. After drinks, we went to a nightclub. Linda, a friend of my sister's, said to me: 'Don't be a priest. That'd be a waste.'

Next day, I journaled: *'Was in fine form this day just ended.'* I studied and felt good about myself, appreciating that we become ourselves by acting on our decisions.

The following day, I skipped Sunday mass, my second time to do so. I went for a cycle instead and enjoyed it. After a luxurious hot bath, I went with my friends Tom and Brendan to a Maura O'Connell concert at the Olympia. She was magnificent; the audience singing along with gusto. Here was life being lived to the full, a vibrant, alternative universe to my preoccupation with religious concepts and sacrifice.

On 1 May, I absented myself from mass and Morning Prayer. I was depressed though and did little study. I rang home to talk to my sister but my mother answered. She spoke about 'a guy who pulled out just before diaconate', as if oblivious to my situation. My journal records my reaction as 'rage' but doesn't record if I let it show.

At spiritual direction on 2 May, I discussed avoiding mass, my critical view of papal teachings, and my rejection of Catholic dogmas like the 'immaculate conception' of Mary, a theological contrivance so that Jesus, supposedly divine, could be born of a woman 'unstained' by 'original sin'. I also had fundamental doubts about the sacramental and clerical systems of the Church.

She wondered if next time I might be closer to a decision.

I journaled: *'Opting for what's "safe" isn't working so well. I feel I'm turned inside out.'*

At first, the image spoke of my inner anguish and pain. But then I saw it as a powerful metaphor for my nascent self. Emerging from within, I was growing in personal integrity, becoming my authentic self, more comfortable in my skin.

Next day, 3 May, I had another liberating image – of walking through glass unscathed. A breakthrough and a breakout. I felt it physically through my body; releasing tension from the gut. My self-imposed religious restrictions fell away, yielding shard by shard. I stepped through, crossing the boundary of my self-confinement, discovering the glass was a mirage.

That sensation encapsulated my liberation, shattering the man-made boundaries of religion and of my mind. I was crossing a threshold, discarding a mask and a shell, stepping into personal freedom.

I went to the career's office in UCD and explored becoming a writer, journalism, editing and publishing. I couldn't sleep that night due to existential questions cascading through my mind.

All options remained open: doing the All Hallows course next year; choosing exclaustration – retaining my identity as a Marist, financial security should I need it, and the option of returning; doing the Higher Diploma in Education, so I would be trained to teach, as a security for me and not a waste of time should I stay in the Marists; looking for a job in publishing in Ireland or London; or temporary employment with an eye to journalism.

During counselling with Ms D – but from my journal it's not clear to me which session it was – it might have happened earlier or later in my process – she pushed me to decide the fundamental life choice that faced me.

'Do you believe you have a vocation?' she asked.

I could still read both interpretations of my life.

'I don't know,' I said.

275

'Get out of your head. What does your gut say?' she asked.

My gut? After all these years, was I to wager my life on my gut? Discarding other people's opinions, my faltering faith, my past nine years. And ignoring my previous decisions to stay and any theological argument. Decide, solely, on my gut!

She asked: 'In this moment, what does your gut say?'

The consequences for me couldn't have been starker – my vocation, identity, work, financial security, my past, present and unknown future; all to be determined by my gut! I became aware of my belly, and my vital organs, churning within.

'I don't know,' I cried in despair.

'I know it's hard. But try. What does your gut say?'

'I don't know…'

'Right now,' she persisted.

The clock ticked. And out of the silence, I answered.

'No,' I whispered, from my gut.

'To be clear, what are you saying?'

'In my gut, I don't believe.'

It was the moment that changed my life. My Berlin Wall between head and gut was breached.

#### #95

I met the Superior for a drink on 4 May 1989. I cried a lot. I was assertive and honest.

'As I see things,' he said, 'you are going to leave, without the Marists being involved in your decision.'

'It's my life,' I said. 'Only I can decide!'

276

'Yes, but your decision is of moment to the Marists. It seems to me you're just going to go off and decide alone for yourself.'

I thought: Isn't that the whole point? I needed to make my honest judgement and act on it. On previous occasions, due to my immaturity, I had allowed him and others to undermine my decision and I stayed.

He agreed it had to be my decision, even if it wasn't the 'right' one.

'My fear,' I replied, 'is that the decision will be taken out of my hands. A deep part of me doesn't believe I have a vocation. Obedience gets me off the hook of taking responsibility for my judgements. Celibacy stops me from exploring my sexuality and hides my lack of confidence in myself as a worthwhile, loving person, able to sustain a happy marriage.'

I told him, again, of my repugnance for teaching and reminded him he had said that I would probably spend the first five years of my priesthood teaching.

'You need to tread the path between sticking to your guns and surrendering yourself,' he said. 'I found it difficult when I was your spiritual director. You had this emotional shield and I didn't know how to interpret you nodding your head.'

My journal of five years earlier, on 6 May 1984, when he admitted he had misjudged and mishandled my aborted weekend to Kenmare, offers an interpretation. Gaining much needed distance from his counsel, I had journaled: *His platitudes were met with my telltale nodding head. He noticed and stopped.'*

Now, on 4 May 1989, he added: 'I was inspired by the experience of directing you. I was struck by your courage.'

And he referred to the moment on 13 November 1988, four weeks before the original date for my diaconate, when, alone in a car while he was gone, I had had a profound inner freedom, imagining a new direction, realising I could choose a different life. I was inwardly free to leave the Marists. When he returned to the car, I had said to him: 'I am open to postponing diaconate.'

'I'm struck by how free you are,' he had replied.

And now, on 4 May 1989, he told me that he too had felt free then and thought that being involved in my decision 'could be great'.

That night, in bed in CUS, my image was *'of having gone through a further pane of glass.'*

I asked myself: *'What's in my gut? Pastoral work in Inchicore this summer? No. Moving to Chanel? No. All Hallows? No. And NO to other people making decisions for my life. Rather, start taking my own gut as my truth.'*

But immediately I wondered: *'What of my gut before?'* My vocational crises, in Spring 1984 and in December 1985, had been resolved by my deeply felt choice to remain a Marist. And what of my choices for final profession and diaconate? Or my choice to enter the Society of Mary in the first place?

Set against those were my decisions to leave in December 1985 and to postpone diaconate on 22 March 1989.

On 6 May I went out for a drink with a confrère from CUS. I cried trying to say to him: 'The hardest thing is giving up my Marist identity, my Marist dream. I fear standing alone.'

He suggested the senior Marist student weekend I attended had been helpful as it helped me explore my motivation for diaconate.

Sunday 7 May was a significant day. I had a pint with my friends Tom and Brendan. I told them of my tears speaking with the Superior and with my confrère about giving up my Marist identity.

'That sounds pretty decisive,' said Tom.

We chatted up some girls. I was aroused by one, took the initiative, got her address and kissed her. It felt good.

I journaled: *'I didn't deceive her. No "sex" apart from a goodnight kiss. She's nice. And I still have vows. And to my list of withdrawals from religious life, I can add "initiative towards dating a girl".'*

I walked home alone thinking: *'My decision: to leave.'*

I journaled: *'My image of myself today was of a gigantic weight, bigger than could ever possibly be necessary for knocking down a whole building with one blow, hitting me! And has it broken the "emotional shield" around me, the game I've been playing for nearly nine years?*

*'I don't want other people making my decisions. Or My Decision. Was it yesterday I'd the image of myself buried in a grave with just my head and shoulders above the gravel and soil?'*

Then came a cry from my doubting heart: *'Help me, God of mercy and love. Mary, mother of Jesus and mine, pray for me.'*

## #96

After a visit home on 8 May 1989, I journaled that my mother was, *'as bitchy and off the wall as ever'*.

I had a drink and chat with my sister. *'She looked beautiful all day – never better. Her decision to quit her job and move to France has made her blossom into an attractive woman.'*

279

We shared memories and feelings, including sadness that mother would soon be selling the family home. She offered me financial support if I needed it.

I journaled: *'I shared where I am, hesitating to say anything, given I'd reversed my decision before. Yet, at present, I'm on the way out. I said I'll miss her and spoke of my blindness as a child to her and thanked goodness I'd at last woken up to the gift she is to me.'*

Before midnight, I journaled: *'Have I, or have I not, decided to leave?'*

I spent 9 May with my pal Tom, my sister and her friend at Glendalough. I journaled: *'Earlier in the day I thought: my tentative decision is to leave. Tonight, in the pub, I knew I have to leave. I belonged with these people – not quiet over a tea in CUS. I felt known and supported by her and Tom. I felt their presence with me in this hard time.'*

I studied *'the photo of me coming down the aisle after my final profession'* and saw *'the look of agony and "For Sale and Sold" on my face'.*

Perplexed, I wondered: *'What of my discernment last year which concluded in favour of diaconate?'*

On 10 May, I met a careers adviser at UCD. 'It's cut-throat competition out there for very, very few jobs,' he warned.

During my counselling session with Ms D on 11 May I told her of my decision to leave and my inhibition about putting my arm around a girl I fancied in the pub. Sticking to my brain, I told myself I still had vows.

She said: 'You are more than your brain now.'

At a party in Milltown Park, I told a fellow student I was 'thinking' of leaving and a fellow Marist of my 'tentative' decision to depart.

280

*'Felt dreadfully depressed most of the day,'* I journaled on 12 May.

I fought hard during the evening meal at CUS to become involved in the conversation. Later, I enjoyed playing snooker in the community room. I journaled: *'Priesthood could be alright. Maybe even Marist priesthood. Even Marist writer? Present thought: exclaustration for a year, and very possibly coming back.'*

I attended an excellent broadcasting seminar on 13 May, and wondered could I specialise in communications as a priest. I thought: *'Terror of unemployment, being poor, making a mistake – and what a mistake!'* And might exclaustration be dishonest, a *'licence to sin'?*

After mass on Pentecost Sunday, 14 May, I journaled: *'So much easier and tempting to write off my whole counselling experience and decision and plod along, be obedient.'*

Next day, I wrote: *'Get into journalism, writing as I am, a man who is a Marist. Although I've taken final profession, I've never really made the fundamental, basic option for Marist priesthood. I've always held off and conceived of an alternative future.'*

I met the Superior on 15 May.

'I've been fooling myself all these years, engaged in self-delusion,' I told him.

He replied: 'It's hardly all self-delusion. A year from now you may see things differently.'

He said that where I invested too much of myself – where I identified with a particular project – people didn't feel free to say no because to reject my idea was to reject me. 'And, if it's rejected, you're flattened,' he said.

But I had to carve out a new ministry for myself given my consistent revulsion at the prospect of teaching, especially as the Marists seemed hell-bent on making me a teacher.

He said I had three options: to stay, to leave, or to decide not to decide.

'Or exclaustration,' I added.

He said I could give retreats for a year. I thought that was crazy given my profound doubts about the faith.

I cried next day talking to Paul and Marie, my 'adopted' parents.

'Teaching is a major obstacle for me,' I said. 'And obedience. I resent people making decisions for me.'

Paul told me he believed in my vocation. He suggested I write to the Provincial about teaching.

Marie suggested: 'Leave things aside until after your exams. Put it in God's hands.'

I met my pal Tom on 16 May. He told me I was wearing a smile but that my eyes revealed a different me.

He said: 'You're like a man who got right up to a precipice and had decided to jump and you're tottering against the thought of it. Maybe Marist priesthood is what you want.'

### #97

My sister left home to live in Paris on 17 May 1989. I was horrified that my mother had bought her the same card as I had, and had written 'verse' on it, just like me.

I was encouraged by my sister's decision to quit her job, leave home and move to France. But I knew I needed to find the courage within myself for the personal decision that faced me.

282

At counselling with Ms D on 18 May, we explored my sexual inhibition with Carrie (not her real name).

'I'm still a Marist,' I said, 'she's my sister's friend, and she intends emigrating.'

'Lame ducks!' retorted Ms D.

I had proposed to meet Carrie on a Thursday. She said Thursdays were out for her. And I had left it at that, feeling rejected. I felt hopeless.

On Friday 19 May, I journaled: *I wanted to be a priest too much. I am not happy. I don't want to give my life to teaching. My motivations were largely unexplored. I needed, rather than chose, the priesthood. It was an urgent need to be a priest – because I felt so inadequate as a man.*

Other reasons I listed for leaving included: the *superficiality of community life*; feeling unnourished by a poor *community prayer life*; and *different ecclesiologies and Christologies* – different ways of understanding the Church and Jesus – held by priests trained before and after the Second Vatican Council.

My *desire for a sexual relationship and for greater intimacy*; my wanting *sons and daughters*; and an inner invitation to take a risk *to stop hiding behind the props of religious life*. These included other people *making decisions for me*, *financial security*, and my *Marist identity* which I saw as a *mask for my maleness* and a *barrier and protection* from facing my lack of confidence in myself to sustain a happy marriage.

I needed to *face, rather than protect myself from, reality* and train myself for a career, earn my own living, and enjoy an intimate relationship.

I saw masturbation as a sign of my loneliness and that I didn't really want religious life; and of my anger with myself for having chosen it. I saw it as *deceit and flight from self*.

283

I regarded my repugnance for teaching as symbolic *'of my not wanting to be a Marist'.* I lacked a sense of belonging within the congregation. As for the vow of poverty, I felt I wasn't living it nor did I want to.

My *'disbelief and agnosticism'* was important and I saw the priesthood as an escape from *'facing my fears'*, including exploring my sexuality, choosing a career I wanted and being willing to stand alone.

I had a *'deep suspicion of self-delusion vis-à-vis my being a Marist'.* I saw applying for diaconate as *'self-deception'* and an *'escape from the necessity of having to make my own decisions and take responsibility for my life.'*

My reasons for staying in the Marists were fewer, less convincing, insufficient and dubious. They included: *'the familiar; financial security; status; decision-making processes within Marists; loyalty; final vows; my consistent choice over nine years; being trained for priesthood and religious life; and Marists are people I know and who know me.'*

Within religious life, I was less likely to mature sexually and I wondered if there might be clandestine *'liaisons'.* Staying seemed the *'safer'* and *'easier'* option in the short term *'but long term (i.e., life!) at what cost?'*

After a 75-mile cycle on Saturday 20 May, I felt good. *'Also,'* I journaled, *'meeting, and not lame ducking, Carrie. Excellent. I'm leaving.'*

I went to the musical Evita with my pal Tom that night. It was brilliant. I journaled: *'I felt well. Felt happy. Hopeful. Confident. Tomorrow, Sunday 21 May, I would have been ordained deacon had I not decided to postpone it. Tonight, I feel good.'*

At 11pm that Sunday, I journaled: *'I cried on my own in my room tonight. I was looking at my sister's painting – feeling black.'* The painting was of a small boat on turbulent waves, a dark vista with angry colours and a threatening sky. Its mood was attuned to mine.

'And I felt sad, lonely, depressed, angry. I saw the boat and remembered dreams I've had about a terminal and a boat. And the boat docking and it was: Get off now or never. If I didn't get back on, the boat went without me. I felt trapped. And later, again, I cried. I was very keyed up when I went down for tea at 9.30pm.

'Today, I would have been ordained deacon had I not postponed it. During the ceremony, I felt glad that I was not going ahead, at least today, with it. Tonight, I prayed: Help me to leave.'

In large handwriting, I journaled: 'Complete the analysis of my situation. Make my final decision. Don't postpone it.'

## #98

On 22 May 1989, I was relieved when I learned that I had not been offered a place on the All Hallows pastoral course.

'So, I'm free,' I journaled. 'After my BA, I didn't want to go straight into theology. After first-year theology, I wanted a break in my studies. Now, for the first time, there isn't a "stalling" time-filler. Now, the challenge is to complete my analysis. In the shower just now, I cried – having, at last, to face my fear of the unknown in leaving the Marists.'

My mind was filled with multiple possibilities, including staying in the Marists and studying journalism. But I crossed that out, presuming that it would be dismissed by the Province as had my dreams of getting into counselling or working for reconciliation in the North.

That afternoon, after some study, I slept heavily, 'I think from psychic and emotional exhaustion'. Paul Toomey rang me to say that if I left, I would be welcome to stay with them.

He said it was a family decision. I cried while on the phone, *'quite a lot, and even more once I'd escaped to my room. At table in CUS, I thought: I don't belong here.'*

The Superior took me to Wilde's *An Ideal Husband* that night. We didn't talk about All Hallows or exclaustration or leaving or options within the Society of Mary. Next morning, he rang, *'to explain that I was satisfactory in every area of the All Hallows interviews except for the psychological test. It seems that my turmoil was evident and that they felt the group functions element of the course would, at this time, be too much for me.'*

He suggested I have a chat with the psychologist who assessed my psychological state and capacity for the course. *'I'll do that,'* I journaled.

On Wednesday 24 May, I journaled: *'My written B.D. is next Wednesday! I got quite a shock when I saw the notice. Six days' maximum study! A Bachelor degree in six days. That's tempting to any gambler. And a challenge. I'll leave aside everything vocational, existential, dramatic and angst-ridden until after 10 June!'*

At my seventeenth counselling session with Ms D on 25 May, I cried relating the story of looking at my sister's painting of the overcast sea. I wondered where Jesus fitted in. I journaled: *'Were tears the recognition of self-delusion or the question of faith? I don't know, perhaps a bit of both. If I am asked to go into teaching, I WILL LEAVE. Eureka! I might have wavered a bit – but I'm sure of that.'*

I told Ms D that the Superior had not accepted my writing off my nine years in the Marists as self-delusion.

'How do you see it?' she asked.

'I do see it as self-delusion,' I said.

'Why not go now?' she asked.

'God – whatever that means – is not involved in the decision. It's a decision at variance with my consistent

286

pattern over nine years. I have final vows – that's a reason for caution. I so recently wanted the diaconate. Am I acting out of anger at God or at myself?'

'Why are you angry with yourself?'

'The fact that I am a Marist? I want to complete my analysis before acting.'

'Will you ever be finished or sure?' she asked. 'Won't you always find another thing to do in the short term? An excuse for not deciding.'

'I wanted to be a priest.'

'Why?'

'For others – to offer meaning and hope, to address the real needs of others.'

'And for you?'

'I want to know where God fits in.'

'And where do you fit in?'

'I fit in if it's a project I believe in. I don't want to be poor – ironically, a reason for staying in the Society of Mary! I don't want celibacy. I don't want obedience. I don't want teaching.'

I journaled: *I was extremely tense when I arrived but felt content when I left.*

I told her I would like some more sessions: 'Here, I am learning to come in touch with who I am.'

She said: 'A crutch? Time does run out.'

I journaled: *I can still conceive of both possibilities.*

On 27 May, I journaled: *So, what do I want? To write. To live in a caring community whose mission I believe in. To have a wife, a sexual relationship, to father children. To watch my wife become "round-bellied at the womb" with my child. To hold my child.*

# IN MY GUT, I DON'T BELIEVE

*'For Marists, a valid question: what's in this for me? I have not found a way within the Marists to use my energies in the service of an ideal.'*

I awoke before 4 a.m. on 28 May and journaled: *'I cannot see how I can stay. Now is surely the time to go.'*

## #99

On 28 May 1989, I skipped Sunday mass again. Next day, I met the Superior.

'I hope you will stay,' he said. 'Would you consider doing a retreat?'

'No,' I replied, amused, liberated and confident in myself; retreats, delays and other peoples' opinions among the shards of glass strewn on the floor behind me.

'What about just taking the summer off – get a job or whatever.'

I had asked for that in April. It was too little too late.

'If I am asked to go into teaching, I will leave.'

'But what if you say that to other things?'

'I will be applying for exclaustration.'

'Why not wait until after the summer to apply for it?'

I called into a confrère's room and cried. I told him I'm fairly definitely heading for exclaustration. Back alone in my room at CUS, I wept again.

I wrote to my sister in Paris telling her my final theology written exams were *'this Wednesday (31st) and Friday (2nd)'*, with the final oral exam on Saturday 10th June. *'I cannot go through with ordination in the near future feeling as I do – in light of my guts having been dissected through counselling. Being turned inside out is a powerful image.*

288

*'I think I will apply for exclaustration. I would remain a Marist for at least a year but I would be free to make my own decisions, work and live where I please. And I would be free to return to the Society of Mary. Counselling is nearly finished – so am I!'*

I journaled: *'I need the space outside religious life to come to know myself better and to make a free decision.'*

Nearing midnight on 29 May, I journaled: *'A very significant day. The feeling, the decision, is coming from within – not as an imposition but a feeling of inexorable necessity, if I am to be true to myself and brave enough to face my fears.'*

Next day, I went for a cycle. I journaled: *'I didn't enjoy it – my vocational dilemma was with me all the way. Setting out, I felt excruciatingly perplexed. At Lough Dan, I thought: don't spend the summer with this decision. Decide!'*

I had my first written paper on 31 May and I was happy with it. On 1 June, the eve of my final written exam, I went to counselling.

'What were you saying "no" to in refusing to do a retreat?' Ms D asked me.

'My fear of spiritualising the clear direction emerging from within myself,' I replied. 'My interpretation of my meeting with the Superior is that it is more important to them that I am willing to teach than that I remain a Marist. I had a stark recognition of this.'

'Did you put that to the Superior?' she asked.

'No.'

'You can't pick and choose,' she said.

'If I take exclaustration, it would be difficult for me to return because of gossip and how cruel we are about one another.'

'Other people again,' she said, 'and what they think or say mattering. You know Aesop's tale of the father, the son and the donkey – fluctuating this way and that through gossip.'

She said it was good that I was beginning to speak directly of my needs.

'What do you think now?' she asked.

'That I should take exclaustration. It's the only way I can be true to myself. Nobody outside of myself is raising the question of my leaving. It's all coming from within me. I may come back to the Marists. Perhaps then I will have enough respect for myself to speak my needs, wishes and thoughts to superiors.'

I journaled: '*On my way over, I felt there was no need for me to have extra sessions with Ms D – that my decision is for exclaustration. Yet, when she asked me had I decided, I told her: parts of me yes, parts of me no.*'

I completed my last written exam on 2 June. It went well. Now, I had only the oral to do.

'*I'd a long cycle today,*' I journaled on 3 June, having cycled to Greystones, Wicklow, Aughavannagh, Donard, Blessington, and back to CUS, some 95 miles.

While cycling, '*I decided I must decide. Last summer was overshadowed with making a decision. I don't want to waste another summer. Plus, that decision, when I made it, didn't give me peace. And from then until now has been Hell.*

'*I could hardly respect myself if I do not seek exclaustration. I am not confident that my needs, wishes, ideas, suggestions have a hope of acceptance in the Society of Mary. A year or two out could be the making of me. Making a decision and acting on it will be formative and character building.*'

During my final spiritual direction, I was so sure I was doing the right thing that '*I felt like writing my letter of application for exclaustration there and then.*'

290

## #100

*I* *think I've decided for exclaustration, I said to myself, and it gradually dawned on me that the first couple of words were obsolete,'* I journaled on 7 June 1989. *'Down in the refectory just now, my eyes filled with the realisation that I've decided.'*

'You would have made a great priest,' a friend said when I told her.

Having told a confrère, he acknowledged the anguish involved and said: 'I admire a man who can make a decision.'

His accolade struck me in its irony and veracity. Exhausted and tense, on 8 June, I met the psychologist who had conducted the tests for All Hallows. He said that my personality was suited to the priesthood.

It was a week of endings: my final spiritual direction, completing my Bachelor of Divinity, deciding for exclaustration, and my final counselling session with Ms D.

I journaled: *'I'm drained. And I need to brace myself for the changes in my life. I thanked her.'*

'Who else must you thank?' she asked.

'The Marists, my friends, my confrères.'

'Anyone else?'

'I don't know.'

'Don't forget to thank yourself,' she said. 'You have done so much work. You have broken your pattern. You are consulting your feelings, your hunches, your opinions.'

She was right. Even if it wasn't the 'right' decision, it was mine. I journaled: *'The key to myself doesn't lie outside myself but within.'*

'I'll miss coming to you,' I told Ms D.

291

I went over to Paul and Marie's, confirmed I had made my decision and they showed me my room. I wrote my letter to the Superior General seeking exclaustration. On 9 June, I gave it to the Superior.

'I hope you will return,' he said. 'Something might yet happen on the Northern Ireland front, according to one of Denis's contacts up there. I regret it has come to this.'

Later, having met the Provincial, I journaled: *He didn't give me reason to believe that the Provincial Council will give its consent! He was startled that I should be thinking in terms of leaving CUS next week.*

Somewhat peeved, he asked: 'Is my function just to rubber stamp your decision?'

*I told him that I don't want to force their hand; that I would find it difficult to stay in CUS after having made my decision; that it isn't a new thing on my agenda; and that I need to get out there now seeking jobs.*

He asked me for a more detailed letter and suggested some specific phrases to include. I knew that if I wasn't granted exclaustration, I would have no option but to leave outright.

The affable Superior of CUS was shocked. He hadn't expected it given my nine years in the Marists.

'So, you won't be teaching,' he said. An avid supporter of priests in schools, he knew of my aversion to being sent teaching. He insisted I was entitled to my holiday money and told me I was welcome to stay in CUS for the summer.

On 9 June, I journaled: *I cried again tonight in my room.* I rang my sister and *'told her of my decision and that I must await the outcome of tomorrow's Provincial Council meeting. My oral exam is tomorrow morning too.'*

I journaled on 11 June: *'Eureka! I got a 2.1 in my B.D. Not bad! It shows my capacity to pull off a good mark at the heart of a personal crisis. That's a huge weight off my mind.'* I had added consistency to success in my three degrees – my academic redemption was complete.

*

Later, I was annoyed that the Provincial *'seems in some way to have stymied things on the exclaustration front'.* The Superior was not free to speak and could say only that the Provincial *'will be in touch with me next week'.*

If exclaustration was delayed for a few months, I wondered would I stay in CUS while waiting. What if it wasn't granted? I journaled: *'Would I request an indult of departure instead? Or would I, in conscience, be able to just walk away regardless – I suspect not.'*

On 12 June 1989, I met the Provincial. The Provincial Council had approved my request for two years' leave of absence.

He gave me £500, reassured me I remained a Marist, that I would be welcome back, and that I was thought highly of by the Province.

I met my mother for a meal in a Dublin restaurant. It was a good encounter. She had sold the family home or was about to do so. She was shocked when I told her exclaustration was for two years, possibly three.

I journaled: *'We spent time together – a sign of reconciliation and…love. Good meal; and we extended it later, partly due to rain, for a drink. I felt very good. I have made my decision.'*

293

# Postscript

Twenty of us entered the novitiate of the Marist Fathers in Dublin in 1980. All but three of us left, before or after ordination. I left the Society of Mary one year into my two years' leave of absence, ten years after I had entered the novitiate.

I taught English and religious education in London for five years, before becoming a professional writer, editor, podcaster and Humanist celebrant. I met Ruth, the love of my life, in 1992. We married in 1993, have a son and daughter, John and Sarah. We celebrated our twenty-seventh wedding anniversary in 2020.

I am grateful to the Marist Fathers for the time I spent as a member of the congregation. However difficult it was to leave, I have never regretted doing so, making the hardest and best decision of my life.

It would take another volume to show the second part of my transition from belief to unbelief – after I left the Marists. I had many more thresholds to pass through before I fully unpacked the significance of my personal realisation that, in my gut, I don't believe.

295

# IN MY GUT, I DON'T BELIEVE

# Interview with my brother Paul

'You never knew where you were going after school or where you'd be waking up,' my brother Paul told me of the period after his mother's death.

A solution had to be found. Just over a year after his mother's death, my father proposed to my mother. Six months later, on 3 September, 1959, they married.

'She told me I killed my mother,' Paul told me, when he himself was a grandfather. 'It was when we were still living in our old house, the house I loved, where my mother had lived, so I couldn't have been older than thirteen. I could have been a lot younger. I was sitting down at table. David was there. She was standing. I'll never forget it. She said it to me twice, once in that house and once when we moved house.

'All my friends lived near our old house. We had great neighbours there. It was where I remembered my mother.

But Pauline said to me: It'll make no difference to you anyway, moving house.'

Paul was forced to wear a trench coat to school. He was a laughing stock.

'Christ! How I hated that coat. The slagging I got over it. It was a big long black coat, down to my ankles. I needed a coat. The coat was in the wardrobe. It came from a Brother William. And I had to wear that going to school. You can imagine the abuse I got with that.

'And I was always wearing my father's boots. At school they called me Boots. They had steel toecaps. They were waterproof and rubber. And they had a fawn-grey toecap – I was like a clown going to school. Even kids from other schools were slagging me.

'I remember her being nasty just for the sake of it. I'd be heading down the stairs to play football. "Where are you going?" she'd ask. When I'd tell her, she'd say: "No you're not." For no reason.

'There was constant tension. If I did anything wrong, she'd tell my father and he'd whack me. Nobody ever whacked like my father. He had a leather belt and he would whack me across my arse. He would make me pull down my trousers. You'd have bruises on your arse for weeks. He would take me out to the passage beside the house and beat me.

'I was afraid of him. Like the Cat Stevens' song, as soon as I could talk, I was told to shut up. I only ever gave my father a hug when I was a child.

'My childhood isn't something I look back on fondly. I think my father married for stability. It was a bad deal. My father did it with the best of intentions. I felt sorry for my father, especially after Clare and you were born. She used to get into moods – bad, bad moods – giving out to people if you looked at her wrong. Always giving out about money.

'I think my father made a mistake not only in marrying her but making me call her Mammy,' reflected Paul, close to his sixtieth birthday. 'My own opinion is that Pauline should never have married at all. She wasn't suitable. She wasn't motherly. She never sat down to talk to you. If she did, it was to give out to you. My family life finished when my mother died.'

'I ran away a fair bit when I was still in primary school. I was eleven or twelve or maybe younger. I would do something wrong and I'd know I'd face a whacking from my father and, if there was some money, I'd take it and run. I just wasn't happy. I'd run away but I wasn't going to a better place. I often spent hours in the toilets in O'Connell Street, sitting there. At that age, I wasn't aware of the dangers of hiding out in public toilets. I wouldn't even have known what sex was. Luckily, I was left alone.

'I ran away for three weeks once, when I was sixteen. I stayed in a garage. A friend used to leave it open for me. Another fellow – he'd bring me in and give me a big feed. I hate myself for running away that time. My father wasn't long after his stroke,' concluded Paul.

That was when I was five and my mother looked out the kitchen window towards the sheds and back lane, her look cold, steely, devoid of compassion. It was the day when Paul was banished from the family and abject fear of my mother first seized hold of me.

# Selected poetry & reflections

*1*

## *Famine*

Famine. Famine. Can I imagine it?
Famine. Either a feast or a famine.
Feasts I know. But famine?

Work drying up, the closest I know.
Money tight. Or doing a fast, perhaps.
But famine. Famine!

Hunger. I've been peckish for a meal.
But everyday persistent aching hunger?
Hunger. Countrywide hunger.

# IN MY GUT, I DON'T BELIEVE

A nation on its knees.
Beggared. The shame of hunger.
Unasked for. Not chosen.
Crops fail. Shock. Fear.

Courage! We are strong.
Crops fail again. And again.
Soup kitchens. Food parcels.
No money for rent.
Disaster.

Bodies shrink. Tall emaciated figures
On Custom House Quay in Dublin:
Our ancestors.

Children dead. Relatives dead. Neighbours dead.
The boat to England, America, anywhere
Away from this godforsaken land
Of hunger and famine.
Famine. Can we imagine it?

Joe Armstrong © 2014

*I delivered my reflection 'Famine' immediately before Taoiseach Enda Kenny's speech at the National Famine Commemoration, Strokestown Park, Co. Roscommon, Sunday 11 May 2014; an annual ceremony, broadcast on RTE television, to commemorate the Great Irish Famine.*

Joe Armstrong

## *2*

# *We are leaves*

We are leaves,
Each of us, leaves.
By the time we realise it
It is already autumn
And comrades have fallen.

One by one
Or in clusters they fell
Leaves that have sheltered us from the wind
Leaves we have loved.

Some were swept from us in their prime
Before their time:
A mother giving birth
Without whose death I could not have been born –
I cannot fathom it.

A young sister on a May morn on her way to work
Lost life and beauty of an instant
Her falling helped us see what we wanted most
We returned home to Ireland to live here for good.

We are leaves,
Each of us, leaves.
Each fallen leaf has left a parting gift for us.

# IN MY GUT, I DON'T BELIEVE

We are leaves,
Each of us, leaves.
Some leave at a time and in a manner of their choosing:
A wonderful teacher, husband and father, taking his
life, whispers that
Nobody has it all together.

A woman, strong, unbending, takes the plane to
Switzerland
Disregarding my attempts to stop her.
She drew a line in the sand and died with dignity
Teaching me anew the need always to respect another's
choice.

We are leaves,
Each of us, leaves.
Each fallen leaf has left a parting gift for us.

A teenager's death opens a chasm and
An adopted son eases the parents' pain,
He, finding loving parents
That he had never known.

A lady's slaying by her sick
Husband teaches me the fragility
Of life and the hidden lives of
Ordinary people we know.

An ancient aunt dies and
Reminds us at her final gathering
That we are connected to a great
And vibrant branch of the living and the dead,

With our memories and our photographs
And our stories, and our cousins and our children
And our children's children and
Generations yet unborn.

We are leaves,
Each of us, leaves.
Each fallen leaf has left a parting gift for us.
Joe Armstrong © 2014

*Commissioned by the Humanist Association of Ireland (HAI) for its first annual commemoration ceremony in January 2015, We Are Leaves is not a depressing litany of the dead. Rather, it is an affirmation of the gift each departed person has given to us, the living. Our challenge is to recognise it and be grateful.*

*As well as the inaugural HAI ceremony, I read it at the funerals of my mother, who died peacefully while asleep aged 91 on 18 February 2015, and my brother David, who took his life a few weeks later, on 23 March 2015.*

*The 'mother giving birth' is my brothers' mother, Joan. The 'young sister' was Susan, my wife's sister, killed tragically in a car crash. The 'teenager' was Mark Toomey, son of my 'adopted parents', Paul and Marie. The 'ancient aunt' was my Auntie Sadie, fondly remembered, matriarch of the wider Armstrong family.*

*3*

# *Stay awhile*

I meander through an ancient cemetery
Can't stay long:
Winter chills my bones
Back shivers despite heavy coat.

All ages lie here.
Each generation like poppy and shamrock
On hungry soil
Falling.

A haunting soldier daubed anew in blood by
Story makers, story fakers.
Magic makers spout myth and tale
Man-made stories all.

We are not a story.

I breathe in peace
Shorn of creed and myth.
In our only now.

'Will I get the priest?' you ask.
No, you're priest enough for me.
Human with human at the hour of my death.

Stay awhile. Soon go and live.
Your time of life is now.

Joe Armstrong © 2018

# Joe Armstrong

*I wrote 'Stay Awhile' for the 2019 annual HAI commemoration ceremony. The dialogue in the opening lines of the last stanza celebrates a conversation with my much-loved father-in-law, Eugene Cassidy and myself. My wife and family thought I was having a heart attack. I wasn't — it was a muscular chest cramp from zealous gardening the previous day. But thinking my time was up, my unbelief was manifest, assured and true. I have come a long way! The 'haunting soldier' refers to a sculpture erected in Dublin to mark the First World War armistice which was vandalised in November 2018.*

*4*

# *My mortality*

What you are
We once were
What we are
You will be.

So reads the letter
Delivered personally to me
In the Capuchin Crypt in Rome.

A weird place:
The bones of 3000 monks
Displayed as
Decoration.

Skulls, hip bones, leg bones, finger bones.
They lay in the ground
Going the way of all flesh.

Dug up
Their flesh, vein, nerve and muscle
Gone the way of all flesh.

Stripped to the bone
Their skeletons
Make their personal appeal
Imploring me not to flee
From my mortality.

Joe Armstrong © 2019

Joe Armstrong

*'My mortality' was inspired by my visit to the Capuchin Crypt, when my wife and I visited Rome in 2019. It displays the bones of more than 3,000 monks, a provocative visual reminder of our mortality. Although I had been there as a 21-year-old Marist student in 1983, by my second visit I was 57. It was an existential moment for me. Life is fleeting. Seize the day. Live your one and only life to the full. Now!*

**\*5\***

# *Covid Earth*

Life, as we know it, has changed.
Humanity is humbled by a microbe.
This morning, I look at the sky, beautiful and blue.
I hear birdsong.
I breathe.

I, for now, am one of the lucky ones.
Inhaling breath, exhaling, inhaling.
Alive, healthy, breathing still.

The earth breathes too,
Much of it relieved by our humbling.
Demand lessened, growth stalled,
The earth made blue again
By our demise.

Joe Armstrong © 2020

*6*

# *The Gathering*

I recently attended the funeral of a lovely human being. Isn't it strange the way a death brings the living together? A call goes out and we receive the news. We set aside our plans for the day, confirm funeral arrangements, tell those who need to be told and head to the funeral.

There, we see familiar faces. Dredge our memory for names. Is that Paddy? Gosh, there's John – how he has aged! Crikey, it's Pete: looks the very same! Goodness, could that be Patricia? Haven't seen her in 20 years. The handshaking, nods and greeting. 'How's your family?' And questions about the deceased: 'Was it fast?' 'Was he in pain?'

The dead gather us. Their last gift to us. Bidding us to meet up again with friends and relatives, people we're fond of or loved. And, perhaps, the odd toxic person. We drift towards those we loved, who accepted us, with whom we journeyed for a while. We're struck people we're fond of are alive. We see them too rarely!

The deceased presides over the gathering. Perhaps with open coffin, we face our inevitable end. 'Would you recognise him?' 'Ah, poor Brian.' Our last sight of him. Then the ceremony. The singing, readings and prayers. You're glad you went. Reconnected with people. It was good to attend. You were part of it. Appreciated those who came up to you. Glad you greeted some you weren't so sure about. Pleased you didn't rise to the bait of the toxic one. You grew beyond him.

We return home contented. We belong to people. We're nourished by renewing friendships; we're reconciled by turning up. We shared chapters in our lives together. We belong to one another. We matter to them. They matter to us. We're happy they're still alive. They know us, maybe very well. We may know them too to their core.

A funeral brings healing. We are re-knit by the gathering. Validated in our choices. Affirmed in our life. Glad, too, for the wider relationships in our lives, for people past and present, friends and loved ones, old and new.

Joe Armstrong © 2009

*In memory of Brian Keenan, Marist priest, 15 July 1943 – 14 August 2009.*

# Acknowledgements

This book has been 25 years in the making.

I thank the following people for their helpful feedback on various drafts: Barney Flannery, Margaret McCann, Evan Hughes, Maeve Donoghue, David McCarthy; Conor Kostick; Aisling Burke, Andreas Byrne, Trudy Byrne, Andy Carter, Edel Corrigan, Ashling Harrison, Jordan Lee McGrath, Paula McGrath, Joy Orpen Kanter, Laura Peters, Jimmy Plenderleith, Lia Mills, Seamus Hosey, Marita Conlon McKenna, Brendan O'Brien, Marianne Gunn O'Connor, and Andrea Martin for legal advice.

I thank the Marist Fathers for accepting me into their congregation as one of their own. They fed, clothed, educated and cared for me. I grew as a person and am the better man for having been a Marist. I have a deep respect for, and hold in the highest regard, each member of the Society of Mary.

I thank my UCD friends, especially Tom Ambrose. I thank Ms D. I thank Chris Tomasino for her astute analysis and insights, and her confidence in me and in this book from the outset. Thanks too to Nicoline Greer, Production

313

Supervisor of my RTE Radio One documentary *From Belief to Unbelief.*

I want to thank Brian McClinton, Editor of *The Irish Freethinker and Humanist* magazine, for being first to publish sections of this book in column form. And I thank my friend and fellow celebrant Eamon Murphy for his encouragement and for checking each column before publication.

I thank my brother Paul, for his love, and my sister Clare, for being a support to me when I was leaving the Marists. I'm grateful too to my brother David, sadly deceased, who let me stay with him in London for several weeks in 1989, after I left the Marists. I thank my 'adopted parents' Paul and Marie Toomey and their family for making me feel part of their family. I thank my parents, Arthur and Pauline, for bringing me into the world and for doing their best.

I thank my son, John, and daughter, Sarah, for being who they are; and all the ways that they enrich my life. I am proud of you both. Thanks too, John, for your invaluable professionalism in designing the book cover. John took a photograph of the front, back and spine of one of my journals for the cover of this book. And that's my final profession cross on the front.

Finally, I thank my amazing wife Ruth, resplendent with rare common sense, who read and gave feedback on every word of this book. Ruth, this book, and all of my work as a writer, would never have been possible without you. Ruth, love of my life, thank you.

# About the Author

Joe Armstrong[1] spent nine years studying for the Roman Catholic priesthood with the Marist Fathers in Dublin in the 1980s. He taught English and religious education in London for five years. He is a writer, podcaster[2] and Humanist celebrant. His RTE Radio One documentary *From Belief to Unbelief*[3] was shortlisted for New York Festivals World's Best Radio awards. A multi-award-winning public speaker, he is author of several books and was a weekly columnist with *The Irish Times* for seven years. Married with two adult children, he lives in Ireland.

---

[1] Author's website: https://joearmstrong.ie/

[2] Author's podcast: https://losingmyreligion.podbean.com/

[3] Author's RTE documentary:
https://www.rte.ie/radio1/doconone/2012/1012/647201-radio-documentary-from-belief-to-unbelief-joe-armstrong-catholic-priesthood/

CPSIA information can be obtained
at www.ICGtesting.com
Printed in the USA
LVHW081707170222
711208LV00015B/995